Berlitz®

Scandinavian

phrase book

Berlitz Publishing Company, Inc.

Princeton   Mexico City   London   Eschborn   Singapore

How best to use this phrase book

This phrase book is designed to provide you with the essential key phrases you'll need for travelling in and around Scandinavia.

● **Colour margins** will help you locate quickly the language that you require.

● Each language is divided into essential **topic sections**. The following content table will help you find your way around:

Basic expressions	Shops, stores & services
Hotel–Accommodation	incl. bank, post, phone
Eating out	Doctor
Travelling around	Time, date, numbers
Sightseeing	Emergency
Relaxing	Guide to pronunciation

● Each expression appears with a transliteration next to it. Simply read this imitated pronunciation as if it were English, stressing the syllables printed in bold type. For further help, consult the **Guide to pronunciation** at the back of each language section.

● In the **Eating out** section, a selection of popular traditional dishes are listed alphabetically, followed by brief explanations, to help you decypher dishes appearing on a menu.

● If you want to find out how to say something in one of the languages, your fastest look-up is via the relevant **Dictionary** section (pages 161-191). This not only gives you the word, but is also cross-referenced to its use in a phrase on a specific page.

● Throughout the book, this symbol ☛ suggests phrases your listener can use to answer you, simply by pointing to the appropriate answer.

ISBN 2-8315-7738-1

Printed – January 2001

Printed in Spain

Danish

WITHDRAWN

Some basic expressions *Anvendelige udtryk*

Yes/No.	**Ja/Nej.**	ya/nigh
Please.	**Vær så venlig.**	vær saw **veh**nlee
Thank you.	**Tak.**	tak
I beg your pardon.	**Undskyld.**	**oon**skewl

Introductions *Præsentationer*

Good morning.	**God morgen.**	goadh**mōā**ern
Good afternoon.	**God dag.**	goadh**dai**
Good evening.	**God aften.**	goadh**af**dern
Good night.	**God nat.**	goadh**nat**
Good-bye.	**Farvel.**	far**vehl**
My name is...	**Jeg hedder...**	yigh **hehd**herr
Pleased to meet you!	**Det glæder mig at træffe Dem!**	dE **glæd**herr migh ah **træf**er dehm
What's your name?	**Hvad hedder De/du?**	vadh **hehd**herr dee/doo
How are you?	**Hvordan har du det?**	vor**dan** har doo dE
Fine, thanks. And you?	**Tak, godt. Og hvordan har du det?**	tak god. oa vor**dan** har doo dE
Where do you come from?	**Hvor kommer du fra?**	vōār **kom**er doo fra
I'm from...	**Jeg er fra...**	yigh ehr fra
Australia	**Australien**	owstral**ēē**ern
Canada	**Canada**	**ka**nada
Great Britain	**Storbritannien**	stoarbritan**yern**
United States	**USA**	oo ehs ah
I'm with my...	**Jeg er her sammen med...**	yigh ehr hehr **sō**mern mehdh
wife	**min kone**	meen **koa**ner
husband	**min mand**	meen man
family	**min familie**	meen fa**mil**yer
children	**mine børn**	**mee**ner børn
parents	**mine forældre**	**mee**ner for**æl**drer
boyfriend/girlfriend	**min kæreste**	meen **kær**sder
I'm here on holiday (vacation).	**Jeg er her på ferie.**	yigh ehr hehr paw **feh**ryer

GUIDE TO PRONUNCIATION/EMERGENCIES, see page 30

Questions *Spørgsmål*

When?	**Hvornår?**	vornawr
How?	**Hvordan?**	vordan
What?	**Hvad?**	vadh
Why?	**Hvorfor?**	vorfor
Who?	**Hvem?**	vehm
Which?	**Hvilken?**	vilkern
Where is/are ...?	**Hvor er ...?**	vōar ehr
Where can I find/ get ...?	**Hvor kan jeg finde/ få ...?**	vōar kan yigh finner/faw
How far?	**Hvor langt?**	vōar langt
How long?	**Hvor længe?**	vōar længer
How much/How many?	**Hvor meget/Hvor mange?**	vōar mighert/vōar manger
Can I have ...?	**Kan jeg få ...?**	kan yigh faw
Can you help me?	**Kan De hjælpe mig?**	kan dee yehlper migh
Is there/Are there ...?	**Er der ...?**	ehr dehr
There isn't/aren't ...	**Der er ikke ...**	dehr ehr igger
There isn't/aren't any.	**Der er ikke nogen.**	dehr ehr igger nōaern

Do you speak ...? *Kan De tale ...?*

What does this/that mean?	**Hvad betyder det her/det der?**	vadh bertewdherr dᴇ hehr/dᴇ dehr
Can you translate this for me?	**Kan De oversætte det her for mig?**	kan dee o°°errsehder dᴇ hehr for migh
Do you speak English?	**Kan De tale engelsk?**	kan dee tōler ehngerlsk
I don't speak (much) Danish.	**Jeg kan ikke tale det (ret meget) dansk.**	yigh kan igger tōler dᴇ (reht mighert) dansk
Could you speak more slowly?	**Kan De tale lidt langsommere?**	kan dee tōler leet langsomerrer
Could you repeat that?	**Kan De gentage det?**	kan dee gehntōer dᴇ
Could you write it down, please?	**Kan De være rar og skrive det ned?**	kan dee væerer rar oa skrēēver dᴇ nehdh
I understand.	**Jeg forstår det.**	yigh forstawr dᴇ
I don't understand.	**Jeg forstår det ikke.**	yigh forstawr dᴇ igger

It's... *Det er...*

better/worse	**bedre/værre**	behdhrer/vehrer
big/small	**stort/lille**	stoart/leeler
cheap/expensive	**billigt/dyrt**	beeleet/dēwrt
early/late	**tidligt/sent**	teedhleet/sɛnt
good/bad	**godt/dårligt**	god/dawleet
hot/cold	**varmt/koldt**	varmt/kolt
old/new	**gammelt/nyt**	gamerlt/newt
right/wrong	**rigtigt/forkert**	rigteet/forkehrt
vacant/occupied	**ledigt/optaget**	lehdheet/optōerdh

Prepositions *Præpositioner*

above	**ovenpå**	o°°ernpaw
after	**efter**	ehfder
at	**ved**	vehdh
before (time)	**før**	før
below	**nedenunder**	nehdhernoonerr
between	**mellem**	mehlerm
down/downstairs	**ned/nedenunder**	nehdh/nehdhernoonerr
from	**fra**	fra
in/inside	**i/indenfor**	ee/inernfor
near	**nær**	nær
on	**på**	paw
outside	**udenfor**	ōōdhernfor
through	**gennem**	gehnerm
to	**til**	til
under	**under**	oonerr
until	**indtil**	intil
up/upstairs	**op/ovenpå**	op/o°°ernpaw
with	**med**	mehdh
without	**uden**	oôdhern

A few more useful words *Nogle flere nyttige ord*

and	**og**	oa
but	**men**	mehn
never	**aldrig**	aldree
not	**ikke**	igger
nothing	**ikke noget**	igger nōaert
now	**nu**	noo
only	**kun**	koon
or	**eller**	ehler
perhaps	**måske**	mosgɛ
soon	**snart**	snart
too (also)	**også**	osser
very	**meget**	mighert

Hotel—Accommodation *Hotel*

I have a reservation.	**Jeg har bestilt værelse.**	yigh har ber**stilt** v**ææ**rerlser
We've reserved 2 rooms/an apartment.	**Vi har bestilt 2 værelser/en lejlighed.**	vee har ber**stilt** to v**ææ**rerlserr/ehn **ligh**leehehdh
Do you have any vacancies?	**Har De nogle ledige værelser?**	har dee n**oa**ler l**e**d**ee**eer v**ææ**rerlserr
I'd like a...	**Jeg vil gerne have et...**	yigh veel **gehr**ner ha eht
single room	**enkeltværelse**	**ehn**kerldv**ææ**rerlser
double room	**dobbeltværelse**	**dob**erldv**ææ**rerlser
with twin beds	**med to senge**	mehdh toa **seh**nger
with a double bed	**med dobbeltseng**	mehdh **dob**erldsehng
with a bath	**med bad**	mehdh badh
with a shower	**med brusebad**	med br**oo**serbadh
Is there...?	**Er der...?**	ehr dehr
air conditioning	**klimaanlæg**	kl**ee**ma **an**læg
a laundry service	**tøjvask**	**toi**vask
a private toilet	**toilet på værelset**	toa**let** paw v**ææ**rerlserdh
a radio/television in the room	**radio/fjernsyn på værelset**	**radio/fyehrn**sewn paw v**ææ**rerlserdh
room service	**service på værelset**	"service" paw v**ææ**rerlserdh
a swimming pool	**svømmebasin**	**svøm**merbass**æ**ng
washing machine	**en vaskemaskine**	ehn **vas**germaskeener
What's the price...?	**Hvad koster det...?**	vadh **kos**derr dE
Is there a camp site near here?	**Er der en campingplads i nærheden?**	ehr dehr ehn **kam**pingplas ee **nær**hEdhern
We'll be staying...	**Vi bliver her...**	vee bl**ee**eerr hehr
overnight only	**en enkel nat**	ehn **ehn**kerlt nat
a few days	**et par dage**	eht par **daer**
a week (at least)	**i (mindst) en uge**	ee (meenst) ehn **øer**

Decision *Beslutning*

May I see the room?	**Kan jeg se værelset?**	kan yigh sE v**ææ**rerlserdh
That's fine. I'll take it.	**Det er godt. Jeg tager det.**	dE ehr god. yigh tar dE
No. I don't like it.	**Jeg kan ikke lide det.**	yigh kan **ig**ger li dE
It's too...	**Det er for...**	dE ehr for...
dark/small	**mørkt/lyst**	mørkt/lewst
noisy	**støjende**	**stoi**erner

NUMBERS, see page 28

Do you have anything...?	**Har De noget...?**	har dee n̄o̅āert
better	**bedre**	behdhrer
cheaper	**billigere**	beel̄e̅e̅errer
quieter	**roligere**	roal̄e̅e̅errer

Navn/Fornavn	Name/First name
Adresse (by, gade, nummer)	Home town/Street/Number
Nationalitet/Stilling	Nationality/Occupation
Fødselsdato/Fødested	Date/Place of birth
Kommer fra.../Skal videre til...	Coming from.../Going to...
Pasnummer	Passport number
Sted/Dato	Place/Date
Underskrift	Signature

General requirements *Almindelige forespørgsler*

The key to room..., please.	**Nøglen til værelse..., tak.**	noilern til v̄ārerlser... tak
Could you wake me at... please?	**Kan De vække mig klokken...?**	kan dee vægger migh kloggern
Where's the...?	**Hvor er...?**	v̄o̅ar ehr
bathroom	**badeværelset**	b̄o̅dherv̄ārerlserdh
dining-room	**spisesalen**	sp̄e̅e̅sersölern
emergency exit	**nødudgangen**	n̄ødhoodhgangern
lift (elevator)	**elevatoren**	ehlehvatoarern
Where are the toilets?	**Hvor er toilettet?**	v̄o̅ar ehr toalehderdh
Where can I park my car?	**Hvor kan jeg parkere min bil?**	v̄o̅ar kan yigh parkεrer meen beel

Checking out *Afrejse*

May I have my bill, please?	**Må jeg bede om regningen?**	maw yigh bε om righningern
Can you get us a taxi?	**Kan De skaffe os en taxa?**	kan dee skaffer os ehn taksa
Could you have our luggage brought down?	**Kunne vi få bagagen ned?**	kooner vee faw baḡo̅shern nehdh
It's been a very enjoyable stay.	**Vi har nydt opholdet meget.**	vee har newt opholerdh mighert

Eating out *Restauranter*

Can you recommend a good restaurant?	**Kan De anbefale en god restaurant?**	kan dee **an**berföler en goadh rehstoa**rang**
I'd like to reserve a table for 4.	**Jeg vil gerne bestille et bord til 4.**	yigh veel **gehr**ner ber**stil**er eht boar til **fee**rer
We'll come at 8.	**Vi kommer klokken 8.**	vee komerr **klog**gern oader
I'd like..., please.	**Jeg vil gerne have...**	yigh veel **gehr**ner ha
breakfast	**morgenmad**	mōaernmadh
lunch	**frokost**	froakost
dinner	**middag**	mid**dai**
What do you recommend?	**Hvad kan De anbefale?**	vadh kan dee **an**berföler
Do you have a set menu/local dishes?	**Er der en dagens ret/nogle lokale retter?**	ehr dehr ehn **daerns** reht/ loakaler **reh**derr
Do you have any vegetarian dishes?	**Er der nogle vegetariske retter?**	ehr dehr **nōa**ler vehgehtarisger **reh**derr

---

Hvad ønsker De?	What would you like?
Jeg kan anbefale det her.	I recommend this.
Hvad ønsker De at drikke?	What would you like to drink?
Vi har ikke...	We don't have...
Ønsker De...?	Would you like...?

Could we have a/an..., please?	**Kan vi få....**	kan vee faw
ashtray	**et askebæger**	eht **asger**bæær
cup	**en kop**	ehn kop
fork	**en gaffel**	ehn **gaf**erl
glass	**et glas**	eht glas
knife	**en kniv**	ehn knēēv
napkin (serviette)	**en serviet**	ehn sehrvēē**eht**
plate	**en tallerken**	ehn talehrkern
spoon	**en ske**	ehn skE

TELLING THE TIME, see page 27

May I have some...?	**Må jeg bede om...**	maw yigh bᴇ om
bread	**noget brød**	n̄o͞aert brødh
butter	**noget smør**	n̄o͞aert smør
lemon	**noget citron**	n̄o͞aert seetroan
oil	**noget spiseolie**	n̄o͞aert spᴇᴇseroalyer
pepper	**noget peber**	n̄o͞aert peh°°er
salt	**noget salt**	n̄o͞aert salt
seasoning	**nogle krydderier**	n̄o͞aler krewdherrᴇ͞ᴇerr
sugar	**noget sukker**	n̄o͞aert soo͞ggerr
vinegar	**noget eddike**	n̄o͞aert ehdhigger

Reading the menu *Læsning af spisekortet*

Børnemenu	Children's menu
Dagens måltid	Meal of the day
Dagens ret/suppe/grønsager	Dish/soup/vegetables of the day
Husets specialiteter	Specialities of the house
Køkkenchefen anbefaler...	The chef recommends...
Serveres med...	Served with...
Vegetar	Vegetarian
Vælg mellem...	Choice of...

desserter	dehs**sehr**derr	desserts
drikkevarer	**drigg**ervarerr	beverages
fisk	fisk	fish
fjerkræ	**fyehr**kræ	poultry
forretter	**forreh**derr	appetizers
frugt	froogt	fruit
grøntsager	**grøn**saer	vegetables
is	ᴇ͞ᴇs	ice cream
koldt bord	kol bordh	smörgåsbord
kylling	**kew**ling	chicken
ost	oast	cheese
pasta	pasta	pasta
salater	sa**lad**err	salads
skaldyr	**skal**dewr	seafood
småretter	**smaw**rehderr	snacks
smørrebrød	**smør**erbrødh	open sandwich
supper	**soob**berr	soups
vildt	veelt	game
vin	vᴇ͞ᴇn	wine
ægretter	**æg**rehderr	egg dishes
øl	øl	beer

Breakfast *Morgenmad*

I'll have a/an/ some...	**Jeg vil gerne have...**	yigh veel **gehr**ner ha
bacon and eggs	**bacon og æg**	"bacon" oa æg
bread	**brød**	brødh
butter	**smør**	smør
cereal	**cornflakes**	"cornflakes"
eggs	**æg**	æg
boiled egg	**kogt æg**	kogt æg
fried eggs	**spejlæg**	**spighl**æg
scrambled eggs	**røræg**	**rør**æg
poached eggs	**pocheret æg**	posh**ē**rerdh æg
jam	**syltetøj/marmelade**	**sewl**dertoi/marmer**lō**dher
rolls	**rundstykker**	**roon**stewggerr
toast	**ristet brød**	**reest**erdh brødh

Starters (Appetizers) *Forretter*

blandet hors d'oeuvre	**blan**erdh "hors d'oeuvre"	assorted appetizers
fyldte tomater	**fewl**der toa**mad**err	stuffed tomatoes
omelet	**oamer**leht	omelet
sildesalat	**seel**ersalat	herring salad
kyllingesalat (**kewl**leengersah**lōt**)		chicken meat, macaroni, tomato slices, green peppers, olives, lettuce and mushrooms
smørrebrød (**smører**brødh)		large, buttered open-faced sandwich covered with one of a variety of delicacies and garnished with various accessories

Soups and stews *Suppe- og labskovsretter*

I'd like some soup.	**Jeg vil gerne have en suppe.**	yigh veel **gehr**ner ha en **soob**ber
aspargessuppe	ah**spars**soobber	asparagus soup
champignonsuppe	sham**pinyong**soobber	mushroom soup
gule ærter	**gōō**ler ærderr	split-pea soup with salt pork
hummersuppe	**hoo**mersoobber	lobster chowder
hønsekødsuppe	**høn**serkødhsoobber	chicken vegetable soup
æblesuppe	**æb**lersoobber	apple soup
labskoves (**lab**sko°°s)		beef, diced potatoes, slices of carrots and onions, served with rye bread
frugtsuppe (**froogt**soobber)		"fruit soup", composed of a variety of dried fruits, served chilled or hot.

Fish and seafood *Fisk og skaldyr*

cod	**torsk**	torsk
perch	**aborre**	ahborer
pike	**gedde**	gehdher
smoked herring	**røget sild**	roierdh seel
sole	**søtunge**	søtoonger
trout	**forel**	foarehl

sild i karry
(seel ee **kö**ree)

herring with curry sauce, served with rice, leeks and dark bread

ålesuppe
(**awl**ersoobber)

sweet-and-sour eel soup, with apples and prunes, served with dark rye bread

boiled	**kogt**	kogt
fried	**stegt**	stehgt
grilled	**grillet**	**greel**erdh
roast	**ovnstegt**	o°°nstehgt
stewed	**stuvet**	**stoo**erdh
underdone (rare)	**letstegt**	**leht**stehgt
medium	**medium**	**meh**deeoom
well-done	**gennemstegt**	**gehn**ermstehgt

Meat *Kød*

I'd like some... **Jeg vil gerne have** yigh veel **gehr**ner ha
noget.../nogle... **nöä**ert.../**nöä**ler

bacon	**bacon**	"bacon"
beef	**oksekød**	**okser**kødh
chicken	**kylling**	**kewl**ling
duck	**and**	an
ham	**skinke**	**skeen**ger
lamb	**lammekød**	**lamer**kødh
pork	**svinekød**	**svēē**nerkødh
veal	**kalvekød**	**kalv**erkødh

engelsk bøf
(**ehng**erlsk bøf)

fillet of beef with onions and boiled potatoes

forloren skildpadde
(for**loa**rern **skeel**padher)

"mock turtle": a very traditional Danish dish consisting of meat from a calf's head with meat balls and fish balls

kalkunragout
(**kal**koon ra**goo**)

jugged turkey in a sweet-and-sour gravy, served with mashed potatoes or chestnuts

æbleflæsk
(**ǣb**lerflæsk)

smoked bacon with onions and sautéed apple rings

Vegetables *Grøntsager*

beans	**bønner**	**bø**nerr
cabbage	**kål**	kawl
carrots	**gulerødder**	goolerrødherr
lettuce	**salat**	salat
mushrooms	**champignoner**	**sham**pinyong
onions	**løg**	loi
peas	**ærter**	**ær**derr
potatoes	**kartofler**	kar**tof**lerr
tomatoes	**tomater**	toa**ma**derr

Cheese *Ost*

danbo (danbo)	a mild, firm cheese with holes, sometimes flavoured with caraway seeds
esrom (ehsrom)	a mild, slightly aromatic cheese of spongy texture
samsø (samsø)	a mild, firm cheese with a sweet, nutty flavour

Fruit and nuts *Frugt og nødder*

apple	**et æble**	eht **æb**ler
cherries	**kirsebær**	**keer**serbær
lemon	**citron**	see**troan**
orange	**en appelsin**	aberl**seen**
pear	**pære**	**pæ**rer
plums	**blommer**	**blom**err
pumpkin	**græskar**	**græs**kar
raspberries	**hindbær**	**heen**bær
strawberries	**jordbær**	**yoar**bær

Desserts–Pastries *Desserter–Bagværk*

eis	ees	ice-cream
chokoladeis	shoakoa**lad**herees	chocolate ice-cream
kage	koer	cake
flødekage	**flød**herkoer	layer cream cake
Napoleonskage	napoaleonskoer	custard slice with jam
Wienerbrød	**vee**nerbrødh	Danish pastry

brune kager (brooner koer)	spicy, thin crisp brown cake with almond decoration; a Christmas favourite
bondepige med slør (boanerpeeer mehdh slør)	"veiled country maid": a mixture of rye-bread crumbs, apple sauce, cream and sugar

Drinks *Drikkevarer*

beer	**øl**	øl
light/dark beer	**lyst/mørkt øl**	lewst/mørkt øl
brandy	**en brandy**	ehn "brandy"
(hot) chocolate	**(varm) chokolade**	(varm) shoakoa**ladher**
coffee	**kaffe**	**kafer**
black/with cream	**sort/med fløde**	soart/mehdh **flødher**
fruit juice	**frugtsaft**	**froogtsaft**
lemonade	**limonade**	leemoan**ōdher**
milk	**mælk**	mælk
mineral water	**mineralvand**	meeneh**ral**van
tea	**te**	tɛ
with milk/lemon	**med mælk/citron**	mehdh mælk/see**troan**
wine	**vin**	vēēn
red/white	**rød/hvid**	rødh/veedh
aquavit	traditional Scandinavian drink; colourless	
(ahkva**veet**)	grain spirit, usually flavoured with carraway,	
	drunk neat and ice-cold	

Complaints–Paying *Klager–Regningen*

The meat is ...	**Kødet er ...**	**kødh**erdh ehr
overdone	**stegt for meget**	stehgt for **migh**ert
underdone	**stegt for lidt**	stehgt for leet
This is too...	**Det her er for ...**	dɛ hehr ehr for
bitter/salty/sweet	**bittert/salt/sødt**	**bid**erdh/salt/søt
That's not what I ordered.	**Det har jeg ikke bestilt.**	dɛ har yigh **igger** ber**stilt**
The food is cold.	**Maden er kold.**	**madh**ern ehr kol
What's taking you so long?	**Hvorfor tager det så lang tid?**	**vor**for tar dɛ saw lang teedh

The bill (check) *Regningen*

I'd like to pay.	**Jeg vil gerne betale.**	yigh veel **gehr**ner ber**tōl**er
What's this amount for?	**Hvad dækker dette beløb?**	vadh **dægg**err **dehd**er be**lōb**
I think there's a mistake in this bill.	**Der er vist en fejl i denne regning.**	deh ehr vist ehn fighl ee **dehn**er **righ**ning
Can I pay with this credit card?	**Kan jeg betale med dette kreditkort?**	kan yigh ber**tōl**er mehdh **dehd**er kreh**dit**kort
We enjoyed it, thank you.	**Vi har nydt det.**	vee har newt dɛ

NUMBERS, see page 28

Travelling around *Rejse omkring*

Plane *I fly*

Is there a flight to Rønne?	**Er der et fly til Rønne?**	ehr dehr eht flew til **røner**
What time should I check in?	**Hvad tid må jeg checke ind?**	vadh teed maw yigh "check"er in
I'd like to ... my reservation.	**Jeg vil gerne ... min bestilling.**	yigh veel **gehr**ner ... meen be**stil**ing
cancel	**annullere**	annoo**lē**rer
change	**ændre på**	**æn**drer paw
confirm	**bekræfte**	ber**kræf**der

Train *Tog*

Where's the railway station?	**Hvor ligger jern- banestationen?**	vōar **lee**gerr **jehrn**bōnerstashonern

INDGANG	ENTRANCE	
UDGANG	EXIT	
INFORMATION	INFORMATION	

Where is/are ...?	**Hvor er ...?**	vōar ehr
booking office	**pladsreserveringen**	**plas**rehsehrvē**ē**ringern
left-luggage office (baggage check)	**bagageopbevar- ingen**	bag**ōsh**eropber**vō**ringern
lost property (lost and found) office	**hittegodskontoret**	**heed**ergoskontō**ā**rerdh
luggage lockers	**bagageboksene**	bag**ōsh**erbokserner
platform 7	**perron 7**	peh**rong** sewv
ticket office	**billetlugen**	bee**lehd**lōō**gern**
waiting room	**venteværelset**	**vehn**dervǣrerlserdh
Where are the toilets?	**Hvor er toilettet?**	vōar ehr toa**lehd**erdh

Inquiries *Forespørgsler*

I'd like a ticket to Copenhagen.	**Jeg vil gerne have en billet til Køben- havn.**	yigh veel **gehr**ner ha ehn bee**lehd** til købern**hown**
single (one-way)	**enkelt**	**ehn**kerlt
return (round trip)	**retur**	reh**tōor**
first/second class	**første/anden klasse**	**fōr**sder/**an**ern **kla**ser
How long does the journey (trip) take?	**Hvor længe tager turen?**	vōar **læ**nger tar **tōo**rern

TELLING THE TIME, see page 27/NUMBERS, see page 28

When is the... train to Århus?	**Hvornår kører det... tog til Århus?**	vornawr kōrerr deht... toa til awrhōōs
first/last/next	**første/sidste/ næste**	fōrsder/seesder/næster
What time does the train to Randers leave?	**Hvad tid afgår toget til Randers?**	vadh teed owgawr to°°erdh til raners
Is this the right train to Aarhus?	**Kører det her tog til Århus?**	kōrerr dɛ hehr toa til awhōōs

Underground (subway) *S-tog*

Where's the nearest underground station?	**Hvor er den nærmeste S-togstation?**	vōar ehr dehn nærmerster ehs toa stashon
Which line should I take to...?	**Hvilket tog skal jeg tage til...?**	vilkert toa skal yigh ta til
Where do I change for...?	**Hvor skal jeg skifte til...?**	vōar skal yigh skeefder til

Bus *Bus*

Which bus goes to the town centre?	**Hvilken bus kører til centrum?**	vilkern boos kōrerr til sentroom
How much is the fare to...?	**Hvor meget koster det til...?**	vōar mighert kosderr dɛ til
Will you tell me when to get off?	**Vil De sige til, hvornår jeg skal af?**	veel dee sēēer til vornawr yigh skal ah

Boat service *Bådfart*

When does the next boat for... leave?	**Hvornår går den næste båd til...?**	vornawr gaw dehn næsder bāwdh til
How long does the crossing take?	**Hvor længe varer overfarten?**	vōar længer vōrerr o°°erfardern
I'd like to take a canal tour/ tour of the harbour.	**Jeg vil gerne tage på en kanaltur/en havnerundfart.**	yigh veel gehrner ta paw ehn kanōltōōr/ehn hownerroondfart

Taxi *Taxa*

Where can I get a taxi?	**Hvor kan jeg få en taxa?**	vōar kan yigh faw ehn taksa
What's the fare to...?	**Hvad koster det til...?**	vadh kosderr dɛ til
Take me to this address.	**Kør mig til denne adresse.**	kōr migh til dehner ahdrehser
Please stop here.	**Stands her.**	stans hehr

Car hire (rental) *Biludlejning*

I'd like to hire (rent) a car.	**Jeg vil gerne leje en bil.**	yigh veel **gehr**ner **ligh**er ehn beel
I'd like it for a day/a week.	**Jeg vil gerne have den en enkel dag/en uge.**	yigh veel **gehr**ner ha dehn ehn **ehnk**erl dai/ehn ōōer
What's the charge per day/week?	**Hvad koster det pr. dag/uge?**	vadh **kos**derr dɛ pehr dai/ōōer
Is mileage included?	**Er det med kilometerpenge?**	ehr dɛ mehdh keeloam**ē**derpehnger

---

Road signs *Vejskilte*

DATOPARKERING	Parking according to date
ENSRETTET	One-way street
JERNBANEOVERSKØRING	Railway level crossing
OMKØRSEL	Diversion, detour
OPHØR AF...	End of restriction
OVERHALING FORBUDT	No overtaking
PAS PÅ	General warning notice
UDKØRSEL	Exit
UJØVN VEJ	Bad road
VEJARBEJDE	Road works

Where's the nearest filling station?	**Hvor er den nærmeste benzinstation?**	vōar ehr dehn **nær**merster behn**seen**stashon
Fill it up, please.	**Fuld tank**	fōol tank
Give me... litres of petrol (gasoline).	**... liter benzin.**	... **leed**err ben**seen**
super (premium)/ regular/unleaded/ diesel	**super/normal/ blyfri/diesel**	super/nor**mal**/**blew**free/ diesel
How can I find this place?	**Hvordan kan jeg finde frem til dette sted?**	vor**dan** kan yigh **fin**ner frehm til **deh**der stehdh
How far is it to... from here?	**Hvor langt er der til... herfra?**	vōar langt ehr dehr til... hehr**fra**
I've had a break-down at...	**Jeg har fået motor-stop ved...**	yigh har **fā**werdh **moa**torstop vehdh
Can you send a mechanic?	**Kan De sende en mekaniker?**	kan dee **sehn**ner ehn mehk**a**neekerr

| Can you mend this puncture (fix this flat)? | **Kan De reparere denne punktering?** | kan dee rehparĒrer dehner poonktehring |

You're on the wrong road.	**De har kørt forkert.**
Go straight ahead.	**Kør ligeud.**
It's down there on the left/right.	**Det ligger der til venstre/højre.**
opposite/behind...	**overfor/bagved...**
next to/after...	**ved siden af/efter...**
north/south/east/west	**nord/syd/øst/vest**

Sightseeing *Seværdigheder*

Where's the tourist office?	**Hvor er turistbureauet?**	vōar ehr tooreestbewroaert
Is there an English-speaking guide?	**Findes der en engelsktalende guide?**	finners dehr ehn ehngerlsktōlernder "guide"
Where is/are the...?	**Hvor er...?**	vōar ehr
art gallery	**kunstgalleriet**	koonstgalereēert
botanical gardens	**den botaniske have**	dehn botaneesger hōver
castle	**borgen**	bōargern
city centre	**byens centrum**	bewerns sentroom
church	**kirken**	keērgern
concert hall	**koncertsalen**	konsehrtsōlern
harbour	**havnen**	hownern
market	**torvet**	tōarverdh
museum	**museum**	moosseoom
palace	**slottet**	sloderdh
shopping area	**indkøbscentret**	inkøbssentrerdh
square	**pladsen/torvet**	plasern/torverdh
tower	**tårnet**	tawrnerdh
town hall	**rådhuset**	rawdhhōōserdh
What are the opening hours?	**Hvornår er der åbent?**	vornawr ehr dehr āwbern
When does it close?	**Hvornår lukkes der?**	vornawr looggers dehr
How much is the entrance fee?	**Hvor meget koster det i entré?**	vōar mighert kosderr dE ee angtrē

NUMBERS, see page 28

Dansk

Landmarks *Landemærker*

bridge	**en bro**	ehn bro
forest/wood	**en skov**	ehn sko^{oo}
garden	**en have**	ehn **hō**ver
hill	**en bakke**	ehn **bagg**er
island	**en ø**	ehn ø
lake	**en sø**	ehn sø
mountain	**et bjerg**	eht byehr
path	**en sti**	ehn stee
river	**en flod**	ehn floadh
sea	**et hav**	eht how
valley	**en dal**	ehn dal
village	**en landsby**	ehn **lans**bew
waterfall	**et vandfald**	eht **van**fal

Relaxing *Forlystelser*

What's playing at the ... Theatre?	**Hvad spiller man på ... Teateret?**	vadh **speel**err man paw ... tEa**trer**dh
Are there any seats for tonight?	**Er der flere pladser tilbage til i aften?**	ehr dehr **fler**err **plass**err til**bō**er til ee **af**dern
How much are the seats?	**Hvor meget koster billetterne?**	vōar **mig**hert **kos**derr bee**leh**derner
I'd like to reserve 2 seats for the show on Friday evening.	**Jeg vil gerne bes- tille 2 billetter til forestillingen fre- dag aften.**	yigh veel **gehr**ner ber**stil**er to bee**leh**derr til fore**steel**ingern **frE**dai **af**dern
Would you like to go out with me tonight?	**Har du lyst til at gå ud med mig i aften?**	har doo lewst til ah gaw ood mehdh migh ee **af**dern
Thank you, but I'm busy.	**Tak, men jeg er desværre optaget.**	tak mehn yigh ehr dehs**værr**er op**ta**erdh
Is there a disco- theque in town?	**Findes der et dis- kotek i byen?**	**fin**ners dehr eht disko**atE**k ee **bew**ern
Would you like to dance?	**Skal vi danse?**	skal vee **dan**ser
Thank you, it's been a wonderful evening.	**Tak, det har været en virkelig hyggelig aften.**	tak dE har **vae**rerdh ehn **veer**kerlee **hewgg**erlee **af**dern

DAYS OF THE WEEK, see page 27

Sports *Sport*

Is there a football (soccer) match anywhere this Saturday?	**Er der en fodbold-kamp et eller andet sted nu på lørdag?**	ehr dehr ehn **fodh**boldkamp eht **ehl**lerr **an**nerdh stehdh noo paw **lør**dai
Can you get me a ticket?	**Kan De skaffe mig en billet?**	kan dee **skō**fer migh ehn bee**leh**d
Where's the nearest golf course?	**Hvor ligger den nærmeste golf-bane?**	vōar **lee**gerr dehn **nær**merster **golf**bōner
Where are the tennis courts?	**Hvor ligger tennis-banerne?**	vōar **lee**gerr "tennis" **bō**nerner
What's the charge per...?	**Hvad koster det pr....?**	vadh **kos**derr de pehr
day/round/hour	**dag/runde/time**	dai/**roon**der/**tee**mer

cycling	**cykling**	**sew**gling
football (soccer)	**fodbold**	**foad**bold
horse racing	**hestevæddeløb**	**hehs**dervædherløb
horse riding	**ridning**	**reedh**ning
swimming	**svømning**	**svøm**ning
tennis	**tennis**	"tennis"

Can one swim in the lake/river?	**Kan man gå i van-det i søen/floden?**	kan man gaw ee **va**nerdh ee **sø**ern/**floa**dhern
Is there a swimming pool here?	**Findes der et svømmebasin her?**	**fin**ners dehr eht **svøm**erbassehng hehr
Is there a skating rink near here?	**Findes der en skøj-tebane her i nærhe-den?**	**fin**ners dehr ehn **skoi**derbōner hehr ee **nær**hēdhern
I'd like to ski.	**Jeg vil gerne stå på ski.**	yigh veel **gehr**ner staw paw ski
downhill/cross-country skiing	**styrtløb/langrend**	**stewrt**løb/**lang**rehn
I want to hire...	**Jeg vil gerne leje...**	yigh veel **gehr**ner **ligh**er
skates	**et par skøjter**	eht par **skoi**derr
skiing equipment	**noget skiudstyr**	**nōa**ert skioodhstewr
skis	**et par ski**	eht par ski
I'd like to hire a... bicycle.	**Jeg vil gerne leje en...**	yigh veel **gehr**ner **ligh**er ehn
5-gear	**cykel med gear**	**sew**gel mehdh geer
mountain	**bjergcykel**	**byerg**sewgel

Shops and services *Butikker og servicevirksomheder*

Where's the nearest...?	**Hvor er den/det nærmeste...**	vōar ehr dehn/deht **nær**merster
bakery	**bager**	**bō**er
bookshop	**boghandel**	**boa**hanerl
butcher's	**slagter**	**slag**derr
chemist's/drugstore	**apotek**	apo**tehk**
dentist	**tandlæge**	**tan**lǣer
department store	**stormagasin**	**stoar**magaseen
grocery	**købmand**	**kø**man
hairdresser's (ladies/men)	**frisør (dame-/herre-)**	free**sør** (damer-/hehrrer-)
newsagent's	**bladhandler**	**bladh**hanlerr
post office	**posthus**	**post**hoos
souvenir shop	**souvenirbutik**	soovern**ēēr**bootik
supermarket	**supermarked**	**sōō**bermarkerdh

General expressions *Almindelige udtryk*

Where's the main shopping area?	**Hvor er forretningskvarteret**	vōar er forreht**nings**kvar**teh**rerdh

---

Can I help you?	**Kan jeg hjælpe med noget?**
What would you like?	**Hvad skulle det være?**
What... would you like?	**Hvilken... ønsker De?**
colour/shape/quality	**farve/form/kvalitet**
I'm sorry, we don't have any.	**Jeg beklager, det har vi ikke.**
We're out of stock.	**Der er udsolgt.**
Shall we order it for you?	**Skal vi bestille det til Dem?**
Anything else?	**Skulle der være andet?**
That's... kroner, please.	**Det bliver... kroner.**
The cash desk is over there.	**Kassen er derovre.**

I'd like a... one.	**Jeg vil gerne have en...**	yigh veel **gehr**ner ha ehn
big	**stor**	stoar
cheap	**billig**	**bee**lee
dark	**mørk**	mørk
good	**god**	goadh

English	Danish	Pronunciation
heavy	**tung**	toong
large	**stor**	stoar
light (weight)	**let**	leht
light (colour)	**lys**	lews
oval	**oval**	oavōl
rectangular	**rektangulær**	**rehkt**angoolær
round	**rund**	roon
small	**lille**	**leeler**
square	**firkantet**	**fēēr**kanderdh
sturdy	**solid**	soleedh
Do you have any...?	**Har De nogen...?**	har dee nōaern
Don't you have anything...?	**Har De ikke noget...?**	har dee **igger** nōaert
cheaper/better	**billigere/bedre**	bee**lēē**errer/**behdh**rer
larger/smaller	**større/mindre**	**størrer/mindr**er
Can I try it on?	**Kan jeg prøve den?**	kan yigh **prøver** dehn
How much is this?	**Hvad koster det?**	vadh **kos**der dɛ
Please write it down.	**Vær rar og skriv det ned.**	vær rar oa skreev dɛ nedh
I don't want to spend more than... kroner.	**Jeg vil ikke bruge mere end... kroner.**	yigh veel **igger brōō**er **mēhr**er ehn... **krōa**nerr
No, I don't like it.	**Det bryder jeg mig ikke om.**	dɛ **brewdh**err yigh migh **igger** om
I'll take it.	**Jeg tager det.**	yigh tar dɛ
Do you accept credit cards?	**Tager De kreditkort?**	tar dee kreh**dit**kort
Can you order it for me?	**Kan De bestille det til mig?**	kan dee be**stil**er dɛ til migh

English	Danish	Pronunciation
black	**sort**	soart
blue	**blå**	blaw
brown	**brun**	broon
green	**grøn**	grøn
grey	**grå**	graw
orange	**orange**	oa**rangsh**er
red	**rød**	rødh
white	**hvid**	veedh
yellow	**gul**	gool
light...	**lyse-**	lewser-
dark...	**mørke-**	mørker-

NUMBERS, see page 28

Chemist's (drugstore) *Apotek*

aspirin	**en æske aspirin**	ehn **æ**sger "aspirin"
condoms	**nogle kondomer**	n**ō̄**aler kond**o**merr
deodorant	**en deodorant**	ehn de**o**d**o**rant
insect spray (killer)	**en insekt-spray**	ehn in**seh**kt"spray"
moisturizing cream	**fugtighedscreme**	f**oo**gteehehdhskrehm
razor blades	**nogle barberblade**	n**ō̄**aler barb**eh**rbl**ō̄**dher
shampoo	**en shampoo**	ehn "shampoo"
soap	**et stykke sæbe**	eht **stew**gger **sæ**ber
sun-tan cream	**noget solcreme**	n**ō̄**aert s**oa**lkrehm
tampons	**nogle tamponer**	n**ō̄**aler tamp**o**nger
toothpaste	**en tandpasta**	ehn **tan**pasta

Clothing *Klæder*

blouse	**en bluse**	ehn bl**ō̄o**ser
bra	**en bh**	ehn be haw
boots	**et par støvler**	eht par st**ø°°**lerr
dress	**en kjole**	ehn **kyo**aler
gloves	**et par handsker**	eht par **han**sgerr
jersey	**en ulden trøje**	ehn **oo**lern tro**ier**
scarf	**et tørklæde**	eht **tørklæ**dher
shirt	**en skjorte**	ehn **skyoar**der
skirt	**en nederdel**	ehn **nehh**derdehl
shoes	**et par sko**	eht par sk**oa**
socks	**et par sokker**	eht par s**ogg**err
swimming trunks	**et par badebukser**	eht par b**ō̄**dherboogserr
swimsuit	**en badedragt**	ehn b**ō̄**dherdragt
T-shirt	**en T-shirt**	ehn "T-shirt"
tights	**et par strømpe-bukser**	eht par **strømper**boogserr
trousers	**et par bukser**	eht par **boogs**err
underpants	**et par underbukser**	eht par **oo**nerboogserr
What's it made of?	**Hvad er det lavet af?**	vadh ehr dɛ **la**verdh ah

cotton	**bomuld**	**bo**mool
denim	**denim**	"denim"
lace	**knipling**	**knip**ling
leather	**læder**	**læ**dherr
linen	**lærred**	**læ**rerdh
silk	**silke**	**see**lker
suede	**ruskind**	**roo**skin
velvet	**fløjl**	floil
wool	**uld**	ool

Grocer's *Madvarer*

I'd like some bread, please.	**Jeg vil gerne have noget brød.**	yigh veel **gehr**ner ha n**ōā**ert brødh
What sort of cheese do you have?	**Hvad slags ost har De?**	vadh slags ost har dee
half a kilo of tomatoes	**et halvt kilo tomater**	eht halt **kee**lo to**mad**err
a litre of milk	**en liter mælk**	ehn **lee**derr mælk
4 slices of ham	**4 skiver skinke**	feerer sk**ēē**verr **skeeng**er
a tin (can) of peaches	**en dåse ferskner**	ehn **daw**ser **fersg**nerr

Miscellaneous *Forskelligt*

I want to buy a/an/some...	**Jeg vil gerne have...**	yigh veel **gehr**ner ha
bottle opener	**oplukker**	**op**loogger
newspaper American/English	**en avis amerikansk/ engelsk**	ehn a**vees** amehree**kansk**/**ehng**erlsk
postcard	**et postkort**	eht **post**kort
torch	**en lommelygte**	ehn **lom**erlewgder
towel	**et håndklæde**	eht **hawn**klædher
I'd like a film for this camera.	**Jeg vil gerne have en film til dette kamera.**	yigh vil **gehr**ner ha ehn film til **dehd**er **ka**merra
black and white	**sort/hvid**	soart/veedh
colour	**farve-**	**farv**er-
Can you repair this camera?	**Kan De reparere dette kamera?**	kan dee rehpar**ēr**er **dehd**er **ka**merra

Souvenirs *Souvenirer*

ceramics	**keramik**	kehra**mēēk**
costumed doll	**en dukke i folke- dragt**	ehn **doog**ger ee **foal**kerdragt
embroidery	**broderi**	broader**ree**
glassware	**en glasting**	ehn **glas**teeng
hand-painted	**håndmalet**	**hawn**mōlert
modern	**moderne**	moa**dēr**nert
knitware	**strikvarer**	**streek**vōrerr
shag-rug	**et rya-tæppe**	eht **rēw**ōtaiber
textiles	**tekstilvarer**	tɛk**steel**vōrerr
hand-printed	**stortryk**	**stoaf**trewg

At the bank *I banken*

Where's the nearest currency exchange office/bank?	**Hvor er det nærmeste vekselkontor/bank?**	vōar ehr dɛ **nær**merster **vehk**serlkontōar /bank
I want to change some dollars/pounds.	**Jeg ønsker at veksle nogle dollars/pund.**	yigh **øns**gerr at **vehks**ler nōaler "dollars"/poon
What's the exchange rate?	**Hvad er vekselkursen?**	vadh ehr **vehks**erlkoorsern
I want to cash a traveller's cheque.	**Jeg ønsker at indløse en rejsecheck.**	yigh **øns**gerr at **in**løser ehn **righ**ser"cheque"

At the post office *Posthus*

I'd like to send this (by)...	**Jeg vil gerne sende det her...**	yigh veel **gehr**ner sehner dɛ hehr
airmail	**(med) luftpost**	(mehdh) **looft**post
express	**expres**	**ehks**prehs
A...øre stamp, please.	**Et...øres frimærke.**	eht... **ø**rers **free**mærker
What's the postage for a postcard/letter to Los Angeles?	**Hvad er portoen for et postkort/brev til Los Angeles?**	vadh ehr **por**tōaern for eht **post**kort/breh°° til "Los Angeles"
Is there any post (mail) for me?	**Er der noget post til mig?**	ehr dehr **nōa**ert post til migh

Telephoning *Telefonering*

Where's the nearest telephone booth?	**Hvor er den nærmeste telefonboks?**	vōar ehr dehn **nær**merster tehler**foan**boks
I'd like a telephone card.	**Jeg vil gerne have et telet.**	yigh veel **gehr**ner ha eht **teh**let
May I use your phone?	**Må jeg låne Deres telefon?**	maw yigh **law**ner dehrers tehler**foan**
Hello. This is...	**Hallo. Det er...**	halloa dɛ ehr
I'd like to speak to...	**Jeg vil gerne tale med...**	yigh veel **gehr**ner **tōl**er mehdh
When will he/she be back?	**Hvornår kommer han/hun tilbage?**	vor**nawr koam**err han/ hoon til**bō**er
Will you tell him/her I called? My name is...	**Vil De sige til ham/ hende, at jeg ringede? Mit navn er...**	veel dee **seeer** til ham/ **heh**ner at yigh **ring**erdher. meet nown ehr

NUMBERS, see page 28

Doctor *Læge*

Where can I find a doctor who speaks English?	**Hvor kan jeg finde en læge, der taler engelsk?**	vōar kan yigh finner ehn lǣer dehr tōlerr ehngerlsk
Where's the surgery (doctor's office)?	**Hvor har lægen konsultation?**	vōar har lǣern konsooltashon
Can I have an appointment...?	**Kan jeg komme...?**	kan yigh komer
tomorrow	**i morgen**	ee mōāern
as soon as possible	**så snart som muligt**	saw snart som mooleet

Parts of the body *Legemsdele*

arm	**armen**	armern
back	**ryggen**	rewggern
bone	**knoglen**	knoalern
ear	**øret**	ōrerdh
eye(s)	**øjet**	oierdh
face	**ansigtet**	anseegderdh
finger	**fingeren**	feengerern
foot	**foden**	fōadhern
hand	**hånden**	hawnern
head	**hovedet**	ho°°erdh
heart	**hjertet**	yehrderdh
knee	**knæet**	knǣerdh
leg	**benet**	behnerdh
lung	**lungen**	loongern
mouth	**munden**	moonern
muscle	**muskelen**	moosglern
neck	**halsen/nakken**	halsern/naggern
nose	**næsen**	nǣsern
shoulder	**skulderen**	skoolererrn
skin	**huden**	hoodhern
stomach	**maven**	mōvern
throat	**halsen**	halsern
tongue	**tungen**	toongern
I've got a/an...	**Jeg har fået...**	yigh har fāwerdh
bruise	**et blåt mærke**	eht blawt mǣrker
burn	**et brandsår**	eht bransāwr
cut	**et snitsår**	eht sneetsāwr
insect bite	**et insektbid**	eht insehktbeedh
rash	**udslæt**	oodhslǣt
sting	**et stik**	eht steek
swelling	**en hævelse**	ehn hǣverlser
wound	**et sår**	eht sāwr

EMERGENCIES, see page 30

Could you have a look at it?	**Kan De se på det?**	kan dee SE paw dE
It hurts.	**Det gør ondt.**	dE gør oant
I feel dizzy.	**Jeg er svimmel.**	yigh err **sveem**erl
I feel...	**Jeg har...**	yigh har
nauseous	**kvalme**	**kvalm**er
shivery	**kuldegysninger**	**kool**ergewsningerr
I have a temperature (fever).	**Jeg har feber.**	yigh har **fehb**err
I'm diabetic.	**Jeg har sukker-syge.**	yigh har **sooggersew**er
Can you give me a prescription for this?	**Kan jeg få en recept på det?**	kan yigh faw ehn reh**sehpt** paw dE
May I have a receipt for my health insurance?	**Må jeg få en kvit-tering til min syge-forsikring?**	maw yigh faw ehn kveet**teh**ring til meen **sew**erforsikring

👉	👈
Hvor længe har De følt Dem sådan?	How long have you been feeling like this?
Hvor gør det ondt?	Where does it hurt?
Jeg tager temperaturen/måler blodtrykket.	I'll take your temperature/ blood pressure.
Jeg vil give Dem en indsprøjtning.	I'll give you an injection.
Jeg vil have en blodprøve/ afføringsprøve/urinprøve.	I want a specimen of your blood/stools/urine.
De skal holde sengen i... dage.	You must stay in bed for... days.
De bør undersøges af en speciallæge.	I want you to see a specialist.

Can you recommend a good dentist?	**Kan De anbefale en god tandlæge?**	kan dee **an**berfoler ehn goadh **tan**lǣer
I have toothache.	**Jeg har tandpine.**	yigh har **tan**pēener
I've lost a filling.	**Jeg har tabt en plombe.**	yigh har tabt ehn **ploamb**er

Time and date *Klokken og dato*

It's...	Den er...	dehn ehr
five past one	fem minutter over et	fehm minooderr o°°er eht
ten past two	ti minutter over to	tee minooderr o°°er toa
a quarter past three	kvart over tre	kvart o°°er treh
twenty past four	tyve minutter over fire	tewver minooderr o°°er feerer
twenty-five past five	fem minutter i halvseks	fehm minooderr ee halsehks
half past six	halvsyv	halsewv
twenty-five to seven	fem minutter over halvsyv	fehm minooderr o°°er halsewv
twenty to eight	tyve minutter i otte	tewver minooderr ee oader
a quarter to nine	kvart i ni	kvart ee nee
ten to ten	ti minutter i ti	tee minooderr ee tee
five to eleven	fem minutter i elleve	fehm minooderr ee ehlver
twelve o'clock	tolv/fireogtyve	toal/feerer oa tewver
in the morning	om morgenen	om moaernern
in the afternoon	om eftermiddagen	om ehfdermiddaern
in the evening	om aftenen	om afdernern
at night	om natten	om naddern

Sunday	søndag	søndai
Monday	mandag	mandai
Tuesday	tirsdag	teersdai
Wednesday	onsdag	oansdai
Thursday	torsdag	toarsdai
Friday	fredag	frehdai
Saturday	lørdag	lørdai
January	januar	yanooar
February	februar	fehbrooar
March	marts	marts
April	april	apreel
May	maj	migh
June	juni	yoonee
July	juli	yoolee
August	august	owgoost
September	september	sehptehmberr
October	oktober	oktoaberr
November	november	noavehmberr
December	december	dehsehmberr

NUMBERS, see page 28

DANISH

yesterday/today	**i går/i dag**	ee gawr/ee dai
tomorrow	**i morgen**	ee mōāern
spring/summer	**forår/sommer**	forawr/somerr
autumn/winter	**efterår/vinter**	ehfderawr/**vin**derr

Numbers *Tal*

0	**nul**	nool
1	**en**	ehn
2	**to**	toa
3	**tre**	treh
4	**fire**	feerer
5	**fem**	fehm
6	**seks**	sehks
7	**syv**	sewv
8	**otte**	oader
9	**ni**	nee
10	**ti**	tee
11	**elleve**	ehlver
12	**tolv**	toal
13	**tretten**	trehdern
14	**fjorten**	fyoardern
15	**femten**	fehmdern
16	**seksten**	sighsdern
17	**sytten**	sewdern
18	**atten**	addern
19	**nitten**	needdern
20	**tyve**	tewver
21	**enogtyve**	ehnotewver
30	**tredive**	trehdhver
40	**fyrre**	førrer
50	**halvtreds**	haltrehs
60	**tres**	trehs
70	**halvfjerds**	halfyehrs
80	**firs**	feers
90	**halvfems**	halfehms
100	**hundrede**	hoonrerdher
1000	**tusind**	tōōsin
100,000	**hundrede tusind**	hoonrerdher tōōsin
1,000,000	**en million**	ehn meelyoan
first	**første**	førsder
second	**anden/andet**	anern/anerdh
third	**tredje**	trehdhyer
once/twice	**en gang/to gange**	ehn gang/toa ganger
a half	**en halv/et halvt**	ehn hal/eht halt

Dansk

Where do you come from? *Hvor kommer De fra?*

Canada	**Canada**	kanada
England	**England**	ehnglan
Finland	**Finland**	finlan
Great Britain	**Storbritannien**	stoarbritanyern
Ireland	**Irland**	irlan
New Zealand	**New Zealand**	"new zealand"
Norway	**Norge**	nōārer
Scotland	**Skotland**	skotlan
South Africa	**Sydafrika**	sewdhafrika
Sweden	**Sverige**	svehrēēer
United States	**USA**	oo ehs ah

Signs and notices *Skilte og opslag*

Åben	Open
Alt optaget	No vacancies
Damer	Ladies
Fare (Livsfare)	Danger (of death)
... forbudt	... forbidden
Forsigtig	Caution
Gratis adgang	Free admittance
Herrer	Gentlemen
Indgangen	Entrance
Information	Information
Ingen adgang/Adgang forbudt	No admittance
I uorden	Out of order
Kasse	Cash desk
Koldt	Cold
Ledig	Vacant
Må ikke berøres	Do not touch
Nødudgang	Emergency exit
Optaget	Occupied
Privat vej	Private road
Reserveret	Reserved
Rygning forbudt	No smoking
Skub	Push
Til leje	To let/for hire
Til salg	For sale
Træk	Pull
Udgang	Exit
Udsalg	Sale
Udsolgt	Sold out
Varmt	Hot
Vent	Please wait
Vil ikke forstyrres	Do not disturb

Emergency *Nødstilfælde*

Call the police	**Tilkald politiet**	tilkal politierdh
Get a doctor	**Tilkald læge**	tilkal lāēer
Go away	**Gå væk**	gaw vehk
HELP	**HJÆLP**	yehlp
I'm ill	**Jeg er syg**	yigh ehr sew
I'm lost	**Jeg er faret vild**	yigh ehr fōōrerdh veel
Leave me alone	**Lad mig være i fred**	ladh migh vāērer ee frehdh
LOOK OUT	**GIV AGT**	giv agt
STOP THIEF	**STOP TYVEN**	stop tewvern
My ... has been stolen.	**Min/Mit ... er ble-vet stjålet.**	meen/meet ... ehr bleh°°erdh styāwlerdh
I've lost my ...	**Jeg har tabt ...**	yigh har tabt
handbag	**min håndtaske**	meen hāwntasger
passport	**mit pas**	meet pas
wallet	**min tegnebog**	meen tighnerboa
Where can I find a doctor who speaks English?	**Hvor kan jeg finde en læge, der taler engelsk?**	vōar kan yigh finner ehn lāēer dehr tōlerr ehngerlsk

Guide to Danish pronunciation *Udtale*

Consonants

Letter	Approximate pronounciation	Symbol	Example	
b, f, l, m, n, v as in English				
c	1) before **e, i, y, œ** and **ø**, like **s** in sit	c	**citron**	seetrōan
	2) before **a, o, u** and a consonant, like **k** in kite	k	**café**	kafē
d	1) when at the end of the word after a vowel, or between a vowel and unstressed **e** or **i**, like **th** in this	dh	**med**	mɛdh
	2) as in English	d	**dale**	dōler
g	1) at the beginning of a word or syllable, like **g** in go	g	**glas**	gals
	2) at the end of a word, usually like **y** in yet; sometimes mute after **a, e, o**	y	**sige**	sēēyer

TELEPHONING, see page 24/DOCTOR, see page 25

hv	like **v** in **v**iew	v	**hvot**	v$\overline{o}$ar
j, hj	like **y** in **y**et	y	**ja**	y$\overline{æ}$
k	1) between vowels, generally like **g** in **g**o	g	**ikke**	igger
	2) otherwise like **k** in **k**ite	k	**kaffe**	kahfer
l	always as in lea**f**, never as in be**ll**	l	**vel**	vehl
ng	as in si**ng**, never as in fi**ng**er, unless **n** and **g** are in separate syllables	ng ngg	**ingen** **ingre-diens**	inge**r**n inggray-dee**ehn**ss
p	1) between vowels, generally like **b** in **b**it	b	**stoppe**	sto**bb**er
	2) otherwise like **p** in **p**ill	p	**pude**	**p**oodher
r	pronounced in the back of the throat, as in French at the beginnings of words, but otherwise often omitted	r	**rose**	r$\overline{o}$a**ss**er
s	always as in **s**ee (never as in ri**s**e)	s	**skål**	skawl
sj	usually like **sh** in **sh**eet (but may also be pronounced like the **ss y** in pa**ss y**ou)	sh	**sjælden**	she**h**lern
t	1) between vowels, generally like **d** in **d**o	d	**lytte**	lew**d**er
	2) otherwise like **t** in **t**o (at the end of a word often mute)	t	**torsk**	toarsk

Vowels

a	1) long, like **a** in car	$\overline{o}$	**klare**	kl$\overline{o}$rer
	2) short, more like **a** in cart	a	**hat**	hat
e	1) when long, as **e** in the French "l**e**s" but longer	$\overline{E}$	**flere**	fl$\overline{E}$rer
	2) short, like **i** in h**i**t	E	**fedt**	fEt
	3) short, also like **e** in m**e**t	eh	**let**	leht
	4) when unstressed, like **a** in **a**bove	er	**hjælpe**	yehlper

i	1) long, like **ee** in b**ee**	$\overline{ee}$	**ile**	$\overline{ee}$ler
	2) short, between **a** in plate and **i** in pin	i	**drikke**	**drig**ger
o	1) when long, like the **oa** sound in b**oa**t, before you bring your lips together to finish the word	$\overline{oa}$	**pol**	p$\overline{oa}$l
	2) when short, more or less the same sound	oa	**bonde**	**boa**ner
	3) when short, also like **o** in l**o**t	o	**godt**	god
u	1) when long, like **oo** in p**oo**l	$\overline{oo}$	**frue**	**fr$\overline{oo}$**er
	2) when short, like **oo** in l**oo**t	oo	**nu**	noo
y	put your tongue in the position for the **ee** of b**ee**, but round your lips as for the **oo** of p**oo**l	$\overline{ew}$ ew	**nyde** **lytte**	**n$\overline{ew}$**dher **lew**der
æ	1) when long, like **ai** in **ai**r	$\overline{æ}$	**sæbe**	**s$\overline{æ}$**ber
	2) when short, like **e** in g**e**t	eh	**ægte**	**eh**gter
ø	put your lips together to whistle but make a noise with your voice instead; can be long or short	$\overline{ø}$ ø	**frøken** **øl**	**fr$\overline{ø}$**gern øl
å	1) when long, like **aw** in s**aw**	$\overline{aw}$	**åben**	**$\overline{aw}$**bern
	2) when short, like **o** in **o**n	aw	**på**	paw

Diphthongs

av, af	like **ow** in n**ow**	ow	**hav**	how
ef, ej, ij, eg	like **igh** in s**igh**	igh	**nej**	nigh
ev	like **e** in g**e**t followed by a short **oo** sound	eh^{oo}	**levned**	**leh^{oo}**erdh
ou, ov	like **o** in g**o**t followed by a short **oo** sound	o^{oo}	**sjov**	sho^{oo}
øi, øj	like **oi** in **oi**l	oi	**øje**	oier
øv	like **ur** in h**ur**t followed by a short **oo** sound	ø	**søvnig**	**sø^{oo}**nee

Finnish

Basic expressions *Perusilmaisut*

Yes/No.	**Kyllä/Ei.**	kewllæ/ayⁱ
Please.	**Olkaa hyvä.**	oalkaa hewvæ
Thank you.	**Kiitos.**	keetoass
I beg your pardon?	**Anteeksi?**	ahntāyksi

Introductions *Esittely*

Good morning.	**(Hyvää) huomenta.**	(hewvǣ) h°°oamayntah
Good afternoon.	**(Hyvää) päivää.**	(hewvǣ) pæⁱvǣ
Good night.	**Hyvää yötä.**	hewvǣ ^{ew}urtæ
Good-bye.	**Näkemiin.**	nækaymeen
Hello/Hi!	**Hei/Terve!**	hayⁱ/tayrvay
My name is...	**Nimeni on...**	nimmayni oan
What's your name?	**Mikä teidän nimenne on?**	mikkæ tayⁱdæn nimmaynnay oan
Pleased to meet you.	**Hauska tutustua.**	hah°°skah tootoostooah
How are you?	**Mitä kuuluu?**	mittæ kōolōo
Very well, thanks. And you?	**Kiitos, hyvää. Entä sinulle?**	keetoass hewvǣ. ayntæ sinnoollay
Where do you come from?	**Mistä päin tulette?**	mistæ pæⁱn toolayttay
I'm from...	**Olen...-sta/...-lta**	oalayn...-stah/...-ltah
Australia	**Australia**	ah°°straaliah
Canada	**Kanada**	kahnahdah
Great Britain	**Iso-Britannia**	isoa-britahnniah
United States	**USA (Yhdysvallat)**	ōōæssaa (ewhdewsvahllaht)
I'm with my...	**Minulla on mukana...**	minnoollah oan mookahnah
wife	**vaimo**	vahⁱmoa
husband	**aviomies**	ahvioamⁱays
family	**perhe**	payrhay
boyfriend	**poikaystävä**	poaⁱkahewstævæ
girlfriend	**tyttöystävä**	tewtturewstævæ
I'm here on business/ vacation.	**Olen täällä liike-matkalla/lomalla.**	oalayn tǣllæ leekaymahtkahllah/loamahllah

PRONUNCIATION, see page 63/EMERGENCIES, see page 62

Questions *Kysymyksiä*

When?/How?	**Milloin?/Kuinka?**	milloa'n/koo'nkah
What?/Why?	**Mitä?/Miksi?**	mittæ/miksi
Who?	**Kuka?**	kookah
Which?	**Mikä?/Kumpi?**	mikkæ/koompi
Where is/are...?	**Missä on/ovat...?**	missæ oan/oavaht
Where can I find/get...?	**Mistä löydän...?**	mistæ lur^{ew}dæn
How far?	**Kuinka kaukana?**	koo'nkah kah^{oo}kanah
How long (time)?	**Kuinka kauan?**	koo'nkah kah^{oo}ahn
How much/many?	**Kuinka paljon/monta?**	koo'nkah pahlyoan/moantah
Can I have...?	**Saanko...?**	saahnkoa
Can you help me?	**Voitteko auttaa minua?**	voa'ttaykoa ah^{oo}ttaa minnooah
Is there/Are there...?	**Onko...?**	oankoa
There isn't/aren't...	**Ei ole...**	ay' oalay
There isn't/aren't any.	**Ei ole yhtään.**	ay' oalay ewhtæn

Do you speak...? *Puhutteko...?*

What does this/that mean?	**Mitä tämä/tuo tarkoittaa?**	mittæ tæmæ/t^{oo}oa tahrkoa'ttaa
Can you translate this for us?	**Voitteko kääntää tämän meille?**	voa'ttaykoa kæntæ tæmæn may'llay
Do you speak English?	**Puhutteko englantia?**	poohoottaykoa aynglahntiah
I don't speak (much) Finnish.	**En puhu (paljon) suomea.**	ayn poohoo (pahlyoan) s^{oo}oamayah
Could you speak more slowly?	**Voisitteko puhua hitaammin.**	voa'sittaykoa poohooah hittaammin
Could you repeat that?	**Voisitteko toistaa sen.**	voa'sittaykoa toa'staa sayn
Could you write it down, please?	**Voisitteko kirjoittaa sen.**	voa'sittaykoa keeryoa'ttaa sayn
I understand.	**Ymmärrän.**	ewmmærræn
I don't understand.	**En ymmärrä.**	ayn ewmmærræ

It's... *Se on...*

better/worse	**parempi/huonompi**	pahraympi/**h**ᵒᵒoanoampi
big/small	**suuri/pieni**	soori/p¹ayni
cheap/expensive	**halpa/kallis**	hahlpah/**kahl**liss
early/late	**aikainen/myöhäi-nen**	ah¹ka¹nayn/mᵉʷurhæ¹nayn
good/bad	**hyvä/huono**	hewvæ/**h**ᵒᵒoanoa
hot/cold	**kuuma/kylmä**	kōōmah/**kewl**mæ
near/far	**lähellä/kaukana**	læhayllæ/**kah**ᵒᵒkahnah
right/wrong	**oikea/väärä**	oa¹kaya/**væ**æræ
vacant/occupied	**vapaa/varattu**	vahpaa/**vah**rahttoo

A few more useful words *Muutama hyödyllinen sana lisää*

a little/a lot	**vähän/paljon**	væhæn/**pahl**yoan
and	**ja**	yah
behind	**-n takana/taakse**	-n **tah**kahnah/**taak**say
below	**-n alla/alle**	-n **ahl**lah/**ahl**lay
between	**-n välissä/välillä**	-n **væ**lissæ/**væl**illæ
but	**mutta**	**moot**tah
down	**alas/alhaalla**	**ahl**ahs/**ahl**haallah
downstairs	**alakerrassa**	**ahl**ahkayrrassah
from	**-n suunnasta**	-n **soon**nahstah
in	**-n sisässä/-llä**	-n **sis**sæssæ/-llæ
inside	**sisään/sisälle**	sis**sæ**n/**sis**sællay
near	**lähellä/lähelle**	**læ**hayllæ/**læ**hayllay
never	**ei koskaan**	ay¹ **koas**kaan
not	**ei**	ay¹
nothing	**ei mitään**	ay¹ **mitt**ǣn
now	**nyt**	newt
only	**vain**	**vah**¹n
or	**tai**	tah¹
outside	**ulkona/ulos**	**ool**koanah/**ool**oas
perhaps	**ehkä**	**ayh**kæ
since	**alkaen**	**ahl**kahayn
soon	**pian**	p¹ahn
then	**sitten**	**sit**tayn
through	**läpi**	**læ**pi
too (also)	**myös**	mᵉʷurss
towards	**-a kohti**	-a **koah**ti
under	**alla/alle**	**ahl**lah/**ahl**lay
up	**ylös/ylhäällä**	**ewl**urss/**ewl**hǣllæ
upstairs	**yläkerrassa**	**ewl**ækayrrahssah
very	**tosi**	**toa**si
with	**-n kanssa**	-n **kahns**sah
without	**ilman**	**il**mahn

Hotel—Accommodation *Hotelli*

I have a reservation.	Minulla on varaus.	minnoollah oan **vahra**°°s
We've reserved 2 rooms.	Olemme varanneet kaksi huonetta.	oalaymmay **vahrahnnayt kahksi** h°°oanayttah
Do you have any vacancies?	Onko teillä vapaita huoneita?	oankoa tay'llæ **vah**pah'tah h°°oanay'tah
I'd like a...	Haluaisin...	hahlooah'sin
single room	yhden hengen huoneen	ewhdayn **hayng**ayn h°°oan**ay**n
double room	kahden hengen huoneen	kahhdayn **hayng**ayn h°°oan**ay**n
with twin beds	jossa on kaksi vuodetta	yaossah oan **kahk**si v°°oadayttah
with a double bed	jossa on kaksoisvuode	yaossah oan **kahk**soa'sv°°oaday
with a bath	jossa on kylpyhuone	yaossah oan kewlpewh°°oanay
with a shower	jossa on suihku	yaossah oan **soo**'hkoo
Is there...?	Onko...	oankoa
air conditioning	ilmastointia	ilmahstoa'ntiah
a private toilet	oma wc	oamah **vay**sāy
a radio/television in the room	huoneessa radio/televisio	h°°oanayssah **rah**dioa/taylayvissioa
a sauna	saunaa	sah°°naa
What's the price...?	Mitä hinta on...?	mittæ **hin**tah oan
Is there a camp site near here?	Onko lähellä leirin-täaluetta?	oankoa læhayllæ lay'rintæahlooayttah
Can we camp here?	Voimmeko leiriytyä tässä?	voa'mmaykoa lay'riewtewæ **tæ**ssæ
We'll be staying...	Viivymme...	veevewmmay
overnight only	vain yhden yön	vah'n **ewh**dayn ew°urn
a few days	muutamia päiviä	mōōtahmiah **pæ**'viæ
a week	viikkon	**vee**koan

Decision *Päätös*

May I see the room?	Saanko nähdä huoneen?	saankoa **næh**dæ h°°oan**ay**n
That's fine. I'll take it.	Tämä on hyvä. Otan sen.	**tæ**mæ oan **hew**væ. **oa**tahn sayn
No. I don't like it.	Ei. En pidä siitä.	ay'. ayn **pi**dæ **see**ttæ
It's too...	Se on liian...	say oan **lee**ahn
dark/small	pimeä/pieni	**pim**°ey°æ/p'ayni
noisy	meluisa	**may**loo'sah

NUMBERS, see page 60

Do you have anything...?	**Onko teillä mitään...?**	oankoa **tay**ˈllæ **mitt**æn
better/bigger	**parempaa/suurempaa**	**pahr**aympaa/**sōō**raympaa
cheaper	**halvempaa**	**hahl**vaympaa
quieter	**rauhallisempaa**	rah°°**hahl**lissaympaa

Sukunimi/Etunimi	Name/First name
Kotikaupunki/Katu/Numero	Home town/Street/Number
Kansallisuus/Ammatti	Nationality/Occupation
Syntymäaika/-paikka	Date/Place of birth
Tulossa/Menossa	Coming from.../Going to...
Passin numero	Passport number
Paikka/Päivä	Place/Date
Allekirjoitus	Signature

General requirements *Yleisiä tarpeita*

The key to room..., please.	**Avain huoneeseen numero..., kiitos.**	**ah**vahˈn h°°oan**ay**ssæyn **noom**ayroa... **kee**toass
Where's the...?	**Missä on...?**	**miss**æ oan
bathroom	**kylpyhuone**	**kewl**pewh°°oanay
dining-room	**ruokasali**	r°°**oak**ahsahli
emergency exit	**hätäuloskäynti**	hætæ**ool**oaskæ°°nti
lift (elevator)	**hissi**	**hissi**
Where are the toilets?	**Missä ovat WC:t?**	**miss**æ **oav**aht **vay**sæyt
Where can I park my car?	**Minne voin pysäköidä autoni?**	**min**nay voaˈn **pew**sækurˈdæ **ah**°°toani

Checking out *Lähtö*

May I have my bill, please?	**Saisinko laskuni.**	**sah**ˈsinkoa **lahs**kooni
Can you get us a taxi?	**Voitteko hankkia meille taksin?**	voaˈ**ttay**koa **hahnk**kiah **may**ˈllay **tahk**sin
It's been a very enjoyable stay.	**Olen viihtynyt erinomaisesti.**	**oal**ayn **veeh**tewnewt **ayr**inoamahˈsaysti

Eating out *Ravintolat*

Can you recommend a good restaurant?	**Voitteko suositella hyvää ravintolaa?**	voa'sittaykoa s°°sittayllah hewvǣ rahvintoalaa
I'd like to reserve a table for 4.	**Varaisin pöydän neljälle.**	vahrahisin p⁾ewdæn nayljællay
We'll come at 8.	**Tulemme kello 8.**	toolaymmay kaylloa kahhdayksahn
I'd like breakfast/ lunch/dinner.	**Saisinko aamiaisen/lounas/päivällinen.**	sah'sinkoa aamiah'ssayn/ loa°°nahss/pæ'vællinnayn
What do you recommend?	**Mitä suosittelisitte?**	mittæ s°°oasittaylissittay
Do you have a set menu/local dishes?	**Onko teillä vakiolistaa/paikallisia erikoisuuksia?**	oankoa tay'llæ vahkioalistaa/ pah'kahllissiah ayrikoa'sōōksiah
Do you have any vegetarian dishes?	**Onko teillä kasvissyöjän annoksia?**	oankoa tay'llæ kahsvissew⁾yæn ahnnoaksiah

---

Mitä saisi olla?	What would you like?
Suosittelen tätä.	I recommend this.
Mitä haluaisitte juoda?	What would you like to drink?
Meillä ei ole...	We don't have ...
Ottaisitteko...?	Would you like ...?

Could we have a/an..., please?	**Voisimmeko saada...**	voa'simmaykoa saadah
ashtray	**tuhkakupin**	toohhkahkoopin
cup	**kupin**	koopin
fork	**haarukan**	haarookahn
glass	**lasin**	lahsin
knife	**veitsen**	vay'tsayn
napkin (serviette)	**lautasliinan**	lah°°tahsleenahn
plate	**lautasen**	lah°°tahsayn
spoon	**lusikan**	loossikkahn

TELLING THE TIME, see page 59

Suomi

May I have some …?	Voisinko saada …?	voa'sinkoa saadah
bread	leipää	lay'pǣ
butter	voita	voa'tah
lemon	sitruunaa	sitrōōnaa
oil	öljyä	urlyewæ
pepper	pippuria	pippooriah
salt	suolaa	sᵒᵒoalaa
seasoning	mausteita	mahᵒᵒstay'tah
sugar	sokeria	soakayriah
vinegar	viinietikkaa	veeniayttikkaa

Reading the menu *Ruokalistan luku*

alkupaloja	ahlkoopahloayah	appetizers
äyriäisiä	æᵉʷriæissiæ	seafood
hampurilaisia	hahmpoorillah'sia	burgers
hedelmiä	haydaylmiæ	fruit
jäätelöä	yǣtaylʳ̄ʳæ	ice cream
jälkiruokia	yælkirrᵒᵒoakiah	desserts
juomat	yᵒᵒamaht	beverages
kalaa	kahlaa	fish
kanaa	kahnaa	chicken
keittoja	kay'ttoayah	soups
lintua	lintᵒᵒah	poultry
munaruokia	moonahrᵒᵒoakiah	egg dishes
olut	oaloot	beer
pasta	pahstah	pasta
riistaa	reestaa	game
salaatteja	sahlaattayyah	salads
seisova pöytä	say'soavahpurᵉʷtæ	smörgåsbord
välipalaa	vælipahlaa	snacks
väliruokia	vælirrᵒᵒoakiah	entrees
vihanneksia	vihahnnayksiah	vegetables
viinit	veenit	wine

Breakfast *Aamiainen*

I'd like…	Saisinko…	sah'sinkoa
bread/butter	leipää/voita	lay'pǣ/voa'tah
cheese	juustoa	yᵒᵒstoaah
eggs	munia	mooniah
ham and eggs	kinkkua ja munia	kinkkooah yah mooniah
jam/rolls	hilloa/sämpylöitä	hilloah/sæampewlur'tæ

Starters (Appetizers) *Alkuruokia*

kaviaaria	**kahv**ʲ**aariah**	caviar
lohta	**loah**tah	salmon
leikkeleitä	**lay**ʲ**kkay**laytæ	cold meats
mätiä	**mæ**tiæ	roe
parsaa	**pahr**saa	asparagus
poronkielitä	**poaroank**ʲ**ay**litæ	reindeer tongue
silakoita	**sillah**koaʲtah	Baltic herring

Soups *Keittoja*

I'd like some soup	**Haluaisin jotain keittoa.**	**hah**looah'sin **yoa**tahʲn **kay**ʲttoah
häränhäntäliemi	**hæ**rænhæntælʲaymi	oxtail soup
hernekeitto	**hayr**naykayʲttoa	pea soup
kalakeitto	**kah**lahkayʲttoa	fish soup
kanakeitto	**kah**nahkayʲttoa	chicken soup
lihamuhennos	**lih**hah**moo**haynnoas	meat stew
pinaattikeitto	**pinn**aattikayʲttoa	spinach soup
kesäkeitto		summer soup; a Finnish speciality of veget-
(kayssaekayʲttoa)		ables, particularly cauliflower, stewed in milk

Fish and seafood *Kalaa ja äyriäisiä*

ankerias	**ahn**kayriahss	eel
hummeri	**hoom**mayri	lobster
kaviaari	**kah**viaari	caviar
kuha	**koo**hah	pike perch
lohi	**loa**hi	salmon
kirjolohi	**kir**yoaloahi	rainbow trout
meriantura	**may**riahntoorah	sole
punakampela	**poo**nahkahmpaylah	plaice
rapu	**rah**poo	crayfish/crawfish
sardiinit	**sahr**deenit	sardines
silakka	**sill**ahkkah	Baltic herring
silli	**sill**i	herring
taimen	**tah**ʲmayn	trout
tonnikala	**toan**nikahlah	tuna
turska	**toors**kah	cod
kalakukko		'fish loaf'; sort of loaf of dark bread with
(kahlahkookkoa)		*muikku* (sometimes perch) and pork inside and baked in the oven
silaakalaatikko		casserole made of alternating layers of potato
(sillahkkahlaatikkoa)		slices, onion and Baltic herring, with an egg and milk sauce, baked in the oven

baked	**uunissa paistettu**	ōōnissah pah'stayttoo
boiled	**keitetty**	kay'tayttew
fried/grilled	**paistettu/grillattu**	pah'stayttoo/grillahttoo
roast	**paahdettu**	paahdayttoo
underdone (rare)	**puolikypsä**	p°°oalikewpsæ
medium	**keski-kypsä**	kayski-kewpsæ
well-done	**hyvin/kypsäksi**	hewvin/kewpsæksi
	paistettu	pah'stayttoo

Meat *Liharuokia*

beef	**naudanlihaa**	nah°°dahnlihaa
chicken	**kana**	kahna
duck	**ankka**	ahnkkah
lamb	**lammasta**	lahmmahstah
pork	**porsaanlihaa**	poarsaanlihaa
veal	**vasikanlihaa**	vahsikkahnlihaa
hanhi	hahnhi	goose
hirvenliha	hirvaynlihah	elk
kaalikääryleet	(kaalikǣrewlāyt)	cabbage leaves stuffed with minced meat and rice
kalkkuna	kahlkkoonah	turkey
karhunpaisti	kahrhoonpah'sti	bear steak
(savustettu) kinkku	(sahvoostayttoo) kinkkoo	(smoked) ham
makkara	mahkkahrah	sausage
palapaisti	pahlahpah'sti	beef ragout
pekonia	paykoaniah	bacon
pihvi	pihvi	steak
piparjuuriliha	pippahyōōrilihah	boiled beef with horseradish sauce
poronkäristys	poaronkæristewss	sautéed reindeer stew
poronliha	poaroanlihah	reindeer meat

Vegetables and salads *Vihanneksia ja salaatteja*

beans	**pavut**	pahvoot
beetroot	**punajuuri**	poonahyōōri
broccoli	**parsakaali**	pahrsakaali
cabbage	**kaali**	kaali
carrots	**porkkanat**	poarkkahnaht
cauliflower	**kukkakaali**	kookkahkaali
cucumber	**kurkku**	koorkkoo
leeks	**purjo(sipuli)**	pooryoa(sippooli)

lettuce	**lehtisalaatti**	layhtisahlaatti
mushrooms	**sieni**	s'ayni
onions	**sipulit**	sippoolit
peas	**herneit**	hayrnäyt
potatoes	**perunat**	payroonaht
swede (rutabaga)	**lanttu**	lahnttoo
tomatoes	**tomaatit**	toamaattit
turnips	**nauriit**	nah°°reet

hapankaalisalaatti	hahpahnkaalisahlaatti	sauerkraut salad
lanttulaatikko	lahnttoolaatikkoa	mashed swede casserole
perunalaatikko	payroonahlaatikkoa	potato bake
pinaattiohukaiset	pinnaattioahookah'sayt	spinach pancakes
porkkanaohukaiset	poarkkahnahoa hookah'sayt	carrot pancakes
rosolli	roasoalli	beetroot salad with salt herring

Fruit *Hedelmiä*

apple	**omena**	oamaynah
banana	**banaani**	bahnaani
blackcurrants	**musta viinimarjat**	moostah veenimahryahit
cherries	**kirsikat**	keersikkaht
grapes	**viinirypäleet**	veenirewpæliäyt
grapefruit	**greippi**	gay'ppi
lemon	**sitruuna**	sitrōōnah
melon	**meloni**	mayloani
orange	**appelsiini**	ahppaylseeni
peach	**persikka**	payrsikkah
pear	**päärynä**	pǣrewnæ
plums	**luumut**	lōōmoot
raspberries	**vadelmat**	vahdaylmaht
strawberries	**mansikat**	mahnsikkaht

karpalo (**kahr**pahloa)	cranberry; also used for making *Polar* liqueur
lakka (**lahk**kah)	Arctic cloudberry; yellow berry growing on the marshes in northern Finland, regarded as the 'queen of berries' in Finland, used in desserts and for making *Lakka* liqueur
mesimarja (**mayssimahr**yah)	Arctic bramble; *Mesimarja* liqueur is well known throughout Finland
mustikka (**moos**tikkah)	bilberry, or whortleberry; one of the commonest berries in Finland, used for a variety of desserts and pastries

Desserts—Pastries *Jälkiruokia—Leivonnaisia*

jäätelö	yäætaylur	ice-cream
marengit	mahrayngit	meringues
mustikkapiirakka	moostikkahpeerahkkah	bilberry pie
omenapiirakka	oamaynahpeerahkah	apple pie
ohukaiset	oahookah'sayt	small pancakes
suklaakakku	sooklaakahkkoo	chocolate cake
vohvelit	voahvaylit	waffles

kiisseli (keessayli) — dish made of any fruit or berries and their juice, thickened with potato flour, usually served cold, often with sugar and/or cream and milk

köyhät ritarit (kur^{ew}hæt rittahrit) — 'poor knights'; bread soaked in milk and then fried, served with jam, berries and whipped cream

puolukkapuuro (p^{oo}oalookkahpooroa) — porridge made with semolina and lingonberries, served cold with milk

Drinks *Juomia*

beer	**olut**	oaloot
(hot) chocolate	**kaakao**	kaahkahoa
coffee	**kahvi**	kahhvi
black	**mustana**	moostahnah
with milk	**maidon kanssa**	mah'doan kahnssah
fruit juice	**hedelmämehu**	haydaylmæmayhoo
lemonade	**limonaatia**	limmoanaatiah
milk	**maito**	mah'to
mineral water	**mineraalivesi**	minnayraalivaysi
fizzy (carbonated)	**hiilihapollista**	heelihahpoallistah
still	**ilman hiilihappoa**	ilmahn heelihahppoah
sugar	**sokeria**	soakayriah
tea	**tee**	tāy
cup of tea	**kuppi teetä**	kooppi tāytæ
with milk/lemon	**maidon/sitruunan kanssa**	mah'doan/sitroonahn kahnssah
wine	**viini**	veeni
red/white	**puna/valko**	poonah/vahlkoa

akvaviitti (ahkvahveetti) — aquavit, flavoured with caraway seed; originally Danish, now also made in Finland

Pöytäviina (pur^{ew}tæveenah) — perhaps the most popular of the cheaper varieties of schnapps; distilled from grain

vodka (voadkah) — competing with Russian and Polish vodka, the Finns make *Dry Vodka* and, in a special bottle, *Finlandia Vodka*

Complaints Valituksia

The meat is ...	Liha on ...	lihah oan
overdone	ylikypsää	ewlikewpsæ
underdone	puolikypsää	p°°oalikewpsæ
This is too ...	Tämä on liian ...	tæmæ oan leeahn
bitter/salty/sweet	kitkerää/suolaista/ makeaa	kitkayræ/s°°alahˈstah/ mahkayaa
That's not what I ordered.	Tämä ei ole sitä, mitä tilasin.	tæmæ ayˈ oalay sittæ mittæ tillahsin
The food is cold.	Ruoka on kylmää.	r°°oakah oan kewlmæ

The bill (check) Lasku

I'd like to pay.	Haluaisin maksaa.	hahlooahˈsin mahksaa
What's this amount for?	Mihin tämä summa liittyy?	mihin tæmæ soommah leettēw
I think there's a mistake in this bill.	Tässä laskussa taitaa olla virhe.	tæssæ lahskoossah tahˈtaa oallah veerhay
Is everything included?	Sisältyykö siihen kaikki?	sissæltēwkur seehayn kahˈkki
Can I pay with this credit card?	Voinko maksaa tällä luottokortilla?	voaˈnkoa mahksaa tællæ l°°attoakoartilla
We enjoyed it, thank you.	Kiitos, pidimme siitä kovasti.	keetoass piddimmay seetæ koavahsti

Snacks—Picnic Välipalat—Piknik

Give me two of these and one of those.	Saisinko kaksi tällaista ja yhden tuollaisen.	sahˈsinkoa kahksi tællahˈstah yah ewhdayn t°°oallahˈsayn
to the left/right	vasemmalle/ oikealle	vahsaymmahllay/ oakayahllay
chips (french fries)	ranskalaisia (peru- noita)	rahnskahlahˈsiah (payroonoaˈtah)
omelet	munakkaan	mooonahkkaan
open sandwich	voileivän	voaˈlayˈvæn
with ham	kinkku	kinkkoo
with cheese	juustovoileivän	yōōstoavoaˈlayˈvæn
piece of cake	palan kakkua	pahlahn kahkkooah
soft drink (soda)	(alkoholittomia) juomia	(ahlkoahoalittoamiah) y°°oamiah

NUMBERS, see page 60

Suomi

Travelling around *Kulkuneuvot*

Plane *Lento*

Is there a flight to Ivalo?	**Onko lentoa Ivaloon?**	oankoa layntoah ivvahlōan
What time should I check in?	**Mihin aikaan minun on ilmoittauduttava?**	mihin ah¹kaahn minoon oan ilmoa¹ttah°°doottahvah
I'd like to … my reservation.	**Haluaisin … varaukseni.**	hahlooa¹siin … vahrahooksayn
cancel	**peruuttaa**	payrōōttaa
change	**muuttaa**	mōōttaa
confirm	**vahvistaa**	vahhvistaa

Train *Juna*

Where's the railway station?	**Missä on rauta-tieasema?**	missæ oan rah°°tahtiayahsaymah

SISÄÄN	ENTRANCE
ULOS	EXIT
LAITUREILLE	TO THE PLATFORMS
NEUVONTA	INFORMATION

Where is/are (the) …?	**Missä on/ovat …?**	missæ oan/oavaht
booking office	**lipunmyynti**	lippoonmēwnti
left-luggage office (baggage check)	**matkatavarasäilytys**	mahtkahtahvahrahsæilewtewss
lost property (lost and found) office	**löytötavaratoimisto**	lur⁰ʷturtahvahrahtoa¹mistoa
luggage lockers	**säilytyslokerot**	sæ¹lewtewsloakayroat
platform 7	**laituri 7**	lah¹toori say¹tsaymæn
reservations office	**paikanvaraus**	pah¹kahnvahrah°°s
ticket office	**lipputoimisto**	lippootoa¹mistoa
waiting room	**odotushuone**	oadoatoosh°°oanay
I'd like a ticket to Pori.	**Saisinko lipun Poriin.**	sah¹sinkoa lippoon poareen
single (one-way)	**menolippu**	maynoalippoon
return (round trip)	**menopaluu**	maynoapahlōō
first/second class	**ensimmäinen/toinen luokka**	aynsimmæ¹nayn/toanayn l°°oakkah

TELLING THE TIME, see page 59

Inquiries *Tiedusteluja*

How long does the journey (trip) take?	**Kuinka kauan matka kestää?**	koo¦nkah kah°°ahn mahtkah kaystǣ
When is the...train to Tampere?	**Milloin Tampereelle lähtee... juna?**	milloa¦n tampayrāȳllay lǣhtāȳ...yoonah
first	**ensimmäinen**	aynsimmǣ¦nayn
last	**viimeinen**	veemay¦nayn
next	**seuraava**	say°°raavah
What time does the train to Turku leave?	**Mihin aikaan Turkuun lähtee juna?**	mihin ah¦kaan toorkōōn lǣhtāȳ yoonah
What time does the train arrive in Mikkeli?	**Mihin aikaan juna saapuu Mikkeliin?**	mihin ah¦kaan yoonah saapōō mikkayleen
Is there a dining car/ sleeping car on the train?	**Onko junassa ravintolavaunua/ makuuvaunua?**	oankoa yoonassah rahvintoalahvah°°nooah/ mahkōōvah°°nooah
Is this the right train to Tampere?	**Onko tämä Tampereen juna?**	oankoa tǣmǣ tahmpayrāȳn yoonah
Porter!	**Kantaja!**	kahntahyah
Can you help me with my luggage?	**Voitteko auttaa kantamisessa?**	voa¦ttaykoa ah°°ttaa kahntahmisayssah

Underground (subway) *Metro*

Where's the nearest underground station?	**Missä on lähin metroasema?**	missǣ oan lǣhin maytroaahsaymah

Bus—Tram (streetcar) *Bussi—Raitiovaunu*

Which tram (streetcar) goes to the town centre?	**Mikä raitiovaunu menee kaupungin keskustaan?**	mikkǣ rah¦tioavah°°noo maynāȳ kah°°poongin kayskoostaan
How much is the fare to...?	**Mitä on maksu... -n/...-lle?**	mittǣ oan mahksoo...-n/ ...-llay
Will you tell me when to get off?	**Sanoisitteko, kun minun täytyy nousta pois?**	sahnoa¦sittaykoa koon minnoon tǣ^ew̄tēw̄ noa°°stah poais
When's the next coach (long-distance bus) to...?	**Milloin lähtee seuraava bussi...-n/ ...-lle?**	milloa¦n lǣh-tāȳ say°°raavah boossi...-n/ ...-llay

TELLING THE TIME, see page 59

Boat service *Vesiliikenne*

When does the next boat for ... leave?	**Milloin lähtee seuraava lautta ...-n/ ...-lle?**	milloa¹n **læh**tāy say°°raavah lah°°ttah ...-n/ ...-llay
How long does the crossing take?	**Kauanko ylitys kestää?**	kah°°ahnkoa ewlittews kaystāē
I'd like to take a cruise/tour of the harbour.	**Haluaisin risteilylle/satamaristeilylle.**	hahlooah¹sin **ris**tay¹lewllay/ sahtahmahristay¹lewllay

Taxi *Taksi*

Where can I get a taxi?	**Mistä voin saada taksin?**	mistæ voa¹n **saa**dah **tahk**sin
What's the fare to ...?	**... – Mitä maksaa ajaa sinne?**	mittæ **mahk**saa ahyaa **sin**nay
Take me to this address.	**Viekää minut tähän osoitteeseen.**	v¹ay**kāē** minnoot tæhæn oasoa¹ttāyssāyn
Please stop here.	**Pysähtykää tässä.**	pewssæhtewkæ tæssæ
Could you wait for me?	**Voitteko odottaa?**	voa¹ttaykoa oadoattaa
I'll be back in 10 minutes.	**Tulen takaisin kymmenessä minuutissa.**	toolayn tahkah¹sin kewmmaynayssæ minnoottissah

Car hire (rental) *Auton vuokraus*

I'd like to hire (rent) a car.	**Haluaisin vuokrata auton.**	hahlooah¹sin v°°oakrahtah ah°°toan
I'd like it for a day/a week.	**Haluaisin sen päiväksi/viikoksi.**	hahl°°ah¹sin sayn pæ¹væksi/ veekoaksi
What's the charge per day/week?	**Mikä on päivämaksu/viikkomaksu?**	mikkæ oan pæ¹væmahksoo/ veekkoamahksoo
Is mileage included?	**Kuinka suuri kilometrimäärä sisältyy hintaan?**	koo¹nkah soori killoamaytrimāēræ sissæltew hintaan
I'd like full insurance.	**Haluaisin täysvakuutuksen.**	hahlooah¹sin tæ°°svahkootooksayn

Where's the nearest filling station?	Missä on lähin bensiiniasema?	missæ oan læhin baynseeniahsaymah
Fill it up, please.	Tankki täyteen, kiitos.	tahnkki tæᵉʷtäyn keetoass
Give me... litres of petrol (gasoline).	Saanko... litraa bensiiniä.	saankoa... litraa baynseeniæ
super (premium)	korkeaoktaanista	koarkayahoaktaahnistah
regular	matalaoktaanista	mahtahlahoaktaahnistah
unleaded	lyijytöntä	lewⁱyewturntæ
diesel	dieselöljyä	dᵗaysaylurlyewæ
How do I get to...?	Miten pääsen...-n/ ...-lle?	mitayn pǣsayn...-n/ ...- llay
How far is it to... from here?	Kuinka kaukana täältä on...?	kooⁱnkah kahᵒᵒkahnah tǣltæ oan
I've had a break-down at...	Autoni meni epä-kuntoon...-n koh-dalla.	aᵒᵒtoani mayni aypækoontōan...-n koahdahllah
Can you send a mechanic?	Voitteko lähettää korjaajan?	voaittaykoa læhayttǣ koaryaayahn
Can you mend this puncture (fix this flat)?	Puhjennut rengas. Voitteko korjata tämän ?	poohyaynnoot rayngahs voaⁱttaykoa koaryahtah tæmæn

---

Road signs *Liikennemerkkejä*

AJA HITAASTI	Drive slowly
AJO SALLITTU OMALLA VASTUULLA	Drive at own risk
ALUERAJOITUS	Local speed limit
KAPEA SILTA	Narrow bridge
KELIRIKKO	Frost damage
KOKEILE JARRUJA	Test your brakes
LIUKAS TIE	Slippery road
NOPEUSRAJOITUS	Speed limit... km
PYSÄKÖINTIPAIKKA	Parking
RYHMITYSMERKKI	Get in lane
TIETYÖ	Road works

Olette väärällä tiellä.	You're on the wrong road.
Ajakaa suoraan eteenpäin.	Go straight ahead.
Se on tuolla vasemmalla/oikealla.	It's down there on the left/right.
Vastapäätä (...-a/...-ta/...-tta)	opposite
...-n takana	behind...
...-n vieressä/...-n jälkeen	next to/after...
pohjoisessa/etelässä	north/south
idässä/lännessä	east/west

Sightseeing *Kiertoajelu*

Where's the tourist office?	**Missä on matkaitoimisto?**	missæ oan ... mahtkahⁱtoaⁱmistoa
Is there an English-speaking guide?	**Onko siellä englantia puhuva opas?**	oankoa sⁱayllæ aynglahntiah poohoovah oapahss
Where is/are the ...?	**Missä on/ovat ...?**	missæ oan/oavaht
botanical gardens	**kasvitieteellinen puutarha**	kahssvitⁱaytäyllinnayn pōōtahrhah
castle	**linna**	linnah
cathedral	**tuomiokirkko**	t^{oo}amioakeerkkoa
city centre/downtown area	**keskusta**	kayskoostah
exhibition	**näyttely**	næ^{ew}ttaylew
harbour	**satama**	sahtahmah
market	**(kauppa)tori**	(kah^{oo}ppah)toari
museum	**museo**	moossayoa
shopping area	**ostoskeskus**	oastoaskayskooss
square	**tori**	toari
tower	**torni**	toarni
zoo	**eläintarha**	aylæⁱntahrhah
When does it open/close?	**Milloin se avataan/suljetaan?**	milloaⁱn say ahvahtaan/soonnoontahⁱsin
How much is the entrance fee?	**Paljonko pääsymaksu on?**	pahl^yoankoa pæsewmahksoo oan

TELLING THE TIME, see page 59/NUMBERS, see page 60

Landmarks *Maamerkkejä*

bridge	**silta**	siltah
forest	**metsä**	maytsæ
fjord	**vuono**	v°°oanoa
glacier	**jäätikkö**	yæetikkur
island	**saari**	saari
lake	**järvi**	yærvi
mountain	**vuori**	v°°oari
path	**polku**	poalkoo
river	**joki**	yoaki
sea	**meri**	mayri
waterfall	**vesiputous**	vaysipootoa°°ss

Relaxing *Yirkistyminen*

What's playing at the... Theatre?	**Mitä ... -teatterissa esitetään?**	mittæ ... tayahttayrissah ayssittaytæen
Are there any seats for tonight?	**Onko täksi illaksi paikkoja?**	oankoa tæksi illahksi pah'kkoayah
What time does it begin?	**Mihin aikaan se alkaa?**	mihin ah'kaan say ahlkaa
I'd like to reserve 2 seats for the show on Friday evening.	**Haluaisin varata 2 paikkaa perjantai-illan näytökseen.**	hahlooah'sin vahrahtah kahksi pah'kkaa payryahntai illahn næ'ᵂturksāyn
Would you like to go out with me tonight?	**Lähtisit(te)kö kanssani ulos tänä iltana?**	læhtissit(tay)kur kahnssahni ooloass tænæ iltahnah
Thank you, but I'm busy.	**Kiitos, mutta minulle ei sovi.**	keetoass moottah minnoollay ay' soavi
Is there a disco-theque in town?	**Onko tässä kau-pungissa diskoa?**	oankoa tæssæ kah°°poongissah diskoaah
Would you like to dance?	**Haluaisitteko tanssia?**	hahlooah'sittaykoa tahnssiah
Thank you, it's been a wonderful evening.	**Kiitos, on ollut ihana ilta.**	keetoass oan oalloot ihhahnah iltah

Sports *Urheilu*

Is there a football (soccer) match anywhere this Saturday?	**Onko jossain jalka-pallo-ottelua tänä lauantaina?**	oankoa yoassah'n yalkahpahlloa-**oatt**aylooah tænæ **lah°°**ahntah'nah
What's the admission charge?	**Mitä on pääsy-maksu?**	mikkæ oan p**ǣ**sew**mahk**soo
Where's the nearest golf course?	**Missä on lähin golf-rata?**	missæ oan læhin golf-**rah**tah
Where are the tennis courts?	**Missä on tennis-kenttiä?**	missæ oan taynnis**kaynt**tiæ

cycle racing	**pyöräkilpailut**	pew^{ur}ræ**kil**pah'loot
football (soccer)	**jalkapallo**	yahl**kah**pahlloa
ice hockey	**jäähockey**	y**ǣ**hoakkay'
(horse-back) riding	**ratsastus**	**raht**sahstooss
mountaineering	**vuoristokiipeily**	v°°oaristoa**kee**pay'lew
speed skating	**pikaluistelu**	pikkahloo'staylooo
ski jumping	**mäkihyppy**	mæki**hewp**pew
skiing	**hiihto**	**heeh**toa
swimming	**uinti**	oo'nti
tennis	**tennis**	taynnis

Can one swim in the lake/river?	**Voiko tuossa jär-vessä/joessa uida?**	voa'koa t°°oassah yærvayssæ/yoa^{ay}ssah oo'dah
Is there a swimming pool here?	**Onko täällä uima-allasta?**	oankoa t**ǣ**llæ oo'mahahllahstah
Is there a skating rink near here?	**Onko täällä lähellä luistinrataa?**	oankoa t**ǣ**llæ læhayllæ loo'stinrahtaa
I'd like to ski.	**Haluaisin hiihtää.**	hahlooah'sin heeht**ǣ**
downhill/cross-country skiing	**laskettelu/murto-maahiihto**	lahskayttaylooo/ moortoamaaheehtoa
I want to hire...	**Olisivatko... vuok-rattavissa?**	oalissivahtkoa... v°°oakrahttahvissah
skates	**luistimet**	loo'stimmayt
skiing equipment	**hiihtovarusteet**	heehtoava**hroost**ayt
skis	**sukset**	sooksayt
I'd like to hire a... bicycle.	**Haluaisin vuok-rata...-pyörän.**	hahlooah'sin v°°oakrahtah...-**pew**^{ur}ræn
5-gear	**vaihde**	va**ĥh**day
mountain	**maasto**	maastoa

DAYS OF THE WEEK, see page 59

Shops, stores and services *Myymälät, tavaratalot ja palvelut*

Where's the nearest...?	**Missä on lähin...?**	missæ oan læhin
baker's	**leipomo**	laypoamoa
bookshop	**kirjakauppa**	keeryuakaᵒᵒuppah
butcher's	**lihakauppa**	lihahkaᵒᵒuppah
chemist's/drugstore	**apteekki**	ahptaȳkki
dentist	**hammaslääkäri**	hahmmahslǣkæri
department store	**tavaratalo**	tahvahrahtaloa
grocer's	**sekatavarakauppa**	saykahtahvahrahkaᵒᵒuppah
hairdresser's (ladies/men)	**kampaaja/parturi**	kahmpaayah/pahrtoori
market	**tori**	toari
newsstand	**lehtikioski**	layhtikioaski
post office	**posti**	poasti
souvenir shop	**matkamuistomyymälä**	mahtkamooˈstoamēwmælæ
supermarket	**valintamyymälä**	vahlintahmēwmælæ

General expressions *Yleisiä ilmauksia*

Where's the main shopping area?	**Missä on tärkein ostosalue?**	missæ oan tærkayˈn oastoasahlooay
Do you have any...?	**Onko teillä...-a?**	oankoa tayˈllæ...-a

Voinko auttaa?	Can I help you?
Mitä saisi olla?	What would you like?
Mitä... saisi olla?	What... would you like?
väriä/muotoa/laatua	colour/shape/quality
Tällä hetkellä meillä ei ole sitä varastossa.	We're out of stock at the moment.
Tilaammeko teille sellaisen?	Shall we order it for you?
Entä muuta?/Saako olla muuta?	Anything else?
... markkaa, olkaa hyvä.	That's... marks, please.
Kassa on tuolla.	The cashier's is over there.

I'd like a . . . one.	**Minulle saisi olla . . .**	minnullay **sah¹si oall**ah
big	**iso**	**iss**oa
cheap	**halpa**	**hahl**pah
dark	**tumma**	**toom**mah
good	**hyvä**	**hew**væ
heavy	**painava**	**pah¹nah**vah
large	**suurta kokoa**	**soort**ah **koak**oah
light (weight)	**kevyt**	**kay**vewt
light (colour)	**vaalea**	**vaal**ayah
rectangular	**suorakulmainen**	s⁰⁰**oarah**koolmah¹nayn
round	**pyöreä**	p**ᵉʷ**urrayæ
small	**pieni**	p¹ayni
square	**neliskulmainen**	**nayl**iskoolmah¹nayn
sturdy	**tanakka**	**tah**nahkkah
Don't you have any-thing . . . ?	**Eikö teillä olisi jotain . . . ?**	aykur **tay¹ll**æ oalissi yoatah¹n
cheaper/better	**halvempaa/parem-paa**	**hahl**vaympaa/**pah**raympaa
larger/smaller	**suurempaa/pie-nempää**	**sōō**raympaa/p¹aynaympǣ
How much is this?	**Paljonko tämä maksaa?**	**pahl**yoankoa tæmæ **mahk**saa
Please write it down.	**Voisitteko kirjoit-taa.**	voa¹**sitt**ayko **keer**yoattaa
I don't want to spend more than . . . marks.	**En halua maksaa enempää kuin . . . markkaa.**	ayn **hah**looah **mahk**saa **ay**naympǣ koo¹n . . . **mahr**kkaa
No, I don't like it.	**Ei, en pidä siitä.**	ay¹ ayn **pidd**æ **seet**æ
I'll take it.	**Otan sen.**	**oat**ahn sayn
Do you accept credit cards?	**Hyväksytteko luot-tokortteja?**	**hew**væksewttaykur l⁰⁰**oatt**oakoa**rtt**ayyah
Can you order it for me?	**Voitteko tilata sen minulle?**	voa¹**tt**aykoa **till**ahtah sayn **min**noollay

black	**mustaa**	**moos**taa
blue	**sinistä**	**sinn**istæ
brown	**ruskeata**	**roos**kayahtah
green	**vihreää**	**vih**rayǣ
grey	**harmaata**	**hahr**maahtah
orange	**oranssia**	**oar**ahnssiah
red	**punaista**	**poo**nah¹stah
white	**valkoista**	**vahl**koa¹stah
yellow	**keltaista**	**kayl**tah¹stah
light . . .	**vaalean . . .**	**vaal**ayahn
dark . . .	**tumman . . .**	**toom**mahn

NUMBERS, see page 60

Chemist's (drugstore) *Apteekki*

aspirin	**aspiriinia**	aahspireeniah
condoms	**kondomeja**	koandoamayyah
deodorant	**deodoranttia**	dayoadoarahnttiah
insect repellent	**hyttysöljyä**	hewttewsurlyewæ
moisturizing cream	**kosteusvoidetta**	koastay°°svoaˈdayttah
razor blades	**partakoneen teriä**	pahrtahkoanayn tayriæ
shampoo	**shampoota**	shahmpoatah
soap	**saippuaa**	saˈppooaa
sun-tan cream	**aurinkovoidetta**	ah°°rinkoavoaˈdayttah
tampons	**tampooneja**	tahmpoanayyah
toothpaste	**hammastahnaa**	hahmmahstahhnaa

Clothing *Vaatetus*

blouse	**puseron**	poosayroan
boots	**saappaat**	saappaat
bra	**rintaliivit**	rintahleevit
dress	**leningin**	layningin
gloves	**hansikkaat**	hahnsikkaat
jersey	**villatakin**	villahtahkin
scarf	**huivin**	hooˈvin
shirt	**paidan**	pahˈdahn
shoes	**kengät**	kayngæt
skirt	**hameen**	hahmāyn
socks	**(nilkka)sukat**	(nilkkah)sookaht
swimming trunks	**uimahousut**	ooˈmahhoa°°soot
swimsuit	**uimapuvun**	ooˈmahpoovoon
T-shirt	**T-paidan**	tāypahˈdahn
tights	**sukkahousut**	sookkahhoa°°soot
trousers	**(pitkät) housut**	(pitkæt) hoa°°soot
Can I try it on?	**Voinko sovittaa sitä?**	voaˈnkoa soavittaa sittæ
What's it made of?	**Mistä se on tehty?**	mistæ say oan tayhtew

cotton	**puuvillaa**	poovillaa
denim	**farkkukangasta**	fahrkkookahngahstah
lace	**pitsiä**	pitsiæ
leather	**nahkaa**	nahhkaa
linen	**pellavaa**	payllahvaa
silk	**silkkiä**	silkkiæ
suede	**mokkaa**	moakkaa
velvet	**samettia**	sahmayttiah
wool	**villaa**	villaa

NUMBERS, see page 60

Grocer's *Elintarvikemyymälä*

What sort of cheese do you have?	**Mitä eri juustolaatuja teillä on?**	mittæ ayri yoostoalaatooya tay'llæ oan
half a kilo of	**puoli kiloa**	p°°oali killoah
tomatoes	**tomaatteja**	toamaattayyah
a litre of milk	**litran maitoa**	litrahn mah'toah
4 slices of ham	**4 siivua kinkkua**	naylyæ seevooah kinkkooah
a tin (can) of peaches	**tölkin persikoita**	turlkin payrsikoa'tah

Miscellaneous *Sekalaista*

I'd like a/an/some ...	**Haluaisin ...-n/-a**	hahlooah'sin ...-n/-a
battery	**pariston**	pahristoan
bottle opener	**pullonavaaja**	poolloanahvaayah
bread	**leipää**	lay'pǣ
newspaper	**sanomalehden**	sahnoamahlayhdayn
American/English	**amerikkalaisen/ englantilaisen**	ahmayrikkahlah'sayn/ aynglantillah'sen
postcard	**postikortin**	poastikoartin
torch	**taskulampun**	tahskoolahmpoon
I'd like a film for this camera.	**Haluaisin filmin tähän kameraan.**	hahlooah'sin filmin tæhæn kahmayraan
black and white	**mustavalkoista**	moostahvahlkoa'stah
colour	**värillistä**	værillistæ
Can you repair this camera?	**Voitteko korjata tämän kameran?**	voa'ttaykoa koaryahtah tæmæn kahmayrahn
I'd like a haircut, please.	**Saisinko tukanleikkuun.**	sah'sinkoa tookahnlay'kko͞on

Souvenirs *Muistoesineitä*

candles	**kyntillät**	kewnttilæt
furs	**turkikset**	toorkiksayt
glass	**lasi**	lahsi
handicrafts	**käsityöt**	kæsit^ew^urt
reindeer hide	**porontalja**	poaroantahlyah
table linen	**pöytä-ja lautasliinat**	pur^ew^tæ-yah lah°°tahsleenaht

At the bank *Pankissa*

Where's the nearest bank/currency exchange office?	**Missä on lähin pankki/valuutan-vaihtopaikka?**	missæ oan læhin **pahnkki/vahlōōtahn**vah**'htoapaihk-kah**
I want to change some dollars/pounds.	**Haluaisin vaihtaa dollareita/puntia.**	hahlooah'sin vah'htaa doallahray'tah/**poon**tiah
I want to cash a traveller's cheque.	**Haluaisin muuttaa matkasekin rahaksi.**	hahlooah'sin mōōttaa **mahtkahshay**kin rahhaahksi
What's the exchange rate?	**Mikä on vaihto-kurssi?**	mikkæ oan **vah'htoakoors**si

At the post office *Posti*

I'd like to send this (by)...	**Lähettäisin tämän...**	læhayttæisin tæmæn
airmail	**lentopostissa**	layntoapoastissah
express	**pikana**	pikkahnah
A... penni stamp, please.	**Saisinko... pennin postimerkin.**	sah'sinkoa... **pay**nnin poastimayrkin
What's the postage for a postcard to Los Angeles?	**Mitä maksaa posti-kortti Los Angele-siin?**	mittæ **mahk**saa poastikoartti loas ahngaylaysseen
Is there any post (mail) for me? My name is...	**Onko minulle pos-tia? Nimeni on...**	oankoa minnoollay poastiah. nimmayni oan

Telephoning *Puhelut*

Where's the nearest telephone booth?	**Missä on lähin puhelinkioski?**	missæ oan læhin poohaylink'oaski
May I use your phone?	**Voinko käyttää puhelintanne?**	voa'nnkoa kæ^{ew}ttæ poohaylintahnnay
Hello. This is...	**Hei. Täällä...**	hay' tællæ
I'd like to speak to...	**Onko... tavatta-vissa?**	oankoa... tahvahttahvissah
When will he/she be back?	**Milloin hän palaa?**	milloa'n hæn pahlaa
Will you tell him/her I called?	**Kertoisitteko hänelle, että soitin?**	kayrtoa'sittaykoa hænayllaay aytæ soa'tin
Would you ask him/her to call me?	**Pyytäisittekö häntä soittamaan minulle?**	pēwtæisittaykur hæntæ soa'ttahmaan minnoollay
Would you take a message, please?	**Voisinko jättää viestin?**	voa'sinkoa yættæ v'aystin

NUMBERS, see page 60

Doctor *Lääkäri*

Where can I find a doctor who speaks English?	**Mistä löytyisi lääkäri, joka puhuu englantia?**	mistæ lur**ew**tewⁱsi **læ**kæri yoakah poohōō ayng**lah**ntiah
Where's the surgery (doctor's office)?	**Missä on lääkärin vastaanotto?**	missæ oan **læ**kærin vahst**aa**no**att**oa
Can I have an appointment...?	**Voinko saada ajan...?**	voaⁱnkoah saadah ahyahn
tomorrow	**huomenna**	h**ōō**amaynnah
as soon as possible	**mahdollisimman pian**	mahh**d**oallissimmahn pⁱahn

Parts of the body *Ruumiinosia*

arm	**käsivarsi**	**kæ**sivahrsi
back	**selkä**	**sayl**kæ
bone	**luu**	l**ōō**
ear	**korva**	**koar**vah
eye(s)	**silmä(t)**	**sil**mæ(t)
face	**kasvot**	**kahs**voat
finger	**sormi**	**soar**mi
foot	**jalka**	**yahl**kah
hand	**käsi**	**kæ**si
head	**pää**	p**ææ**
heart	**sydän**	**sew**dæn
knee	**polvi**	**poal**vi
leg	**sääri**	**sææ**ri
mouth	**suu**	s**ōō**
muscle	**lihas**	**lih**hahss
nose	**nenä**	**nay**næ
shoulder	**olkapää**	**oal**kahp**ææ**
skin	**iho**	**ih**hoa
stomach (inside/ outside)	**maha/vatsa**	**mahh**ah/**vaht**sah
throat (inside/ outside)	**kurkku/kaula**	**koork**koo/kah**ōō**lah
tongue	**kieli**	kⁱ**ayl**i
I've got a/an...	**Minulle on tullut...**	**min**noollay oan **tool**loot
bruise	**mustelma**	**moos**taylmah
burn	**palohaava**	**pahl**oahaavah
cut	**(viilto)haava**	**(veel**toa)haavah
insect bite	**hyönteisen purema**	h**ew**urntaysayn **poor**aymah
rash	**ihottumaa**	**ih**hoattoomah
sting	**pistos**	**pist**oass
swelling	**turvotusta**	**toor**voatoostah
wound	**haava**	**haa**vah

DAYS OF THE WEEK, see page 59

Could you have a look at it?	**Voisitteko katsoa sitä?**	voa'sittaykoa **kaht**soah sittæ
It hurts.	**Siihen koskee.**	**see**hayn koas**kay**
I feel...	**Minulla on...**	minnoollah oan
dizzy	**huimausta**	hoo'mah°°stah
nauseous	**pahoinvointia**	pahhoa'n**voa**'ntiah
shivery	**puistatuksia**	poo'stahtooksiah
I'm diabetic.	**Minulla on soker-itauti.**	minnoollah oan soakayritah°°ti
Can you give me a prescription for this?	**Voitteko antaa minulle reseptin tätä varten?**	voa'ttaykoa **ahn**taa minnoollay **ray**sayptin tætæ **vahr**tayn
May I have a receipt for my health insurance?	**Voinko saada kui-tin sairausvakuu-tustani varten?**	voa'nkoa saadah koo'tin sah'rah°°svahkoo̅toostahni vahrtayn

---

Kuinka kauan teillä on ollut näitä oireita?	How long have you been feeling like this?
Mihin koskee?	Where does it hurt?
Mittaan lämpönne/verenpaineen.	I'll take your temperature/blood pressure.
Annan teille ruiskeen.	I'll give you an injection.
Tarvitsen teiltä veri/uloste/virtsanäytteen.	I want a specimen of your blood/stools/urine.
Teidän täytyy pysyä vuoteessa... päivää.	You must stay in bed for... days.
Annan teille lähetteen erikoislääkärille.	I want you to see a specialist.

Can you recommend a good dentist?	**Voitteko suositella hyvää hammaslää-käriä?**	voa'sittaykoa s°°asittayllah hewvvæ hahmmahsl**æ̅**kæriæ
I have toothache.	**Hammastani sär-kee.**	hahmmahstahni **sær**kay
I've lost a filling.	**Minulta on pudon-nut paikka.**	minnoolтah oan poodoannoot pah'kkah

Time and date *Kello ja päivämäärät*

It's...	Se on...	say oan
five past one	viittä yli yksi	veettæ ewli ewksi
ten past two	kymmentä yli kaksi	kewmmayntæ ewli kahksi
a quarter past three	neljännestä/vartin yli kolme	naylyænnaystæ/**vahr**tin ewli koalmay
twenty past four	kahtakymmentä yli neljä	kahhtahkewmmayntæ ewli naylyæ
twenty-five past five	viittä vaille puoli kuusi	veettæ vah¹llay p°°oali kōōssi
half past six	puoli seitsemän	p°°oali say¹tsaymæn
twenty-five to seven	kahtakymmentäviittä vaille seitsemän	kahhtahkewmmayntæveettæ vah¹llay say¹tsaymæn
twenty to eight	kahtakymmentä vaille kahdeksan	kahhtahkewmmayntæ vah¹llay kahhdayksahn
a quarter to nine	viisitoista minuuttia vaille yhdeksän	veesitoa¹stah minoottiah vah¹llay ewhhdayksæn
ten to ten	kymmentä vaille kymmenen	kewmmayntæ va¹llay kewmmaynayn
five to eleven	viittä vaille yksitoista	veettæ vah¹llay ewksitoa¹stah
twelve o'clock (noon/ midnight)	kaksitoista (keskipäivällä/ keskiyöllä)	kahksitoa¹stah (kayskipæ¹vællæ/ kayski°°urllæ)
in the morning	aamulla	aamoollah
afternoon/evening	päivällä/illalla	pæ¹vællæ/illahllah
during the day	päivällä	pæ¹vællæ
at night	yöllä	°°urllæ
yesterday/today	eilen/tänään	ay¹layn/yænāān
tomorrow	huomenna	h°°oamaynnah
spring/summer	kevät/kesä	kayvæt/kayssæ
autumn/winter	syksy/talvi	sewksew/tahlvi

Sunday	sunnuntai	soonnoontah¹
Monday	maanantai	maanahntah¹
Tuesday	tiistai	teestah¹
Wednesday	keskiviikko	kayskiveekkoa
Thursday	torstai	toarstah¹
Friday	perjantai	payryahntah¹
Saturday	lauantai	lah°°ahntah¹

NUMBERS, see page 60

January	**tammikuu**	tahmmikkōō
February	**helmikuu**	haylmikōō
March	**maaliskuu**	maalisskōō
April	**huhtikuu**	hoohtikkōō
May	**toukokuu**	toaᵒᵒkoakōō
June	**kesäkuu**	kayssækōō
July	**heinäkuu**	hayⁱnækōō
August	**elokuu**	ayloakōō
September	**syyskuu**	sēwskōō
October	**lokakuu**	loakahkōō
November	**marraskuu**	mahrrahskōō
December	**joulukuu**	yoaᵒᵒlookōō

Numbers *Luvut*

0	**nolla**	noallah
1	**yksi**	ewksi
2	**kaksi**	kahksi
3	**kolme**	koalmay
4	**neljä**	naylyæ
5	**viisi**	veessi
6	**kuusi**	kōōssi
7	**seitsemän**	sayⁱtsaymæn
8	**kahdeksan**	kahhdayksahn
9	**yhdeksän**	ewhdayksæn
10	**kymmenen**	kewmmaynayn
11	**yksitoista**	ewksitoaⁱstah
12	**kaksitoista**	kahksitoaⁱstah
13	**kolmetoista**	koalmaytoaⁱstah
14	**neljätoista**	naylyætoaⁱstah
15	**viisitoista**	veessitoaⁱstah
16	**kuusitoista**	kōōssitoaⁱstah
17	**seitsemäntoista**	sayⁱtsaymæntoaⁱstah
18	**kahdeksantoista**	kahhdayksahntoaⁱstah
19	**yhdeksäntoista**	ewhdayksæntoaⁱstah
20	**kaksikymmentä**	kahksikewmmayntæ
21	**kaksikymmentä-yksi**	kahksikewmmayntæewksi
30	**kolmekymmentä**	koalmaykewmmayntæ
40	**neljäkymmentä**	naylyækewmmayntæ
50	**viisikymmentä**	veessikewmmayntæ
60	**kuusikymmentä**	kōōssikewmmayntæ
70	**seitsemänkymmentä**	sayⁱtsaymænkewmmayntæ

| 80 | **kahdeksankym-** **mentä** | kahdayksahn**kewm**mayntæ |
| 90 | **yhdeksänkymmen-** **tä** | ewhdayksænn**kewm**mayntæ |

100/1000	**sata/tuhat**	**sah**tah/**too**haht
100,000	**satatuhatta**	**sah**tah**too**hahttah
1,000,000	**miljoona**	mil**yoo**nah

first	**ensimmäinen**	**ayn**simmæinayn
second	**toinen**	toa'nayn
third	**kolmas**	**koal**mahss

| once | **kerran** | **kay**rrahn |
| twice | **kahdesti** | **kahh**daysti |

| a half | **puolikas** | p°°oalikkahs |

Where do you come from? *Mistä tulette?*

Denmark	**Tanska**	**tahns**kah
England	**Englanti**	**ayng**lahnti
Finland	**Suomi**	s°°oami
Great Britain	**Iso-Britannia**	isoa-**brit**ahnniah
Ireland	**Irlanti**	**eer**lahnti
New Zealand	**Uusi-Seelanti**	**oo**si-**say**lahnti
Norway	**Norja**	**noar**yah
Scotland	**Skotlanti**	**skoat**lahnti
South Africa	**Etelä-Afrikka**	eatalæ-**ahf**rikkah
Sweden	**Ruotsi**	r°°oatsi

Signs and notices *Kylttejä ja varoituksia*

Alennusmyynti/Ale	Sale
Avoinna	Open
Varokaa koiraa	Beware of the dog
Ei saa koskea	Do not touch
Epäkunnossa	Out of order
Hätä/Varauloskäytävä	Emergency exit
(Hengen)vaara	Danger (of death)
Hissi	Lift
Kassa	Cash desk
...kielletty	...forbidden

Kuuma	Hot
Kylmä	Cold
Miehille	Gentlemen
Naisille	Ladies
Neuvonta	Information
Odottakaa	Please wait
Pääsy kielletty	No admittance
Sisään(käynti)	Entrance
Täynnä	No vacancies
Tupakointi kielletty	No smoking
Työnnä	Push
Ulos(käynti)	Exit
Vapaa	Vacant
Vapaa pääsy	Free admittance
Varattu	Occupied
Varattu	Reserved
Varo(kaa)	Caution
Vedä	Pull
Yksityistie	Private road

Emergency *Hätätilanne*

Call the police.	Kutsukaa poliisi.	kootsookaa poaleessi
Get a doctor.	Hakekaa lääkäri.	hahkaykaa lǣkæri
Go away!	Menkää tiehenne!	maynkǣ t'aynaynnay
HELP!	Apua!	ahpooah
I'm ill.	Olen sairas.	oalayn sah'rahs
I'm lost.	Olen eksynyt.	oalayn ayksewnewt
Leave me alone!	Jättäkää minut rauhaan!	yættækǣ minnoot rah°°haan
LOOK OUT!	Varokaa!	vahroakaa
STOP THIEF!	Ottakaa varas kiinni!	oattahkaa vahrahs keenni
My ... has been stolen.	...-ni on varastettu	-ni oan vahrahstayttoo
I've lost my ...	Olen kadotta-nut ...-ni.	oalayn kahdoattahnoot ...-ni
handbag/passport	käsilaukku/passi	kæssilah°°kkooni/pahssi
wallet	lompakko	loampahkkoa

TELEPHONING, see page 56

Guide to Finnish pronunciation *Ääntäminen*

Consonants

Letter	Approximate pronunciation	Symbol	Example	
k, m, n, p, t, v as in English				
d	as in rea**d**y, but sometimes very weak	d	**taide**	tahⁱday
g	in words of Finnish origin, only found after **n**; **ng** is pronounced as in si**ng**er	ng	**sangen**	sahngayn
h	as in **h**ot, whatever its position in the word	h	**lahti**	lahhti
j	like **y** in **y**ou	y	**ja**	yah
l	as in **l**et	l	**talo**	tahloa
r	always rolled	r	**raha**	rahhah
s	always as in **s**et (never as in pre**s**ent)	s/ss*	**sillä**	sillæ
			kiitos	keetoass

Vowels

a	like **a** in car; short or long	ah / aa	**matala** / **iltaa**	mahtahlah / iltaa
e	like **a** in late; but a pure vowel, not a diphthong; short or long	ay / ay̅	**kolme** / **teevati**	koalmay / tay̅vati
i	like **i** in p**i**n (short) or **ee** in see (long); **ir** + consonant like **i** in pin (short)	i / ee / eer	**takki** / **siitä** / **kirkko**	tahkki / seetæ / keerkoa
o	a sound between **aw** in law and **oa** in coat; short or long	oa / o̅a̅	**olla** / **kookas**	oallah / ko̅a̅kahss
u	like **oo** in pool; short or long	oo / o̅o̅	**hupsu** / **uuni**	hoopsoo / o̅o̅ni
y	like **u** in French s**u**r or **ü** in German **ü**ber; say **ee** as in see, and round your lips while still trying to pronounce **ee**; it can be short or long	ew / e̅w̅	**yksi** / **syy**	ewksi / se̅w̅

*To make doubly sure that the Finnish **s** receives its correct pronunciation as **s** in English s**e**t, and not as a z sound in pre**s**ent, we often use **ss** in our phonetic transcriptions. Similarly, we sometimes employ a double consonant after **i** to ensure this is pronounced like **i** in p**i**n, and not like **i** in k**i**te. In these cases you can quickly check with the Finnish spelling whether you should pronounce a single or a double consonant.

ä	like **a** in hat; short or long	æ	**äkkiä**	**aekkiæ**
		ǣ	**hyvää**	**hewv**ǣ
ö	like **ur** in f**ur**, but without any **r** sound, and with the lips rounded; short or long	ur	**tyttö**	tewttur
		ūr	**likööri**	**likkū**rri

N.B. The letters **b, c, f, q, š, sh, w, x, z, ž** and **å** are only found in words from foreign languages, and they are pronounced as in the language of origin.

Diphthongs

In Finnish, diphthongs occur only in the first syllable of a word, except those ending in **-i**, where they can occur anywhere. They should be pronounced as a combination of the two vowel sounds represented by the spelling. The list below shows you how the Finnish diphthongs are written in our imitated pronunciation.

The first vowel is pronounced louder in the following diphthongs:

ai = ah^i	**iu** = i^{oo}	**äi** = æ^i
au = ah^{oo}	**oi** = oa^i	**äy** = æ^{ew}
ei = ay^i	**ou** = oa^{oo}	**öi** = ur^i
eu = ay^{oo}	**ui** = oo^i	**öy** = ur^{ew}
ey = ay^{ew}	**yi** = ew^i	

The second vowel is louder in:

ie = ^{i}ay	**uo** = ^{oo}oa	**yö** = ^{ew}ur

Double letters

Remember that in Finnish *every* letter is pronounced, therefore a letter written double is pronounced long. Thus, the **kk** in ku**kk**a should be pronounced like the two **k** sounds in the words thi**ck c**oat. Similarly the **aa** in k**aa**tua should be pronouced long (like **a** in English c**a**r). These distinctions are important, not least because ku**k**a has a different meaning to ku**kk**a and k**a**tua a different meaning to k**aa**tua.

Icelandic

Basic expressions *Nokkur orð og orðasambönd*

Yes/No.	**Já/Nei.**	yow/nei
Please.	**Afsakið.**	avsakidh
Thank you.	**Takk fyrir.**	takk firir
I beg your pardon?	**Afsakið?/Geturðu endurtekið?**	avsakidh/geduru endurtekidh

Introductions *Kynningur*

Good morning/Good afternoon.	**Góðan dag/Góðan dag.**	goadhan dag/goadhan dag
Good night.	**Góða nótt.**	goadha noat
Hello/Hi.	**Halló/Hæ.**	halloa/huy
Good-bye.	**Bless.**	bless
May I introduce...?	**Má ég kynna...?**	mow yeg kinna
My name is...	**Ég heiti...**	yeg heidi
Pleased to meet you.	**Gaman/Ánægjulegt að sjá þig.**	gaman/ownuyyulekt adh sjow thig
What's your name?	**Hvað heitirðu?**	kvadh heidiru
How are you?	**Hvernig hefurðu það?**	kvernig hefuru thadh
Fine thanks. And you?	**Ég hef það ágætt en þú?**	yeg hef tha owguytt en thoo
Where do you come from?	**Hvaðan ertu?**	kvadhan ertu
I'm from...	**Ég er frá...**	yeg er frow
Australia	**Ástralíu**	owsrtaleeyu
Britain	**Bretlandi**	bretlandi
Canada	**Kanada**	kanada
Ireland	**Írlandi**	eerlandi
USA	**Bandaríkjunum**	bandareekyunum
I'm with my...	**Ég er með...**	yeg er medh
wife	**konunni minni**	konunni minni
husband	**manninum mínum**	manninum meenum
family	**fjölskyldunni**	fyu(r)lskildunni
boyfriend	**vini mínum**	vini meenum
girlfriend	**vinkonu minni**	vinkonu minni
I'm on vacation/on business.	**Ég er á ferðalagi/í viðskiptaerindum.**	yeg er ow ferdhalayi/ee vidhskiftaerindum

GUIDE TO PRONUNCIATION, see page 95/EMERGENCIES, page 94

ICELANDIC

Questions *Spurnigar*

Where?	**Hvar?**	kvar
How?	**Hvernig?**	**kver**nig
When?	**Hvenær?**	**kve**nuyr
What?	**Hvað?**	kvadh
Why?	**Hvers vegna?**	kvers **vegna**
Who?	**Hver?**	kver
Which?	**Hvaða?**	**kva**dha
Where can I get...?	**Hvar fæ ég...?**	kvar fuy yeg
How far?	**Hversu langt?**	**kver**su lowngt
How long?	**Hversu lengi?**	**kver**su lengi
How much?	**Hvað mikið?**	kvadh mikidh
May I?	**Má ég?**	mow yeg
Can I have...?	**Get ég fengið...?**	get yeg **fen**gidh
Can you help me?	**Geturðu hjálpað mér?**	**ge**duru **hyowl**padh meer
Is there/Are there...?	**Er/Eru...?**	er/eru
There isn't/aren't...	**Það er ekki/eru ekki...**	thadh er **echi**/eru **echi**
There isn't/aren't any.	**Það er enginn/eru enginn.**	thadh er **einginn**/eru **einginn**

Do you speak...? *Talarðu...?*

Do you speak English?	**Talarðu ensku?**	**ta**laru ensku
What does this mean?	**Hvað þýðir þetta?**	kvað **thee**dhir **thet**ta
Can you translate this for me?	**Geturðu þýtt þetta fyrir mig?**	**ge**duru **theett thet**ta firir mig
Could you speak more slowly?	**Gætirðu talað hægar?**	**guy**dirdhu **ta**ladh **huy**gar
Could you repeat that?	**Gætirðu endurtekið?**	**guy**dirdhu endur**te**kidh
Could you write it down, please?	**Gætirðu vinsamlega skrifað þetta niður?**	**guy**dirdhu **vin**samlega **skri**fadh **thet**ta **ni**dhur
I understand.	**Ég skil.**	yeg skil
I don't understand.	**Ég skil ekki.**	yeg skil **echi**

Íslensk

It's...	Það er...	thadh er
better/worse	**bedra/verra**	**bedra/ver**ra
big/small	**stór/lítill**	stoar/**lee**didl
cheap/expensive	**ódýrt/dýrt**	oadeert/deert
early/late	**snemma/seint**	**snem**ma/seint
good/bad	**gott/slæmt**	gott/sluymt
hot/cold	**heitt/kalt**	heitt/kalt
near/far	**nálægt/langt í burtu**	**now**luygt/langt ee **bur**tu
old/young	**gamalt/ungt**	**ga**malt/oongt
right/wrong	**rétt/rangt**	reett/rowngt
vacant/occupied	**laus/upptekin**	löis/**upp**tekin

A few useful words *Nokkur algeng orð*

a little/a lot	**lítið/mikið**	**lee**didh/**mi**kidh
and	**og**	og
behind	**á eftir**	ow **ef**tir
below	**fyrir neðan**	firir **ne**dhan
between	**á milli**	ow **mid**li
but	**en**	en
down	**niður**	**ni**dhur
downstairs	**niðri**	**ni**dhri
during	**á meðan**	ow **me**dhan
from	**frá**	frow
inside	**inni**	**in**ni
near	**nálægt**	**now**luygt
never	**aldrei**	**al**drei
not	**ekki**	**ech**i
nothing	**ekkert**	**ech**ert
now	**núna**	**noo**na
only	**aðeins**	**adh**eins
or	**eða**	**edh**a
outside	**úti**	**oo**di
perhaps	**ef til vill**	ef til vidl
since	**síðan**	**seed**han
soon	**bráðum**	**brow**dhum
then	**þá**	thow
through	**í gegnum**	ee **geg**num
too (also)	**líka**	**lee**ka
towards	**í áttina til**	ee **owt**tina til
under	**undir**	**un**dir
up	**upp**	upp
upstairs	**uppi**	**upp**i
very	**mjög**	myu(r)g
with	**með**	medh
without	**án**	own

Hotel—Accommodation *Hótel og gisting*

My name is...	**Ég heiti ...**	yeg **heidi**
I've a reservation.	**Ég á pantað herbergi.**	yeg ow **pantadh herbergi**
We've reserved two rooms.	**Við pöntuðum tvö herbergi.**	vidh **pu(r)ntudhum tvu(r) herbergi**
Here's the confirmation.	**Hér er staðfestingin.**	heer er **stadhfestingin**
Do you have any vacancies?	**Eru laus herbergi?**	eru löis **herbergi**
I'd like a... room.	**Ég vildi fá ... herbergi.**	yeg **vildi** fow **herbergi**
single	**einsmanns**	**eins**manns
double	**tveggja manna**	**tveggya manna**
with twin beds	**með tveim rúmum**	medh tveim **roomum**
with a double bed	**með hjónarúmi/ tvíbreiðu rúmi**	medh **hyoa**naroomi/ **tvee**breidhu **roomi**
with a bath	**með baði**	medh **badhi**
with a shower	**með sturtu**	medh **sturtu**
with a balcony	**með svölum**	medh **svu(r)lum**
with a view	**með útsýni**	medh **oodseeni**
Is there...?	**Er...?**	er
air conditioning	**loftræstikerfi**	**loft**ruystikervi
a private toilet	**einkasnyrting**	**einka**snirting
a radio/television in the room	**útvarp/sjónvarp í herberginu**	**oodvarp/syoan**varp ee **herberginu**
a sauna	**gufubað**	**guvu**badh
What's the price...?	**Hvað kostar ...?**	kvadh **kostar**
Is there a campsite near here?	**Er tjaldstæði í nágrenninu?**	er **tyaldstuydhi** ee **now**grenninu
Can we camp here?	**Megum við tjalda hér?**	**meigum** vidh **tyalda** hyer
We'll be staying...	**Við verðum...**	vidh **verdhum**
overnight only	**aðeins yfir nóttina**	**adheins** ivir **noattina**
a few days	**í nokkra daga**	ee **nokkra daga**
a week (at least)	**í viku (að minnsta kosti)**	ee **viku** (adh **minnsta kosti**)

Decision *Ákvörðun*

May I see the room?	**Má ég sjá herbergið?**	mow yeg syow **herbergidh**
That's fine. I'll take it.	**Það er ágætt. Ég ætla að taka það.**	thadh er **owguytt.** yeg **uyt**la adh **taka** thadh

NUMBERS, see page 92

No. I don't like it.	**Nei. Mér líkar það ekki.**	nei. myer **lee**kar thadh **e**chi
It's too...	**Það er of...**	thadh er of
cold/hot	**kalt/heitt**	kalt/heitt
dark/small	**dimmt/lítið**	dimmt/**lee**didh
noisy	**hávaðasamt**	**how**vadhasamt
Do you have anything...?	**Áttu eitthvað...?**	**owt**tu eitt**k**vadh
better/bigger	**betra/stærra**	**bed**ra/**stuy**rra
cheaper/quieter	**ódýrara/rólegra**	oa**dee**rara/**roa**legra

Nafn/Skírnarnafn	Name/First name
Heimabær/Gata/Númer	Home town/Street/Number
Þjóðerni/Starf	Nationality/Occupation
Dagsetning/Fæðingarstaður	Date/Place of birth
Koma frá.../Fara til...	Coming from.../Going to...
Vegabréfsnúmer	Passport number
Staður/Dagsetning	Place/Date
Undirskrift	Signature

General requirements *Almennar kröfur*

The key to room..., please.	**Get ég fengið lykil að herbergi...**	ged yeg **feng**idh **li**kil adh **her**bergi
Where's the...?	**Hvar er...?**	kvar er
bathroom	**baðherbergi**	**badh**herbergi
dining-room	**borðstofa**	**bordh**stova
emergency exit	**neyðarútgangur**	neidharood**gown**gur
lift (elevator)	**lyfta**	**lif**ta
Where are the toilets?	**Hvar er snyrtingin?**	kvar er **snir**tingin
Where can I park my car?	**Hvar má ég leggja bílnum?**	kvar moa yeg **leg**gya **beel**num

Checking out *Að skrá sig út*

May I have my bill, please?	**Get ég fengið reikninginn?**	get yeg **feng**idh **reik**ninginn
Can you get us a taxi?	**Geturðu ná í leigubíl fyrir okkur?**	**ge**durdhu nowdh ee **leig**ubeel **fi**rir **och**ur
It's been a very enjoyable stay.	**Dvölin hefur verið ánægjuleg.**	**dvö(r)**lin hefur **ve**ridh **own**uyyuleg

Eating out *Borðað úti*

Can you recommend a good restaurant?	**Geturðu mælt með góðum veitingastað?**	gedurdhu muylt medh goadhum **veit**ingastadh
I'd like to reserve a table for 4.	**Ég ætla að panta borð fyrir fjóra.**	yeg **uyt**la adh **pan**ta bordh firir **fyo**ara
We'll come at 8.	**Við komum klukkan átta.**	vidh **kom**um **kluk**kan **owt**ta
What do you recommend?	**Með hverju mælirðu?**	medh **kver**yu **muy**lirdhu
Do you have a set menu/local dishes?	**Eruð þið með fastan matseðil/þjóðarréttir?**	erudh thidh medh **fast**an **mat**sedhil/**thyo**adharryetti
Do you have vegetarian dishes?	**Eruð þið með grænmetisrétti?**	erudh thidh medh **gruyn**metisreetti

---

Hvað má bjóða þér?	What would you like?
Ég mæli með þessu.	I recommend this.
Hvað viltu fá að drekka?	What would you like to drink?
... er ekki til.	We don't have ...
Viltu/Má bjóða þér ...?	Would you like ...?

Could we have a/an..., please?	**Gætum við fengið...?**	**guy**dun vidh **fen**gidh
ashtray	**öskubakki**	u(r)skubachi
cup	**bolli**	**bod**li
fork	**gaffall**	**gaff**adl
glass	**glas**	glas
knife	**hnífur**	**hnee**vur
napkin (serviette)	**servétta**	**ser**vyetta
plate	**diskur**	**disk**ur
spoon	**skeið**	skeidh

TELLING THE TIME, see page 91/NUMBERS, page 92

Íslensk

May I have some...?	**Get ég fengið...?**	ged yeg **fen**gidh
bread	**brauð**	bröidh
butter	**smjör**	smyu(r)
lemon	**sítróna**	**seed**roana
oil	**olía**	oleea
pepper	**pipar**	**pi**bar
salt	**salt**	salt
seasoning	**krydd**	kridd
sugar	**sykur**	**si**gur
vinegar	**edik**	**e**dig

Reading the menu *Að lesa matseðilinn*

ábætisréttir	**ow**buytisreettir	desserts
ávextir	**ow**vekstir	fruit
bjór	bjoar	beer
borðvín	**bordh**veen	wine
borgarar	**bor**garar	burgers
drykkir	**drik**kir	drinks
eggjaréttir	**egg**yareettir	egg dishes
fiskréttir	**fisk**reettir	seafood
fiskur	**fisk**ur	fish
forréttir	**for**reettir	hors-d'œuvre
fuglakjöt	**fug**lakyu(r)d	poultry
grænmeti	**gruyn**medi	vegetables
hrísgrjón	**hrees**gryoan	rice
ís	ees	ice cream
kjöt	kyu(r)d	meat
kjúklingur	**kyook**lingur	chicken
milliréttir	**mid**liryettir	entrées
ostar	**os**dar	cheese
pastaréttir	**pas**tareettir	pasta
sætabrauð	**suyt**abröidh	pastries
salöd	**sal**u(r)d	salads
smáréttir	**smowr**yettir	snacks
súpur .	**soo**bur	soups
villibráð	**vid**librowdh	game
vín	veen	wine

Starters *Forréttir*

blönduð sjávarréttarsúpa	blu(r)ndudh syow-vareetasooba	mixed seafood soup
djúpsteiktar rækjur	dyoopsteiktar ruykyur	deep-fried prawns
graflax	gravlaks	marinated salmon
humar súpa	humarsooba	lobster soup
rækju súpa	ruykyusooba	prawn soup
reyktur lax	reiktur laks	smoked salmon
villigæsapate	vidliguysapade	wild goose paté
blandaðir sjávarréttir (blandadhir syowvareettir)		mixed seafood plate of prawn, lobster and scallop

Soups *Súpur*

I'd like some soup	Ég ætla að fá súpu.	yeg uytla adh fow soobu
humar súpa	humar sooba	lobster soup
kjötsúpa	kyu(r)tsooba	soup with meat and vegetables
rækju súpa	ruykyu sooba	shrimp soup
sjávarréttasúpa	syowvarreettarree-tarsooba	mixed seafood soup
tómatsúpa	toamadsooba	tomato soup
uxahalasúpa	uksahalasooba	oxtail soup

baked	bakað	bakadh
boiled	soðið	sodhidh
fried	steikt	steikt
grilled	glóðað	gloadhadh
roast	steikja	steikya
stewed	soðið í langan tíma	sodhidh ee langan teema
underdone (rare)	lítið steikt	leedidh steikt
medium	miðlungs steikt	midhlungs steikt
well-done	vel steikt	vel steikt

Fish and seafood *Fiskur og fiskréttir*

cod	**þorskur**	thoskur
crayfish/crawfish	**krabbadýr**	krabbadeer
haddock	**ýsa**	eesa
halibut	**lúða**	loodha
lobster	**humar**	humar
mussel	**kræklingur**	kruyklingur
plaice	**rauðspretta**	röidhspretta
prawn	**rækja**	ruykya
scallop	**hörpuskelfiskur**	hu(r)rpuskelfiskur
sole	**sólflúru**	soalflooru
trout	**silung**	silung

skata	skate; mostly eaten in December, particularly
(**ska**da)	the day before Christmas Eve.

Meat *Kjöt*

I'd like some...	**Ég ætla að fá...**	yeg **uyt**la adh fow
bacon	**beikon**	beikon
beef	**nautakjöt**	nöitakyu(r)d
chicken	**kjúklingur**	kyooklingur
duck	**önd**	u(r)nd
goose	**gæs**	guys
(smoked) ham	**(reykt) svínakjöt**	reikt sveenakyu(r)d
lamb	**lambakjöt**	lambakyu(r)d
pork	**svínakjöt**	sveenakyu(r)d
sausage	**bjúgu**	byooyu
steak	**steik**	steik
turkey	**kalkún**	kalkoon
veal	**kálfakjöt**	kowlvakyu(r)d
lambakótelettur	lambakoadelettur	lamb chop
nautalundir	nöitalundir	fillet of beef
nautasteik	nöitasteik	beef steak

hangikjöt	typical Icelandic dish of smoked lamb; the
(**han**gikyu(r)d)	traditional Christmas dish.

rjúpa	ptarmigan; game bird usually only eaten at
(**ryoo**ba)	Christmas time.

Vegetables *Grænmeti*

beans	**baunir**	böinir
beetroot	**rauðrófa**	röidhroava
broccoli	**spergilkál**	spergilkowl
cabbage	**kál**	kowl
carrots	**gulrætur**	gulruytar
cucumber	**agúrka**	agoorga
gherkin	**gúrka**	goorga
leek	**blaðlaukur**	bladhlöikur
lentils	**linsubaunir**	linsuböinir
mushroom	**sveppur**	sveppur
onion	**laukur**	löigur
peas	**baunir**	böinir
potatoes	**kartöflur**	kartu(r)blur
rice	**hrísgrjón**	hreesgryoan
swede (rutabaga)	**rófa**	roava
tomato	**tómatur**	toamadur
turnips	**næpa**	nuyba

ávaxtasalad	owvakstasalad	fruit salad
eggjakaka	eggyakaka	omelette
grænt salad	gruyn salad	green salad
gulrótarsalad	gulroadarsalad	carrot salad

| **grænmetisbaka** | vegetable pie; served warm, made from a |
| (**gruyn**metisbaka) | selection of seasonal vegetables. |

Fruit *Ávextir*

apple	**epli**	epli
banana	**banani**	banani
blackcurrants	**sólber**	soalber
grapes	**vínber**	veenber
grapefruit	**greipávöxtur**	greibowvu(r)kstur
lemon	**sítróna**	seetroana
melon	**melóna**	meloana
orange	**appelsína**	appelseena
plum	**plóma**	ploama
raspberries	**hindber**	hindber
strawberries	**jarðaber**	yardhaber

bláber	blowber	blueberries
krækiber	kruygiber	crowberries
rifsber	rivsber	redcurrants

Desserts–Pastries *Eftirréttir–Kökur*

ávaxtakaka	**ow**vakstakaka	gateau
ís	ees	ice-cream
jarðarber með rjóma	**yard**haber medh **ryoa**ma	strawberries and whipped cream
ostakaka	**osd**akaka	cheese cake
ostar	**osd**ar	mixed cheese plate
súkkulaði kaka	**soo**kuladhi **kaka**	chocolate cake

Drinks *Drykkir*

(hot) chocolate	**(heitt) súkkulaði**	**(heitt) soo**kuladhi
coffee	**kaffi**	**kaffi**
black	**svart**	svart
with milk	**með mjólk**	medh **myoalk**
fruit juice	**ávaxtadjús**	**ow**vakstadyoos
orange	**appelsínudjús**	**app**elseenudyoos
apple	**epladjús**	**ep**ladyoos
lemonade	**sítrónudrykkur**	**see**troanudrichur
mineral water	**sódavatn**	**soa**davatn
fizzy (sparkling)	**með gosi**	medh **gosi**
still	**án goss**	own **gosi**
tea	**te**	te
cup of tea	**tebolli**	**te**bodli
with milk	**með mjólk**	medh **myoalk**
iced tea	**íste**	**ees**te
beer	**bjór**	**byoar**
gin and tonic	**gin og tónik**	gin og **toa**nik
liqueur	**líkjör**	**leek**yu(r)r
port	**púrtvín**	**poort**veen
rum	**romm**	romm
sherry	**sherrí**	**syer**ree
wine	**vín**	veen
red/white	**rauðvín/hvítvín**	**röidh**veen/**kveet**veen
vodka	**vodka**	**vod**ka
brennivín	Icelandic schnapps (sometimes called 'Black Death')	
(brenniveen)		
neat (straight)	**óblandað**	**oab**landadh
on the rocks	**á ís**	ow ees
with a little water	**með smávegis af vatni**	medh **smow**vegis av **vatni**
Cheers!/To your health!	**Skál!**	skowl

Complaints and paying *Kvartanir og greiðsla*

The meat is...	**Kjötið er ...**	kyu(r)tidh er
overdone	**of steikt**	ov steikt
underdone	**of lítið steikt**	ov leedidh steikt
This is too...	**Þetta er of ...**	thetta er of
bitter/salty/sweet	**beiskur/saltur/ sætur**	beiskur/saltur/suydur
That's not what I ordered.	**Ég pantaði ekki þetta.**	yeg pantadhi ekki thetta
The food is cold.	**Maturinn er kaldur.**	madurinn er kaldur

The bill (check) *Reikninginn*

I'd like to pay.	**Ég ætla að borga.**	yeg uytla adh borga
What's this amount for?	**Fyrir hvað er þessi upphæð?**	firir hvadh er thessi upphuydh
I think you made a mistake in the bill.	**Ég held að reik- ningurinn sé ekki réttur.**	yeg held adh reiknin- gurinn see ekki reetur
Can I pay with this credit card?	**Get ég borgað með þessu greiðslu- korti?**	get yeg borgadh medh thessu greidhslukorti
Is service included?	**Er þjónustugjald innifalið?**	er thyoanustugyald innifalidh
We enjoyed it, thank you.	**Þetta var góð máltíð.**	thetta var goadh mowlteedh

Snacks—Picnic *Smáréttir—Lautarferð*

Give me two of these and one of those.	**Ég ætla að fá tvo af þessum og einn af þessu.**	yeg uytla adh fow tvo av thessum og eidn av thessu
to the left/right	**til vinstri/hægri**	til vinstri/huygri
above	**fyrir ofan**	firir ovan
below	**fyrir neðan**	firir nedhan
chips (french fries)	**franskar kartöflur**	franskar kartu(r)blur
soft drink (soda)	**gosdrykkir**	gosdrikkir
omelette	**eggjakaka**	eggyakaka
open sandwich	**brauðsneið**	bröidhsneidh
with ham	**með skinku**	medh skinku
with cheese	**með osti**	medh osdi
piece of cake	**kökusneið**	ku(r)kusneidh

NUMBERS, see page 92

Travelling around *Ferðast*

Plane *Flugvél*

Is there a flight to Reykjavík?	**Er flogið til Reykjavíkur?**	er **flog**idh til **reik**yaveekur
What time do I check in?	**Klukkan hvað á ég að skrá mig inn?**	**kluk**kna kvað ow yeg adh skrow mig inn
I'd like to... my reservation on flight no. ...	**Ég vil gjarnan... pöntun mín í flug númer...**	yeg vil **gyar**na... **pu(r)**ntun meen ee flug **noo**mer
cancel	**aflýsa**	av**lee**sa
change	**breyta**	**brei**ta
confirm	**staðfesta**	**stadh**festa

Coach (long-distance bus) *Rúta (Lanferðabíll)*

Where's the coach station?	**Hvar er brautastöðin?**	kvar er **bröi**darstu(r)dhin

---

INNGANGUR	ENTRANCE
ÚTGANGUR	EXIT
TIL BRAUTARPALLA	TO THE COACH BAYS
UPPLÝSINGAR	INFORMATION

Where is/are (the)...?	**Hvar er/eru...?**	kvar er/eru
left-luggage office (baggage check)	**farangursgeymsla (farangurssko-ðun)**	farowngursgeimsla (**fa**rowngursskodhun)
lost property (lost and found) office	**tapað fundið**	**ta**padh **fun**didh
luggage lockers	**farangursskápar**	farowngursskowbar
reservations office	**pantanir**	**pan**tanir
ticket office	**miðasala**	**mi**dhasala
waiting room	**biðstofa**	**bidh**stova
I want a ticket to Akureyri.	**Ég ætla að fá miða til Akureyrar.**	yeg **uyt**la adh fow **mi**dha til **a**kureirar
single (one-way)	**aðra leiðina**	**adh**ra **leidh**ina
return (roundtrip)	**báðar leiðir/fram og til baka**	**boadh**ar **leidh**ir/fram og til **ba**ka
first/second class	**fyrsta/annað farrými**	**fir**ta/**an**nadh **far**reemi

TELLING THE TIME, see page 91

Inquiries *Fyrirspurnir*

How long does the journey (trip) take?	Hvað tekur ferðin langan tíma?	kvadh tekur ferdhin langan teema
When is the... coach to Húsavík?	Hvenær fer... rútan til Húsavikur?	kvenuyr fer... roodan til hoosaveekur
first/next	fyrst/næst	first/nuyst
last	síðast	seedhast
What time does the coach to Akranes leave?	Hvenær fer rútan til Akraness?	kvenuyr fer roodan til akraness
What time does the coach arrive in Keflavík?	Hvenær kemur rútan til Keflavíkur?	kvenuyr kemur roodan til keblaveekur
Is this the right coach for Ísafjöður?	Er þetta rútan til Ísafjarðar?	er thetta roodan til eesafyardhar
Porter!	Burðarmaður!	burdharmadhur
Can you help me with my luggage?	Geturðu hjápað mér með farangurinn?	gedurdhu hyowlpadh mör medh farowngurinn

Bus—Tram (streetcar) *Strætó—Sporvagn*

What bus do I take to the centre?	Hvaða strætó tek ég niður í bæ?	kvadha struydoa tek eeg nidhur ee buy
How much is the fare to...?	Hvað kostar...?	kvadh kostar
Will you tell me when to get off?	Viltu segja mér hvenær ég á að fara út úr strætisvagninum?	viltu segya meer kvenuyr yeg ow adh fara oot oor struydisvagninum
When's the next coach (long-distance bus) to Geysir?	Hvenær er næsta rúta (langferðabíll) að Geysi?	kvenuyr er nuysda rooda (langferdhabeedl) adh geisi

Boat service *Báta þjónusta*

When does the next boat for... leave?	Hvenær fer næsti bátur til...?	kvenuyr fer nuysdi bowdur til
How long does the crossing take?	Hvað tekur ferðin langan tíma?	kvadh tekur ferdhin lowngan teema
I'd like to take a tour of the harbour.	Ég vildi gjarnan fara í ferð um höfnina.	yeg vildi gyarnan fara ee ferdh um hu(r)bnina

TELLING THE TIME, see page 91/NUMBERS, see page 92

Taxi *Leigubíll*

Where can I get a taxi?	**Hvar næ ég í leigu-bíl?**	kvar nuy yeg ee **lei**gubeel
How much is it to ...	**Hvað kostar til ...**	kvadh **kos**tar til
Take me to this address.	**Viltu gjöra svo vel að aka mér á þennan stað.**	**vil**tu **gyu**(r)a svo vel adh **a**ka meer ow **then**nan stadh
Please stop here.	**Viltu gjöra svo vel að stoppa hér.**	**vil**tu **gyu**(r)a svo vel adh **stop**pa heer
I'll be back in 10 minutes.	**Ég kem eftir tíu mínútur.**	yeg kem **ef**tir **tee**yu **mee**noodur

Car hire *Bíla leiga*

I'd like to hire (rent) a car.	**Ég ætla að leigja bíl.**	yeg **uyt**la adh **leig**ya beel
I'd like it for a day/week.	**Ég vildi hafa hann í einn dag/eina viku.**	yeg **vil**di **ha**fa hann ee einn dag/**ei**na **vi**ku
What's the charge per day/week?	**Hvað kostar á dag/í viku?**	kvað **kos**tar ow dag/ee **vi**ku
Is mileage included?	**Er kílómetragjald innifalið?**	er **kee**loametragyald **in**nifalidh

---

Road signs *Vegvísar*

Akið hægt	Drive slowly
Akið á eigin ábyrgð	Drive at own risk
Athugið hemlana	Test your brakes
Bílastæði	Parking
Farið á þessa akrein	Get in lane
Frost skemmdir	Frost damage
Hálir vegir (hálka)	Slippery road
Hámarkshraði ... km	Speed limit ... km
Kröpp beygja	Road works
Lausamöl	Loose gravel
Malarvegur	Dangerous bend
Þröng brú	Narrow bridge
Tímabundinn hámarkshraði	Local speed limit

Where's the nearest filling station?	**Hvar er næsta ben-sínstöð?**	kvar er **nuys**ta **ben**seenstu(r)dh
Full tank, please.	**Fylla, takk.**	**fid**la, takk

Give me... litres of petrol (gasoline).	**Ég ætla að fá...** **lítra af bensíni.**	yeg **uyt**la adh fow... **leet**ra af **ben**seeni
super (premium)/ regular/unleaded/ diesel	**súper/venjulegt/ blýlaust/dísel**	**soo**ber/**ven**yulegt/**blee**löist/ **dee**sel
Where can I park?	**Hvar má ég leggja?**	kvar moa yeg **legg**ya
How do I get to...?	**Hvernig kemst ég til...?**	**kver**nig kemst yeg til
How far is it to... from here?	**Hvað er langt héðan til...?**	kvadh er langt **hye**dhan til
I've had a breakdown at...	**Bíllinn bilaði við/í...**	**beed**linn bi**ladh**i vidh/ee
Can you send a mechanic?	**Geturðu sent viðgerðarmann?**	**ge**rurdhu sent **vidh**gerdharmann
Can you mend this puncture (fix this flat)?	**Geturðu gert við sprungið dekk?**	**ge**turdhu gert vidh **sprung**idh dekk
Please check the...	**Vinsamlega athugið...**	**vin**samlega **ath**ugidh
anti-freeze	**frostlögur**	**frost**lu(r)gur
battery	**rafgeymir**	**rav**geimir
brake fluid	**bremsuvökvi**	**brem**suvu(r)kvi
oil/coolant	**olía/kælivökvi**	**ol**eea/**kuy**livu(r)vi
wheel chains	**keðjur**	**kedh**yur
windscreen water	**gluggaúði**	**glugg**aoodhi
Would you check the tyre pressures?	**Viltu mæla loftið í dekkinu?**	**vil**tu **muy**la **loft**idh ee **dech**inu

---

You're on the wrong road.	**Þú ert ekki á réttum vegi.**
Go straight ahead.	**Haltu beint áfram.**
It's down there on the...	**Það er þarna niður til...**
left/right	**vinstri/hægri**
next to/after...	**næsta við/ fyrir aftan...**
north/south	**norður/suður**
east/west	**austur/vestur**
Turn left at the traffic lights.	**Beygðu til vinstri við umferðaljósin.**

NUMBERS, see page 92

íslensk

Sightseeing *Skoðunarferð*

Where's the tourist office?	**Hvar er ferðaskrif-stofan?**	kvar er ferdhaskrifstofan
What are the main points of interest?	**Hverjir eru athyglisverðustu staðirnir?**	**kver**ir **eru athyglisverdhustu stadhirnir**
Is there an English-speaking guide?	**Er leiðsöguma-ðurinn enskumæ-landi?**	er **leidh**su(r)gumadhurinn enskumuylandi
Where is/are the...?	**Hvar er/eru...?**	kvar er/eru
beach	**strönd**	stru(r)nd
botanical gardens	**grasagarðurinn**	**gras**agardhurinn
cathedral	**dómkirkja**	**doam**kirkya
city centre	**miðbær**	**midh**buyr
exhibition	**sýning**	**see**ning
harbour	**höbn**	hu(r)bn
market	**markaður**	**marka**dhur
museum	**safn**	safn
shops	**verslanir**	**vers**lanir
zoo	**dýragarður**	**deera**gardhur
When does it open?	**Hvenær er opnað?**	kven**uyr** er **op**nadh
When does it close?	**Hvenær er lokað?**	kven**uyr** er **lo**kadh
How much is the entrance fee?	**Hvað kostar inn?**	kvað **kos**tar inn

Landmarks *Kennileiti*

bridge	**brú**	broo
fjord	**fjörður**	**fyu(r)**dhur
geyser	**goshver**	**gosk**ver
glacier	**jökull**	**yu(r)**kudl
island	**eyja**	eiya
lake	**stöðuvatn**	**stu(r)**dhuvadn
mountain	**fjall**	fyadl
path	**stígur**	**stee**gur
river	**á**	ow
sea	**sjór**	syoar
waterfall	**foss**	foss
wood	**skógur**	**skoa**gur

TELLING THE TIME, see page 91

Entertainment *Skemmtanir*

What's showing at the cinema tonight?	**Hvað er í bíó í kvöld?**	kvadh er ee **bee**oa ee kvu(r)ld
What's playing at the theatre?	**Hvað er í leikhúsinu í kvöld?**	kvadh er ee **leik**hoosinu ee kvu(r)ld
How much are the seats?	**Hvað kostar miðinn?**	kvað **kos**tar midhinn
What time does it begin?	**Hvenær byrjar það?**	**kve**nuyr **bir**yar thadh
Are there any seats left for tonight?	**Eru einhverjir miðar til í kvöld?**	eru ein**kver**yir **mid**har til ee kvu(r)ld
I'd like to reserve 2 seats for the show on Friday evening.	**Ég ætla að láta taka frá tvo miða á föstudagssýninguna.**	yeg **uyt**la adh **low**da taka frow tvo **midh**a ow **fu(r)s**dudagsseeninguna
Would you like to go out with me tonight?	**Viltu koma út með mér í kvöld?**	**vil**tu **ko**ma oot medh myer ee kvu(r)ld
Thank you, but I'm busy.	**Takk fyrir en ég er upptekin.**	Tach **fir**ir en yeg er **upp**tekin
Is there a discotheque in town?	**Er diskótek í bænum?**	er **dis**koatek ee **buy**num
Would you like to dance?	**Viltu dansa?**	**vil**tu **dan**sa
Thank you. It's been a wonderful evening.	**Takk fyrir. Þetta var dásamlegt kvöld.**	takk **fir**ir. **thet**ta var **dow**samlegt kvu(r)ld

Sports *Íþróttir*

Is there a football (soccer) match anywhere this Saturday?	**Er fótboltaleikur einhvers staðar á laugardaginn?**	er **foad**boltaleikur **eink**vers **stadh**ar ow **löig**ardaginn
What's the admission charge?	**Hvað kostar inn?**	kvað **kos**tar inn
Where's the nearest golf course?	**Hvar er næsti golf-völlur?**	kvar er **nuys**di golfvu(r)dlur
Where are the tennis courts?	**Hvar eru tennis-vellirnir?**	kvar eru **ten**nisvedlirnir

cycle racing	hjólreiðakeppni	hjoalreidhakeppni
fishing	veiðar	veidhar
football (soccer)	fótbolti	foadbolti
ice hockey	ís hokkí	ees hochee
(horse-back) riding	útreiðar	oodreidhar
mountaineering	fjallganga	fyadlgownga
speed skating	skautahlaup	sköidahlöip
ski jumping	skíðastökk	skeedhastu(r)ch
skiing	skíðamennska	skeedhamennska
swimming	sund	sund
tennis	tennis	tennis

Can one swim in the lake/river?	Má synda í vatninu/ánni?	mow sinda ee vadninu/ownni
Is there a swimming pool here?	Er sundlaug hér?	er sundlöig hyer
Is there a skating rink near here?	Er skautasvell hér í nágrenninu?	er sköidasvedl hyer ee nágrenninu
I'd like to ski.	Mig langar á skíði.	mig lowngar ow skeedhi
downhill/cross-country skiing	brun/skíðaganga	brun/skeedhagownga
I want to hire ...	Ég ætlaði að leigja ...	yeg uytladhi adh leigya
skates	skautar	skaöidar
skiing equipment	skíðaútbúnaður	skeedhaoodboonadhur
skis	skíði	skeedhi
I'd like to hire a ... bicycle.	Ég vildi leigja ... hjól.	yeg vildi leigya hjoal
5-gear	fimm-gíra	fimm-geera
mountain	fjalla	fyadla

Shops, stores and services *Verslanir og þjónusta*

Where's the nearest...?	**Hvar er næsta...?**	kvar er nuysta
baker's	**bakarí**	bakaree
bookshop	**bókaverslun**	boakaverslun
butcher's	**kjötbúð**	kyu(r)tboodh
chemist's	**apótek**	aboatek
delicatessen	**verslun með tíl- búna rétti**	verslun medh tilboona reetti
dentist	**tannlæknir**	tannluyknir
department store	**stórmarkaður**	stoarmarkadhur
grocery	**grænmetisverslun**	gruynmetisverslun
hairdresser	**hárgreiðslustofa**	howrgreidhslustofa
liquor store	**vínbúð**	veenboodh
newsagent	**blaðasala**	bladhasala
post office	**pósthús**	poasthoos
souvenir shop	**minjagripaverslun**	minyagripaverslun
supermarket	**stórmarkaður**	stoarmarkadhur

General expressions *Almennar spurningar*

Where's the main shopping area?	**Hvar er aðal verslunarsvæðið?**	kvar er adhal verslunarsvuydhidh
Do you have any...?	**Eru til...?**	eru til

Can I help you?	**Get ég aðstoðað þig?**
What would you like?	**Hvað viltu?**
What... would you like?	**Hvað... mundirðu vilja?**
colour/shape/quality	**litur/lögun/gæði**
We're out of stock at the moment.	**Varan er uppseld í augnablikinu.**
Shall we order it for you?	**Eigum við að panta þetta fyrir þig?**
Anything else?	**Er það eitthvað annað?**
That's... crowns, please.	**Þetta kostar... krónur, takk fyrir.**
The cash desk is over there.	**Kassinn er þarna.**

big	**stór**	stoar
cheap	**ódýr**	oadeer
dark	**dimmur**	dimmur
good	**góður**	goadhur
heavy	**þungur**	thoongur
large	**stór**	stoar
light (weight)	**létt**	leett
light (colour)	**ljós**	lyoas
rectangular	**rétthyrndur**	reetthirndur
round	**kringlóttur**	kringloattur
small	**lítill**	leedidl
square	**ferhyrndur**	ferhirndur
Can you show me this/that?	**Geturðu sýnt mér þetta?**	geturdhu seent myer thetta
Do you have anything...?	**Eru til...?**	eru til
cheaper/better	**ódýrara/betra**	oadeerara/bedra
larger/smaller	**stærra/minna**	stuyrra/minna
Can I try it on?	**Má ég máta?**	mow yeg mowda
Where's the fitting room?	**Hvar er mátunarklefinn?**	kvar er mowdunarklefinn
How long will it take?	**Hvað tekur það langan tíma?**	kvadh tekur thadh lowgan teema
How much is this?	**Hvað kostar þetta?**	kvadh kostar thetta
Please write it down.	**Viltu gjöra svo vel að skrifa það niður.**	viltu gyu(r)a svo vel adh skrifa thadh nidhur
No, I don't like it.	**Nei, mér líkar það ekki.**	nei, myer leekar thadh ekki
I'll take it.	**Ég ætla að fá þetta.**	yeg uytla adh fow thetta
Do you accept credit cards?	**Tekurðu greiðslukort?**	tekurdhu greidhslukort
Can you order it for me?	**Geturðu pantað það fyrir mig?**	geturdhu pantadh thadh firir mig

black	**svart**	svart
blue	**blátt**	blowtt
brown	**brúnt**	broont
green	**grænt**	gruynt
grey	**grátt**	growtt
orange	**appelsínugult**	appelseenugult
red	**rautt**	röitt
yellow	**gult**	gult
white	**hvítt**	kveett

NUMBERS, see page 92

Chemist's (drugstore) *Apótek*

aspirin	**aspirín**	aspereen
condoms	**smokkar**	smochar
deodorant	**svitakrem**	svidakrem
insect repellent/spray	**skordýra fæla/eitur**	skordeera fuyla/eidur
moisturizing cream	**rakakrem**	ragakrem
razor blades	**rakvélablöð**	ragveelablu(r)dh
shampoo	**sjampó**	syampoa
sun-tan cream	**sól krem**	soal krem
soap	**sápa**	sowba
tampons	**tíðatappar**	teedhatappar
toothpaste	**tannkrem**	tannkrem

Clothing *Fatnaður*

blouse	**blússa**	bloossa
boots	**stígvél**	steegvyel
bra	**brjóstahaldari**	bryoastahaldari
coat	**kápa**	kowba
dress	**kjóll**	kjoadl
fur hat	**loðhattur**	lodhhattur
gloves	**hanskar**	hanskar
jersey	**prjónapeysa**	pryoanapeisa
scarf	**slæða**	sluydha
shirt	**skyrta**	skirda
shoes	**skór**	skoar
skirt	**pils**	pils
socks	**sokkar**	sokkar
swimming trunks	**sundskýla**	sundskeela
swimsuit	**sundbolur**	sundbolur
T-shirt	**stuttermabolur**	stuttermabolur
tights	**sokkabuxur**	sokkabuksur
trousers	**síðbuxur**	seedhbuksur
underpants	**undirbuxur**	undirbuksur
What's it made of?	**Úr hverju er það?**	oor kveryu er thadh

cotton	**bómull**	boamudl
denim	**denímefni**	deneemebni
lace	**blúnda**	bloonda
leather	**leður**	ledhur
linen	**lín**	leen
silk	**silki**	silki
suede	**rúskinn**	rooskinn
velvet	**flauel**	flöiel
wool	**ull**	udl

Grocer's *Grænmetisverslun*

What sort of cheese do you have?	**Hvaða ostategundir eru til?**	kvadha osdategundir eru til
half a kilo of apples	**hálft kíló af epplum**	howlft keeloa af epplum
a litre of milk	**einn mjólkurlíter**	einn myoalkurleeter
4 slices of ham	**fjórar sneiðar af skinku**	fyoarar sneidhar av skinku
a tin (can) of peaches	**ein dós af ferskjum**	ein doas av ferskyum

Miscellaneous *Almennar*

I want to buy...	**Ég ætla að fá...**	yeg uytla adh fow
batteries	**rafhlöður**	rafhlu(r)dhur
film	**filmu**	filmu
newspaper	**dagblað**	dagthladh
English/American	**enskt/bandarískt**	enskt/bandareest
torch	**blys**	blis
I'd like... film for this camera.	**Ég ætla að fá... filmu í þessa myndavél.**	yeg uytla adh fow filmu ee thessa mindavyel
black and white	**svart hvíta**	svart kveeda
colour	**lit**	lit
I'd like a haircut.	**Ég ætla að láta klippa mig.**	yeg uytla adh lowta klippa mig

Souvenirs *Minjagripir*

askur
(asgur)
carved wooden dinner bowl that Icelanders traditionally used as plates.

keramik
(keramik)
ceramics; bowls, vases, cups and plates made by Icelandic artists.

lopapeysa
(lobapeisa)
lopi sweater; an ordinary handknitted sweater made of Icelandic wool.

sauðskinsskór
(söidhskinsskoar)
shoes made of sheep skin; small imitations of the kind of shoes traditionally worn in Iceland.

silfurskartgripir
(silvurskartgribir)
silver jewellery; made to old designs by Icelandic silversmiths.

þjóðbúningsdúkka
(thyoadh-booningsdoocha)
national doll; dolls of different sizes dressed in various costumes. The costumes depend on social status and period in history.

Þórshamar
(thoarshamar)
Thorshammer; a small statue of the Nordic God Thor holding his hammer.

At the bank *Í bankanum*

Where's the nearest bank?	**Hvar er næsti banki?**	kvar er **nuysti bown**ki
I want to change some dollars/pounds into krona.	**Ég ætla að skipta nokkrum dollurum/ pundum í krónur.**	yeg **uytla** adh **skipta nokkrum dollurum/ pundum** ee **kroanur**
What's the exchange rate?	**Hvað er gengið?**	kvadh er **gengið**

At the post office *Á pósthúsinu*

I want to send this by...	**Ég ætla að senda þetta með...**	yeg **uytla** adh **senda thetta** medh
airmail	**flugpósti**	**flugpoasti**
express	**hraðpósti**	**hradhpoasti**
registered mail	**ábyrgðarpósti**	owbirgdharpoasti
I want... -krona stamps.	**Ég ætla að fá... króna frímerki.**	yeg **uytla** adh fow... **kroana freemerki**
What's the postage for a letter/postcard to the United States?	**Hvað er póstburðargjald fyrir bréf/ póstkort til Banda- ríkjanna?**	kvadh er **poastburdhaegyald** firir breef/**poastkort** til **bandareekyanna**
Is there any mail for me? My name is...	**Er einhver póstur til mín? Ég heiti...**	er **einkveer poas**tur til meen. yeg **heiti**...
Can I send a telegram/fax?	**Get ég sent skeyti/ símbréf?**	get yeg sent **skeidi/ seembreef**

Telephoning *Sími*

Where's the nearest public phone?	**Hvar er næsti símaklefi?**	kvar er **nuysdi seemaklevi**?
May I use your phone?	**Má ég hringja?**	mow yeg **hringya**
Hello. This is... speaking.	**Halló. Þetta er... sem talar.**	halloa. **thetta** er... sem talar
I want to speak to...	**Get ég fengið að tala við...**	get yeg **fengidh** adh tala vidh
When will he/she be back?	**Hvenær kemur hann/hún aftur?**	**kvenuyr kemur hann/hoon aftur**
Will you tell him/her that I called?	**Viltu segja honum/ henni að ég hringdi?**	**viltu segya honum/henni** adh yeg **hreengdi**
Would you take a message, please?	**Viltu gjöra svo vel að taka skilaboð?**	**viltu gyu(r)a svo vel** adh **taka skilabodh**

NUMBERS, see page 92

Doctor *Læknir*

Where can I find a doctor who speaks English?	**Hvar er ensku-mælandi læknir?**	kvar er **ensk**umuylandi **luyk**nir
Where's the surgery (doctor's office)?	**Hvar er lækna-stofan?**	kvar er **luyk**nastovan
Can I have an appointment…?	**Get ég fengið tíma…?**	get yeg **fengidh teema**
tomorrow	**á morgun**	ow **morgun**
as soon as possible	**eins fljótt og mögulegt er**	eins flyoatt og **mu(r)gulegt er**

Parts of the body *Líkamshlutar*

arm	**handleggur**	**hand**leggur
back	**bak**	bak
bone	**bein**	bein
ear	**eyra**	**eir**a
eye	**auga**	**öig**a
face	**andlit**	**andl**id
finger	**fingur**	**fing**ur
foot	**fótur**	**foa**dur
hand	**hönd**	hu(r)nd
head	**höfuð**	**hu(r)**vudh
heart	**hjarta**	**hyart**a
knee	**hné**	hnye
leg	**fótleggur**	**foad**leggur
lung	**lunga**	**loong**a
mouth	**munnur**	**munn**ur
muscle	**vöðvi**	**vu(r)**dhvi
nerve	**taug**	töig
nose	**nef**	nev
shoulder	**öxl**	u(r)ksl
skin	**húð**	hoodh
stomach	**magi**	**may**i
throat	**háls**	howls
tongue	**tunga**	**toong**a
I've got a/an…	**Ég er með…**	yeg er medh
bruise	**mar**	mar
burn	**brunasár**	**brin**asowr
cut	**skurð**	skurdh
insect bite	**skordýrabit**	**skord**eerabid
rash	**útbrot**	**ood**brod
sting	**sár eftir stungu**	aowr **ev**tir **stoon**gu
swelling	**bólga**	**boal**ga
wound	**sár**	sowr

Could you have a look at it?	**Gætirðu litið á það?**	guydirdhu litidh ow thadh
It hurts.	**Ég finn til.**	yeg finn til
I feel...	**Mér líður...**	myer **leedhur**
dizzy	**Mig svimar**	mig **svimar**
nauseous	**Mér er flögurt**	myeer er **flu(r)gurt**
shivery	**Ég er með skjálfta**	yeg er medh **skyowlfda**
I'm diabetic.	**Ég er sykursjúkur.**	yeg er **sigursyoogur**
Can you give me a prescription for this?	**Get ég fengið lyfseðil fyrir þetta?**	ged yeg **fengið lifsedhil firir thetta**
May I have a receipt for my health insurance?	**Get ég fengið kvittun fyrir sjúkratryggingunni?**	ged yeg **fengidh knittun** firir **syookratriggingunni**

How long have you been feeling like this?	**Hvað lengi hefur þér liðið svona?**
Where does it hurt?	**Hvar finnurðu til?**
I'll take your temperature/blood pressure.	**Ég ætla að mæla þig/blóðþrýstinginn.**
I'll give you an injection.	**Ég ætla að sprauta þig.**
I want a specimen of your blood/stools/urine.	**Ég þarf að fá blóð/hægðar/þvagsýni**
You must stay in bed for... days.	**Þú verður að vera í rúminu í... daga.**
I want you to see a specialist.	**Ég vil gjarnan hitta sérfræðing.**

Can you recommend a good dentist?	**Geturðu mælt með góðum tannlækni?**	gedurdhu muylt medh goadhum **tannluykni**
I have toothache.	**Ég er með tannpínu.**	yeg er medh **tannpeenu**
I've lost a filling.	**Það hefur dottið fylling úr tönn.**	thadh hevur **dottidh filling** oor tu(r)nn

Time and date *Klukkan og dagsetning*

It's...	Hún er...	hoon er
five past one	**fimm mínútur yfir eitt**	fimm **mee**noodur ivir eitt
ten past two	**tíu mínútur yfir tvö**	teeyu **mee**noodur ivir tvu(r)
a quarter past three	**korter yfir þrjú**	korter ivir thryoo
twenty past four	**tuttugu mínútur yfir fjórir**	tuttugu **mee**noodur ivir fjórir
twenty-five past five	**tuttugu og fimm mínútur yfir fimm**	tuttugu og fimm **mee**noodur ivir fimm
half past seven	**hálf átta**	howlf **owt**ta
twenty to eight	**tuttugu mímútur í átta**	tuttugu **mee**noodur ee **owt**ta
twenty-five to nine	**tuttugu og fimm mínútur í níu**	tuttugu of fimm **mee**noodur ee neeyu
ten to ten	**tíu mínútur í tíu**	teeyu **mee**noodur ee teeyu
five to eleven	**fimm mínútur í ellefu**	fimm **mee**noodur ee **el**levu
noon/midnight	**hádegi/miðnætti**	**how**degi/**midh**nuytti
in the morning	**um morgun**	um **mor**gun
during the day	**um daginn**	um **dag**inn
in the evening	**um kvöldið**	um **kvu(r)l**didh

Sunday	**sunnudagur**	**sun**nudagur
Monday	**mánudagur**	**mown**udagur
Tuesday	**þriðjudagur**	**thridh**yudagur
Wednesday	**miðvikudagur**	**midh**vikudagur
Thursday	**fimmtudagur**	**fimm**tudagur
Friday	**föstudagur**	**fu(r)**studagur
Saturday	**laugardagur**	**löi**gardagur
January	**janúar**	**yan**ooar
February	**febrúar**	**feb**rooar
March	**mars**	mars
April	**apríl**	**ap**reel
May	**maí**	**ma**ee
June	**júní**	**yoo**nee
July	**júlí**	**yoo**lee
August	**ágúst**	**owg**oost
September	**september**	**sept**ember
October	**október**	**ok**toaber
November	**nóvember**	**noa**vember
December	**desember**	**de**sember

NUMBERS, see page 92

ICELANDIC

Íslensk

at night	**um nóttina/á nót-tinni**	um **noatt**ina/ow **noatt**inni
yesterday	**í gær**	ee gyuyr
today	**í dag**	ee dag
tomorrow	**á morgun**	ow **mor**gun
spring	**vor**	vor
summer	**sumar**	**su**mar
autumn (fall)	**haust**	höist
winter	**vetur**	**ve**tur

Numbers *Tölur*

0	**núll**	nooll
1	**einn**	eidn
2	**tveir**	tveir
3	**þrír**	threer
4	**fjórir**	**fyoa**rir
5	**fimm**	fimm
6	**sex**	seks
7	**sjö**	syu(r)
8	**átta**	**owt**ta
9	**níu**	**nee**yu
10	**tíu**	**tee**yu
11	**ellefu**	**edle**vu
12	**tólf**	toalf
13	**þrettán**	**thret**town
14	**fjórtán**	**fyoar**town
15	**fimmtán**	**fimm**town
16	**sextán**	**seks**town
17	**sautján**	**söid**yown
18	**átján**	**owd**yown
19	**nítján**	**need**yown
20	**tuttugu**	**tuttu**gu
30	**þrjátíu**	**thryow**teeyu
40	**fjörtíu**	**fyu(r)**teeyu
50	**fimmtíu**	**fimm**teeyu
60	**sextíu**	**seks**teeyu
70	**sjötíu**	**syu(r)**teeyu
80	**áttatíu**	**owt**tateeyu
90	**níutíu**	**nee**teeyu
100	**hundrað**	**hun**dradh
101	**hundrað og einn**	**hun**dradh og eidn
200	**tvöhundruð**	**tvu(r)**hundrudh
500	**fimmhundruð**	**fimm**hundrudh
1,000	**þúsund**	**thoo**sund
100,000	**hundrað þúsund**	**hun**dradh **thoo**sund
1,000,000	**milljón**	**mill**yoan

first	**fyrsti**	**firsti**
second	**annar**	**annar**
third	**þriðji**	**thridhyi**
once	**einu sinni**	**einu sinni**
twice	**tvisvar**	**tvisvar**
three times	**þrisvar**	**thrisvar**
a half	**hálfur**	**howlvur**
a quarter	**fjórðungur**	**fyoardhungur**
one third	**einn þriðji**	**eidn thri-dhyi**

Where do you come from? *Hvaðan kemurðu?*

Australia	**Ástralíu**	**ows**traleeyu
Canada	**Kanada**	**kanada**
Denmark	**Danmörku**	**dan**mu(r)rku
England	**Englandi**	**eng**landi
Finland	**Finnlandi**	**finn**landi
Great Britain	**Stóra Bretlandi**	stoara **bred**landi
Iceland	**Íslandi**	**ees**landi
Ireland	**Írlandi**	**eer**landi
New Zealand	**Nyja Sjálandi**	neeya **syow**landi
Norway	**Noregi**	**nor**eigi
Scotland	**Skotlandi**	**skod**landi
South Africa	**Suður Afríku**	sidhur **afree**ku
Sweden	**Svíþjóð**	**svee**thyosdh
USA	**Bandaríkjunum**	**ban**dareekyunum

Signs and notices *Merki og tilkynningar*

Aðgangur bannaður	No admittance
Aðgangur ókeypis	Free admittance
... bannað	... forbidden
Bilað	Out of order
Draga	Pull
Einkavegur	Private road
Ekkert laust	No vacancies
Frátekið	Reserved
Gjaldkeri	Cash desk
Hætta (lífshætta)	Danger (of death)
Heitt	Hot
Herrasnyrting	Gentlemen (toilets)

Inngangur	Entrance
Kalt	Cold
Kvennasnyrting	Ladies (toilets)
Laust	Vacant
Lifta	Lift
Neyðarútgangur	Emergency exit
Opið	Open
Reykingar bannaðar	No smoking
Snertið ekki	Do not touch
Upplýsingar	Information
Upptekið	Occupied
Útgangur	Exit
Útsala	Sale
Varist hundinn	Beware of the dog
Varúð	Caution
Vinsamlega bíðið	Please wait
Yta	Push

Emergency *Neyðarástand*

Call the police	**Hringið í lögregluna**	hringidh ee lu(r)gregluna
Get a doctor	**Náið í lækni**	noaidh ee luykni
Go away	**Farið í burtu**	faridh ee burtu
HELP	**Hjálp**	hyowlp
I'm ill	**Ég er lasin**	yeg er lasin
I'm lost	**Ég er villtur (villt)**	yeg er viltur (vilt)
Leave me alone	**Látið mig í friði**	lowdidh mig ee fridhi
LOOK OUT	**Varúð**	varoodh
STOP THIEF	**Stöðvið þjófinn**	stu(r)dhvidh thyoavinn
My ... have been stolen.	**... minni hefur verið stolið.**	minni hefur veridh stolidh
I've lost my ...	**Ég hef týnt ... minni.**	yeg hef teent ... minni
handbag	**töskunni**	tu(r)skunni
passport	**vegabréfinu**	vagabreevinu
luggage	**farangrinum**	farowngrinum
wallet	**veskinu**	veskinu

TELEPHONING, see page 88/DOCTOR, see page 89

Guide to Icelandic pronunciation

In Icelandic the first syllable is always stressed. There is hardly any intonation, so there is no difference between the intonation of questions and statements.

Consonants

Letter	Approximate pronunciation	Symbol	Example	
b,d,f, g,h,m, n,p,t,v	as in English			
ð	like **th** in together	dh	**með**	medh
h	when preceding **v** then like **k** in **k**eep	k	**hvar**	kvar
j	like **y** in **y**et	y	**já**	yow
k	1) at the beginning of a word like **k** in **k**eep	k	**kápa**	**kow**pa
	2) double **k** in the middle of a word is like **ch** in Scottish lo**ch**	ch	**ekki**	echi
l	1) at the beginning of a word like **l** in **l**eg	l	**lá**	low
	2) double **l** like **dl** of we**dl**ock	dl	**hella**	he**dl**a
ng	as in si**ng** never as in fi**ng**er	ng	**ganga**	**gow**nga
pp	close to **b** in **b**ed with a slight aspiration; not like **pp** in ski**pp**ed	b(h)	**keppa**	ke**bh**a
r	more like the Scottish **r** (hard **r** or rolling **r**) than the English one, it is always pronounced; it is never like **r** in arm	r	**rúm**	room
s	always like **s** in **s**ee (never like **s** in ri**s**e)	s	**skál**	skowl
þ	like **th** in **th**ought	th	**þá**	thow

Vowels

Note that the vowels with accents – **á, é, í, ó, ú, ý** – are pronounced quite differently from those without.

a	always short like **a** in cat	a	**gaf**	gaf
á	like **ow** in now	ow	**fá**	fow
e	like **e** in get	e	**ef**	ef
é	like the word **yeah**	ye	**él**	yel
i	like **i** in did	i	**il**	il
í	like **ee** in see	ee	**ís**	ees
o	like **o** in got	o	**oft**	oft
ó	like **oa** in goat	oa	**hóll**	hoadl
u	like **u** in put, but with the lips rounded	u	**upp**	uph
ú	like **oo** in pool	oo	**út**	oot
y	like **i** in did	i	**frysta**	frista
ý	like **ee** in see	ee	**ýsa**	eesa
æ	like **uy** in guy	uy	**særa**	suyra
ö	like **ur** in fur, but with the lips rounded and without the r-sound	u(r)	**öl**	u(r)l

Diphthongs

| au | there is no exact equivalent in English; quite like the **ur** of fur, followed by the **i** of did | öi | **sundlaug** | **sund**löig |
| ei, ey | like **a** in game | ei | **heim** | heim |

Norwegian

Basic expressions *Vanlige uttrykk*

Yes/No.	**Ja/Nei.**	yaa/næ
Please.	**Vær (så) snill å .../..., takk.**	vær (saw) snil aw/... tahk
Thank you.	**Takk.**	tahk
I beg your pardon?	**Unnskyld?**	**ewn**shewl

Introduction *Presentasjon*

Good morning.	**God morgen.**	goo**mawer'n**
Good afternoon.	**God dag.**	goo**daag**
Good night.	**God natt.**	goo**naht**
Goodbye.	**Adjø.**	ah**dyūr**
Hello/Hi!	**Hallo/Hei!**	hah**lōō**/hæi
My name is...	**Mitt navn er...**	mit nahvn ær
What's your name?	**Hva heter du?**	vah **hāy**terr dew
Pleased to meet you!	**Hyggelig å treffes!**	**hew**gerli aw **tref**ferss
How are you?	**Hvordan står det til?**	**voo'**dahn stawr deh til
Very well, thanks. And you?	**Bare bra, takk. Og med deg?**	**baa**rer braa tahk. o(g) meh(d) dæi
Where do you come from?	**Hvor kommer du fra?**	voor **kom**mer dew fraa
I'm from...	**Jeg kommer fra...**	yæi **kom**mer fraa
Australia	**Australia**	ou**straa**leeah
Canada	**Kanada**	**kah**nahdah
Great Britain	**Storbritannia**	**stoor**brittahneeah
United States	**USA**	ēw-ehss-**aa**
I'm with my...	**Jeg er her med...**	yæi ær hær meh(d)
wife	**min kone**	meen **kōō**ner
husband	**min mann**	meen mahn
family	**min familie**	meen fah**mee**lyer
boyfriend	**min venn**	meen vehn
girlfriend	**min venninne**	meen veh**nin**ner
I'm here on business/ vacation.	**Jeg er her i forret-ninger/på ferie.**	yæi ær hær ee for**reht**ningerr/paw **fāy**ryer

PRONUNCIATION/EMERGENCIES, see page 126

Questions *Spørsmål*

When?	**Når?**	nor
How?	**Hvordan?/Hvor?**	voo'dahn/voor
What?/Why?	**Hva?/Hvorfor?**	vaa/voorfor
Who?/Which?	**Hvem?/Hvilken?**	vehm/vilkern
Where is/are...?	**Hvor er...?**	voor ær
Where can I find...?	**Hvor finner jeg...?**	voor finnerr yæi
How far?	**Hvor langt?**	voor lahngt
How long?	**Hvor lenge?**	voor lehnger
How much/many?	**Hvor mye/mange?**	voor mewer/mahnger
Can I have...?	**Kan jeg få...?**	kahn yæi faw
Can you help me?	**Kan du hjelpe meg?**	kahn dew yehlper mæi
Is there/Are there...?	**Er det...?**	ær deh
There isn't/aren't...	**Det er ikke...**	deh ær ikker

Do you speak...? *Snakker du...?*

What does this/that mean?	**Hva betyr dette/det?**	vaa bertewr dehter/deh
Can you translate this for us?	**Kan du oversette dette for oss?**	kahn dew awvershehter dehter for oss
Do you speak English?	**Snakker du engelsk?**	snahkerr dew ehngerlsk
I don't speak (much) Norwegian.	**Jeg snakker ikke (så bra) norsk.**	yæi snahkerr ikker (saw braa) noshk
Could you speak more slowly?	**Kan du snakke litt langsommere?**	kahn dew snahker lit lahngsommerrer
Could you repeat that?	**Kan du gjenta det?**	kahn dew yehntah deh
I understand.	**Jeg forstår.**	yæi foshtawr
I don't understand.	**Jeg forstår ikke.**	yæi foshtawr ikker

It's... *Det er...*

better/worse	**bedre/verre**	baydrer/væer
big/small	**stor/liten**	stoor/leetern
cheap/expensive	**billig/dyr**	billi/dewr
early/late	**tidlig/sen**	teeli/sayn
good/bad	**bra/dårlig**	braa/dawr'li
hot/cold	**varm/kald**	vahrm/kahl

near/far	**nær/fjern**	nǣr/fyǣ'n
right/wrong	**riktig/feil**	rikti/fæil
vacant/occupied	**ledig/opptatt**	lāydi/optaht

A few more useful words *Noen flere nyttige ord*

a little/a lot	**lite/mye**	leeter/mēwer
above	**over**	awverr
after	**etter**	ehterr
and	**og**	o(g)
at	**ved**	veh(d)
before	**før**	fūrr
behind	**bak**	baak
below	**under**	ewnerr
between	**mellom**	mehlom
but	**men**	mehn
down	**ned**	nāy(d)
downstairs	**nede**	nāyder
from	**fra**	fraa
in	**i**	ee
inside	**inne**	inner
near	**nær**	nǣr
never	**aldri**	ahldri
next to	**ved siden av**	veh(d) seedern ahv
none	**ingen**	ingern
not	**ikke**	ikker
nothing	**ingenting, ikke noe**	ingernting, ikker nōōer
now	**nå**	naw
on	**på**	paw
only	**bare**	baarer
or	**eller**	ehlerr
outside	**ute**	ēwter
perhaps	**kanskje**	kahnsher
since	**siden**	seedern
soon	**snart**	snaa't
then	**da**	dah/daa
through	**gjennom**	yehnom
too	**også**	osso
towards	**mot**	mōōt
under	**under**	ewnerr
until	**til**	til
up	**opp**	op
upstairs	**oppe**	opper
very	**meget**	māygert
with	**med**	meh(d)
without	**uten**	ēwtern
yet	**ennå**	ehnaw

Hotel—Other accommodation *Hotell*

I have a reservation.	**Jeg har bestilt rom.**	yæi haar ber**stilt** room
We've reserved 2 rooms.	**Vi har bestilt 2 rom.**	vee haar ber**stilt** 2 room
Do you have any vacancies?	**Har dere noen ledige rom?**	haar **dāy**rer **nōō**ern **lāy**deeyer room
I'd like a...	**Jeg vil gjerne ha et...**	yæi vil **yǣ'**ner eht
single room	**enkeltrom**	**ehng**kerltroom
double room	**dobbeltrom**	**dobb**erltroom
with twin beds	**med to senger**	meh(d) tōō **sehng**err
with a double bed	**med dobbeltseng**	meh(d) **dobb**erltsehng
with a bath	**med bad**	meh(d) baad
with a shower	**med dusj**	meh(d) dewsh
Is there...?	**Fins det...?**	finss deh
air conditioning	**air-conditioning**	**āyr**-kondisherning
a private toilet	**toalett på rommet**	tooah**leht** paw **room**mer
a radio/television in the room	**radio/TV på rommet**	**raad**yoo/**tāy**veh paw **room**mer
a sauna	**badstue/sauna**	**bah**stew/**sou**nah
How much does it cost...?	**Hvor mye koster det...?**	voor **mēw**er **kost**err deh
Is there a camp site near here?	**Er det en camping-plass i nærheten?**	ær deh ehn **kæmp**ing-plahss ee **nǣr**hehtern
Can we camp here?	**Kan vi campe her?**	kahn vee **kæmp**er hǣr
We'll be staying...	**Vi blir...**	vee bleer
overnight only	**bare natten over**	**baar**er **nah**tern **aw**verr
a few days	**ett par dager**	eht pahr **daag**err
a week	**en uke**	ehn **ēw**ke

Decision *Beslutning*

May I see the room?	**Kan jeg få se rommet?**	kahn yæi faw sāy **room**mer
That's fine. I'll take it.	**Det er bra. Jeg tar det.**	deh ær braa. yæi taar deh
No. I don't like it.	**Nei. Jeg liker det ikke.**	næi. yæ **leek**err **ik**ker
It's too...	**Det er for...**	deh ær for
dark/small	**mørkt/lite**	murrkt/**lee**ter
noisy	**støyende**	**stoy**erner

NUMBERS, see page 124

Do you have anything...?	**Har dere noe...?**	haar d**ay**rer n**oo**er
better/bigger	**bedre/større**	b**ay**drer/st**u**rrer
cheaper	**rimeligere**	r**ee**merleeyerrer
quieter	**roligere**	r**oo**leeyerrer

Etternavn/Fornavn	Name/First name
Hjemsted	Home town
Nasjonalitet/Yrke	Nationality/Occupation
Fødselsdato/Fødested	Date/Place of birth
Passnummer	Passport number
Dato for ankomst til Norge/ Skandinavia	Date of arrival in Norway/ Scandinavia
Hensikt med oppholdet	Reason for visit
Underskrift	Signature

General requirements *Allmenne forespørsler*

The key to room..., please.	**Nøkkelen til rom...,takk.**	**nu**rkerlern til room... tahk
Where's the...?	**Hvor er...?**	voor ær
bathroom	**badet**	b**aa**der
dining-room	**spisesalen**	sp**ee**sserssaalern
emergency exit	**nødutgangen**	n**u**dewtgahngern
lift (elevator)	**heisen**	h**æ**issern
Where are the toilets?	**Hvor er toalettet?**	voor ær tooahl**eh**ter
Where can I park my car?	**Hvor kan jeg park-ere bilen?**	voor kahn yæi pahrk**ay**rer b**ee**lern

Checking out *Avreise*

May I have my bill, please?	**Kan jeg få regn-ingen?**	kahn yæi faw **ræ**iningern
Can you get us a taxi?	**Kan du skaffe oss en drosje?**	kahn dew sk**ah**fer oss ehn dr**o**sher
It's been a very enjoyable stay.	**Det har vært ett meget hyggelig opphold.**	deh haar væ't eht m**ay**gert h**ew**gerli **o**phol

Eating out *Mat og drikke*

Can you recommend a good restaurant?	**Kan du anbefale en bra restaurant?**	kahn dew **ahn**berfaaler ehn braa rehstew**rahng**
I'd like to reserve a table for 4.	**Jeg vil gjerne bestille et bord til 4.**	yæi vil **yæ**'ner ber**still**er eht bōōr til 4
We'll come at 8.	**Vi kommer kl. 8.**	vee **komm**err **klok**kern 8
I'd like breakfast/lunch/dinner.	**Jeg vil gjerne ha frokost/lunsj/middag.**	yæi vil **yæ**'ner haa **frōō**kost/lurnsh/**mid**dah(g)
What do you recommend?	**Hva kan du anbefale?**	vaa kahn dew **ahn**berfaalerr
Do you have a set menu/local speciality?	**Har dere en meny/lokal spesialitet?**	haar **dāy**rer ehn meh**new**/lookaal spehsseeahli**tāyt**
Do you have any vegetarian dishes?	**Har dere noen vegetariske retter?**	haar **dāy**rer **nōō**ern vehger**taa**risker **reh**terr

---

Hva skal det være?	What would you like?
Jeg kan anbefale dette.	I recommend this.
Hva vil du/dere ha å drikke?	What would you like to drink?
Vi har ikke ...	We don't have ...
Vil du ha ...?	Would you like ...?

Could we have a/an ..., please?	**Kan vi få ...?**	kahn vee faw
ashtray	**et askebeger**	eht **ahs**kerbāygerr
cup	**en kopp**	ehn kop
fork	**en gaffel**	ehn **gahf**erl
glass	**et glass**	eht glass
knife	**en kniv**	ehn kneev
napkin (serviette)	**en serviett**	ehn sehrv**yeht**
plate	**en tallerken**	ehn tah**lær**kern
spoon	**en skje**	ehn shāy

NUMBERS, see page 124

May I have some...?	**Kan jeg få litt...?**	kahn yæi faw lit
bread	**brød**	brur
butter	**smør**	smurr
oil	**olje**	olyer
pepper	**pepper**	pehperr
salt	**salt**	sahlt
seasoning	**krydder**	krewderr
sugar	**sukker**	sookkerr
vinegar	**eddik**	ehdik

Reading the menu *Å lese spisekartet*

dessert	dehssær	dessert
drikker	drikkerr	drinks
fisk	fisk	fish
forretter	forrehterr	appetizers
frukt	frewkt	fruit
fugl	fewl	poultry
hovedretter	hooverdrehterr	main courses (entrées)
is(krem)	ees(krāym)	ice cream
kaker	kaakerr	pastries/cakes
kjøtt	khurt	meat
koldtbord	koltboor	smorgasbord
leskedrikk	lehskerdrik	soft drinks
ost	oost	cheese
pastaretter	pahstahrehterr	pasta dishes
risretter	reesrehterr	rice dishes
salatbar	sahlaatbaar	salad bar
smørbrød	smurrbrur	open sandwiches (smørbrød)
supper	sewperr	soups
varme smørbrød	vahrmer smurrbrur	sandwiches with hot meat, fish, etc.
varmretter	vahrmrehterr	hot dishes
vilt	vilt	game

Breakfast *Frokost*

I'd like...	**Jeg vil gjerne...**	yæi vil yǣ'ner
bread/butter	**brød/smør**	brur/smurr
cheese	**ost**	oost
eggs	**egg**	ehg
ham and eggs	**skinke og egg**	shingker o(g) ehg
jam	**syltetøy**	sewltertoy
roll	**et rundstykke**	eht rewnstewker

Starters (Appetizers) *Forrett*

blåskjell	**blaw**shehl	mussels
froskelår	**frosk**erlawr	frogs' legs
gåselever	**gaws**serlehverr	goose liver
snegler	**snæi**lerr	snails
sursild	**sēw**shil	marinated herring
østers	**ur**stersh	oysters
ål i gelé	awl ee sheh**lāy**	jellied eel

Soups *Supper*

I'd like some soup.	**Jeg vill gjerne ha en suppe.**	yæi vil y**ǣ**'ner haa ehn sewper
betasuppe	**bāy**tahsewper	thick meat-and-vegetable soup
fiskesuppe	**fisk**ersewper	fish soup
grønnsaksuppe	**grurn**saaksewper	vegetable soup
gul ertesuppe	gewl **æ**'tersewper	yellow pea soup
hummersuppe	**hoom**merrsewper	lobster soup
neslesuppe	**nehsh**lersewper	nettle soup
oksehalesuppe	**ook**serhahlersewper	oxtail soup

Fish and seafood (shellfish) *Fisk og skalldyr*

ansjos	ahng**shōōss**	marinated sprats
blekksprut	**blehk**sprēwt	octopus
blåskjell	**blaw**shehl	mussels
brasme	**brahs**mer	bream
flyndre	**flewn**drer	flounder
gjedde	**yeh**der	pike
hellefisk	**heh**lerfisk	halibut
hummer	**hoom**merr	lobster
hyse	**hēw**sser	haddock
kamskjell	**kahm**shehl	scallop
karpe	**kahr**per	carp
kolje	**kol**yer	haddock
krabbe	**krah**ber	crab
laks	**lahkss**	salmon
tunfisk	**tēwn**fisk	tuna

gravet laks/gravlaks
(**graa**vert lahkss/
graavlahkss)
salt-and-sugar-cured salmon flavoured with dill; often served with sliced potatoes in a white sauce

seibiff med løk
(**sæi**bif meh(d) lūrk)
fried fillets of coalfish (pollack) with onions, served with boiled potatoes and vegetables or salad

spekesild
(**spāy**kersil)
salted herring; served with boiled potatoes, onion rings, pickled beetroot, butter and often cabbage or mashed swedes (rutabaga)

baked	**bakte**	bahkt
boiled	**kokt**	kookt
fried	**stekt**	stehkt
grilled	**grillet/grillstekt**	**grill**ert/**gril**stehkt
roast	**ovnsstekt**	**ovns**stehkt
underdone (rare)	**råstekt**	**raw**stehkt
medium	**medium stekt**	**māy**diewm stehkt
well-done	**godt stekt**	got stehkt

Meat *Kjøtt*

I'd like some...	**Jeg vil gjerne ha...**	yæi vil y**ǣ'**ner haa
beef	**oksekjøtt**	**ook**serkhurt
chicken/duck	**kylling/and**	**khew**ling/ahn
lamb	**lammekjøtt**	**lah**merkhurt
pork	**svinekjøtt**	**svee**nerkhurt/**kahl**verkhurt
veal	**kalvekjøtt**	
biff	bif	beef steak
gås	gawss	goose
kalkun	kahl**kewn**	turkey
pølse	**purl**ser	sausage
spekeskinke	**spāy**kershingker	smoked, cured ham
svineribbe	**svee**nerribber	sparerib
elgstek	**ehlg**stāyk	roast elk
kjøttpudding	**khurt**pewding	meat loaf
lungemos	**loong**er**mōōs**	minced pork lungs and onions
medisterkaker	meh**dis**terrkaakerr	small pork-and-veal hamburgers
medisterpølse	meh**dis**terrpurlser	pork-and-veal sausage
okserulader	**ook**serrewlaaderr	braised beef rolls
reinsdyrmedaljonger	**ræinsdēw**-rmehdahlyongerr	small round fillets of reindeer

Vegetables and salads *Grønnsaker og salater*

beans	bønner	burnerr
beetroot	rødbeter	rūrbehterr
cabbage	kål	kawl
carrots	gulrøtter	gewlrurterr
cauliflower	blomkål	blomkawl
cucumber	agurk	ahgewrk
leeks	purre	pewrer
lettuce	hodesalat	hōōdersahlaat
mushrooms	sopp	sop
onions	løk	lūrk
peas	erter	æ'terr
potatoes	poteter	pootāyterr
spinach	spinat	spinnaat
swede (rutabaga)	kålrabi/kålrot	kawlraabi/kawlrōōt
tomatoes	tomater	toomaaterr
turnips	nepe	nāyper

agurksalat (ahgewrksahlaat)	cucumber salad, usually with a vinegar-sugar dressing
blandet salat (blahnert sahlaat)	mixed salad (lettuce, tomatoes, cucumber, etc., with oil-and-vinegar dressing); accompanies many main courses
sildeball (sillerbahl)	potato dumplings with a filling of minced salted herring, onion, bacon and flour; served with pickled beetroot
størje-/tunfisksalat (sturryer-/tēwnfisk sahlaat)	tuna fish salad – Norwegian version of salad Niçoise
skalldyrsalat (skahldēwrsahlaat)	seafood salad (mostly mussels and prawns, but also lobster or crab)

Fruit *Frukt*

apple	eple	ehpler
arctic cloudberries	multer	mewlterr
banana	banan	bahnaan
blackberries	bjørnebær	byūr'nerbær
cherries	kirsebær	khisherbær
cranberries	tyttebær	tewterbær
gooseberries	stikkelsbær	stikkerlsbær

grapes	druer	drewerr
black	blå	blaw
white	grønne	grurner
grapefruit	grapefrukt	graypfrewkt
lemon	sitron	sitroon
melon	melon	mehloon
orange	appelsin	ahperlseen
peach	fersken	fæshkern
pear	pære	pærer
plums	plommer	ploommerr
raspberries	bringebær	bringerbær
rowanberries	rognebær	rongnerbær
strawberries	jordbær	yoorbær
wild strawberries	markjordbær	mahrkyoorbær

Dessert *Dessert*

(varm) eplekake med krem	(vahrm) ehplerkaaker meh(d) kraym	(hot) apple pie with whipped cream
frityrstekt camembert med solbærsyltetøy	fritewshtehkt kahmangbær meh(d) soolbærsewltertoy	deep-fried camembert with blackcurrant jam
fruktkompott	frewktkoompot	stewed fruit
is(krem)	eess(kraym)	ice cream
mandelkake	mahnderlkaaker	almond cake
multer med krem	mewlterr meh(d) kraym	arctic cloudberries with whipped cream
pannekaker	pahnerkaakerr	pancakes
riskrem	reeskraym	creamed rice with red berry sauce
rødgrøt	rurgrurt	fruit pudding with cream
vafler med syltetøy	vahflerr meh(d) sewltertoy	waffles with jam

Hoffdessert (hofdehssær)	layers of meringue and whipped cream, topped with chocolate sauce and toasted almonds
pære Belle Helene (pærer behl hehlayn)	poached pears with vanilla ice cream and chocolate
tilslørte bondepiker (tilshurter boonnerpeekerr)	layers of stewed apples, biscuit (cookie) crumbs, sugar and whipped cream

Drinks *Drikkevarer*

A bottle of mineral (spring) water, please.	En flaske naturlig mineralvann, takk.	ehn flahsker nahtew'li minerraalvahn tahk
fizzy (sparkling)	med kullsyre	meh(d) kewlsewrer
still (natural)	uten kullsyre	ewtern kewlsewrer
apple juice	eplesaft	ehplersahft
aquavit	akevitt	ahkervit
beer	øl	url
(hot) chocolate	(varm) sjokolade	(vahrm) shookoolaader
coffee	kaffe	kahfer
espresso	en espresso	ehn ehsprehssoo
with cream	med fløte	meh(d) flurter
grapefruit juice	grapefruktjuice	graypfrewktyewss
lemonade	sitronbrus	sitroonbrewss
(glass of) milk	(et glass) melk	(eht glahss) mehlk
sugar	sukker	sookkerr
tea	te	tay
a cup of	en kopp	ehn kop
with lemon	med sitron	meh(d) sitroon
with milk	med melk	meh(d) mehlk
vodka	vodka	vodkah
whisky	whisky	viski
wine	vin	veen
red/white wine	rødvin/hvitvin	rurveen/veetveen
May I have the wine list, please?	Kan jeg få se vin-kartet?	kahn yæi faw say veenkah'ter
neat (straight)	bar	baar
on the rocks	med is	meh(d) eess
with water	med vann	meh(d) soodah

Complaints *Klager*

The meat is...	Kjøttet er...	khurter ær
overdone	for mye stekt	for mewer stehkt
underdone	for lite stekt	dor leeter stehkt
This is too...	Dette er for...	dehter ær for
bitter/salty/sweet	beskt/salt/søtt	behskt/surt/sahlt
That's not what I ordered.	Dette er ikke det jeg bestilte.	dehter ær ikker deh yæi berstilter
The food is cold.	Maten er kald.	maatern ær kahl

The bill (check) *Regningen*

I'd like to pay.	**Jeg vil gjerne betale.**	yæi vil y**ææ**'ner ber**taa**ler
What's this amount for?	**Hva står dette beløpet for?**	vah stawr **deh**ter ber**lūr**per for
I think there's a mistake in this bill.	**Jeg tror det er en feil på regningen.**	yæi tr**ōō**r deh ær ehn fæil paw **ræi**ningern
Is everything included?	**Er alt inkludert?**	ær ahlt inklew**dāy**'t
Can I pay with this credit card?	**Kan jeg betale med dette kredittkortet?**	kahn yæi ber**taa**ler meh(d) **deh**ter kreh**dit**-ko'ter
We enjoyed it, thank you.	**Det var meget godt.**	deh vaar **māy**gert got

Snacks—Picnic *Småretter—Picnic*

I'll have one of those.	**Jeg vil gjerne ha en av dem.**	yæi vil y**ææ**'ner haa ehn ahv dehm
to the right/left	**til høyre/venstre**	til **hoyr**er/**vehn**strer
above/below	**ovenfor/nedenfor**	**aw**vernfor/**nāy**dernfor
Danish pastry	**et wienerbrød**	eht **vee**nerrbr**ūr**
doughnut	**en smultring**	ehn **smewlt**ring
fish pudding	**fiskepudding**	**fisk**erpewding
fried sausage	**en grillpølse**	ehn **gril**purlser
liver sausage	**leverpølse**	**leh**verrpurlser
(slice of) pizza	**en (skive) pizza**	ehn (**shee**ver) **pit**sah
a potato pancake	**lompe**	**loom**per
soft drink	**leskedrikk**	**lehs**kerdrik
spring (egg) roll	**vårrull**	**vaw**rrewl

fastelavnsbolle (fahster**laavns**boller)	lenten bun; bun cut in half, filled with whipped cream and topped with icing (confectioners') sugar
kransekake (**krahn**serkaaker)	cone-shaped pile of almond-macaroon rings decorated with icing (frosting), marzipan flowers, etc.

NUMBERS, see page 124

Travelling around *På reise*

Plane *Fly*

Is there a flight to Tromsø?	**Går det et fly til Tromsø?**	gawr deh eht flew til troomsur
What time should I check in?	**Når må jeg sjekke inn?**	nor maw yæi shehker in
I'd like to... my reservation.	**Jeg vil gjerne... reservasjon.**	yæi vil yǣ'ner rehssævahshōōnern
cancel	**annullere**	ahnewlāyrer
change	**endre**	ehndrer
confirm	**bekrefte**	berkrehfter

Train *Tog*

Where's the railway station?	**Hvor er jernban-estasjonen?**	voor ær yǣ'nbaanerstahshōōnern
Where is/are (the)...?	**Hvor er...?**	voor ær
booking office	**billettkontoret**	billehtkoontōōrer
left-luggage office (baggage check)	**bagasjeoppbevar-ingen**	bahgaasheropbervaaringern
lost property (lost and found) office	**hittegodskontoret**	hittergoodskoontōōrer
luggage (baggage) lockers 2	**oppbevaringsbok-sene**	opbervaaringsbokserner
platform 2	**perrong 2**	pehrong 2
ticket office	**billettluken**	billehtlewkern
waiting room	**venterommet**	vehntersaalern

INNGANG	ENTRANCE
UTGANG	EXIT
INFORMASJON	INFORMATION

I'd like a ticket to...	**Jeg vil gjerne ha en billett til...**	yæi vil yǣ'ner ehn billeht til
single (one-way)	**enkeltbillett**	ehngkerltbilleht
return (round-trip)	**tur-returbillett**	tewr-rehtewrbilleht
first/second class	**første/andre/annen klasse**	furshter/ahndrer/aaern klahsser

Inquiries *Forespørsler*

When is the... train to Halden?	**Når går... tog til Halden?**	nor gawr... tawg til hahldern
first/last/next	**første/siste/neste**	furshter/nehster/sister

NUMBERS, see page 124

What time does the train to Oslo leave?	Når går toget til Oslo?	nor gawr **taw**ger til **oosh**loo
Is there a dining car/sleeping car on the train?	Fins det en spisevogn/sovevogn på toget?	finss deh ehn **spee**sservongn/**saw**vervongn ee **taw**ger
Is this the train to Geilo?	Er dette toget til Geilo?	ær **deh**ter **taw**ger til **yæi**loo
I'd like a time-table, please.	Jeg vil gjerne ha en rutetabell.	yæei vil **yæ'**ner haa ehn r̄ew̄tertahbehl

Underground (subway) *T-bane*

| Where's the nearest underground station? | Hvor er nærmeste T-banestasjon? | voor ær **nærm**ehster **tāy**baanerstahshoo&n |
| Where do I change for...? | Hvor må jeg bytte for å komme til...? | voor maw yæi **bew**ter for aw **kom**mer til |

Bus—Tram (Streetcar) *Buss—Trikk*

Which tram (streetcar) goes to the town centre?	Hvilken trikk går til sentrum?	**vil**kern trik gawr til **sehn**trewm
How much is the fare to...?	Hvor mye koster det til...?	voor m̄ew̄er **kos**terr deh til
Will you tell me when to get off?	Kan du si fra når jeg skal gå av?	kahn dew see fraa nor yæi skahl gaw ahv

Boat service *Båt*

When does the next boat/ferry for... leave?	Når går båten/fergen til...?	nor gawr **baw**tern/**fær**ggern til
How long does the crossing take?	Hvor lang tid tar overfarten?	voor lahng teed taar **aw**verrfah'rtern
I'd like to take a boat trip.	Jeg vil gjerne ta en båttur.	yæi vil **yæ'**ner taa ehn **bawt**t̄ew̄r

Taxi *Drosje/Taxi*

Where can I get a taxi?	Hvor kan jeg få tak i en drosje?	voor kahn yæi faw taak ee ehn **dro**sher
What's the fare to...?	Hva koster det til...?	vaa **kos**terr deh til
Take me to this address.	Kjør meg til denne adressen?	kh̄ūrr mæi til **deh**ner ah**dreh**ssern
Please stop here.	Stans her.	stahnss hǣr

Car hire (rental) *Bilutleie*

I'd like to hire (rent) a car.	**Jeg vil gjerne leie en bil.**	yæi vil yǣ'ner læier ehn beel
I'd like it for a day/a week.	**Jeg vil ha den en dag/en uke.**	yæi vil haa dehn ehn daag/ehn ēwker
What's the charge per day/week?	**Hvor mye koster det pr. dag/uke?**	voor mēwer kosterr deh pær daag/ēwker
Is mileage included?	**Er kjørelengden inkludert?**	ær khūrrerlehngdern inklewdāy't
I'd like full insurance.	**Jeg vil ha full forsikring.**	yæi vil haa fewl foshikring

---

Road signs *Trafikkskilt*

ALL STANS FORBUDT	No stopping
FERIST	Cattle grid
GRUSVEI	Gravelled road
INNKJØRSEL FORBUDT	No entry
KJØR SAKTE	Drive slowly
MØTEPLASS	Road passing place
FORBIKJØRING FORBUDT	No overtaking (passing)
OMKJØRING	Diversion (Detour)
PARKERING (FORBUDT)	(No) Parking
RASFARE	Falling rocks
SVAKE KANTER	Soft shoulders
TOLL	Customs
UTKJØRSEL	Exit
VEIARBEID/VEGARBEID	Roadworks

Where's the nearest filling station?	**Hvor er nærmeste bensinstasjon?**	voor ær nærmehster behnseenstahshōōn
Fill it up, please.	**Full tank, takk.**	fewl tahngk tahk
Give me... litres of petrol (gasoline).	**... liter bensin, takk.**	... leeterr behnseen tahk
super (premium)/ regular/unleaded/ diesel	**super/normal/ blyfri/diesel**	sēwperr/noormaal/ blēwfree/deesserl
How do I get to...?	**Hvordan kommer jeg til...?**	voo'dahn kommerr yæi til
How far is it to... from here?	**Hvor langt er det til... herfra?**	voor lahngt ær deh til... hærfrah

I've had a break-down at...	**Jeg har fått motor-stopp ved...**	yæi haar fot **mōō**tooshtop veh(d)
Can you send a mechanic?	**Kan du sende en mekaniker?**	kahn dew **seh**ner ehn meh**kaa**nikkerr
Can you mend this puncture (fix this flat)?	**Kan du reparere denne punkter-ingen?**	kahn dew reh**pah**rayrer **deh**ner poong**tay**-ringern

---

Du har kjørt feil.	You're on the wrong road.
Kjør rett frem.	Go straight ahead.
Det er der borte til høyre / venstre.	It's down there on the right/left.
midt imot/bak...	opposite/behind...
ved siden av/etter...	next to/after...
nord/sør	north/south
øst/vest	east/west

Sightseeing *Sightseeing*

Where's the tourist office?	**Hvor er turistkon-toret?**	voor ær tew**rist**-koont**ōō**rer
Is there an English-speaking guide?	**Fins det en engelsk-talende guide der?**	finss deh ehn **ehng**erlsk-taalerner "guide" **dær**
Where is/Where are the...?	**Hvor er...?**	voor ær
botanical gardens	**den botaniske hagen**	dehn boo**taa**nisker **haa**gern
castle	**slottet**	**shlot**ter
cathedral	**domkirken**	**dom**khirkern
city centre	**sentrum**	**sehn**trewm
exhibition	**utstillingen**	**ēwt**stillingern
harbour	**havnen**	**hahv**nern
market	**torghandelen**	**torg**hahnderlern
museum	**museet**	mewss**ay**er
shopping area	**handlestrøket**	**hahn**dlerstrūrker
square	**plassen/torget**	**plah**ssern/**tor**gger
tower	**tårnet**	**taw**'ner
zoo	**dyrehagen**	**dēw**rerhaagern
When does it open/close?	**Når åpner/stenges det?**	nor **awp**ner/**stehng**err deh

TELLING THE TIME, see page 123

Landmarks *Landemerker*

farm	**en bondegård**	ehn **boon**ergawr
fjord	**en fjord**	ehn f**yoo**r
forest	**en skog**	ehn sk**oo**g
island	**en øy**	ehn oy
meadow	**en eng**	ehn ehng
mountain	**et fjell**	eht fyehl
path	**en sti**	ehn stee
river	**en elv**	ehn ehlv
sea	**en sjø**	ehn sh**ū**r
valley	**en dal**	ehn daal
waterfall	**en foss**	ehn foss

Relaxing *Underholdning*

What's playing at the... Theatre?	**Hva spilles på... Theatret?**	vah **spill**erss paw... t**ā**y**aa**trer
Are there any tickets for tonight?	**Fins det fremdeles billetter for i kveld?**	finss eh frehm**dāy**lerss bill**eh**terr til ee kvehl
What time does it begin/finish?	**Når begynner/ slutter det?**	nor ber**yew**nerr/**shlew**ter deh
I'd like to reserve 2 tickets for the show on Friday evening.	**Jeg vil gjerne bes- tille 2 billetter til forestillingen på fredag kveld.**	yæi vil y**æ'**ner ber**still**er 2 bill**eh**terr til **faw**rerstillingern paw **frā**ydah(g) kvehl
Would you like to go out with me tonight?	**Skal vi gå ut i kveld?**	skahl vee gaw **ēw**t ee kvehl
Thank you, but I'm busy.	**Takk, men jeg er dessverre opptatt.**	tahk mehn yæi ær dehs**vær**er **op**taht
Is there a discotheque in town?	**Fins det et diskotek i byen?**	finss deh eht diskoot**āy**k ee **bēw**ern
Would you like to dance?	**Skal vi danse?**	skahl vee **dahn**ser
Thank you, it's been a wonderful evening.	**Takk, det har vært en veldig hyggelig kveld.**	tahk deh haar væ't ehn **vehl**di **hew**gerli kvehl

TELLING THE TIME/DAYS OF THE WEEK, see page 123

Norsk

Sports *Sport*

Is there a football (soccer) match anywhere this Saturday?	**Er det en fotball-kamp noe sted på lørdag?**	ær deh ehn **foot**bahlkahmp nooer stay(d) paw lur'dah (g)
What's the admission charge?	**Hva koster inn-gangsbilletten?**	vah **kost**err **ing**ahngsbillehtern
Is there a golf course/ tennis court nearby?	**Fins det en golf-bane/tennisbane i nærheten?**	finss deh ehn **golf**baaner/ **teh**nisbaaner ee **nær**hehtern

bicycling	**sykling**	**sewk**ling
football (soccer)	**fotball**	**foot**bahl
fishing	**fiske**	**fisk**er
ice hockey match	**ishockeykamp**	**ees**hokkikahmp
rowing	**roing**	**roo**ing
sailing	**seiling**	**sæ**iling
speed skating	**skøyteløp**	**shoy**terlurp
ski jumping	**skihopping**	**shee**hopping
swimming	**svømming**	**svur**ming

Can one swim in the lake/river?	**Kan man svømme i (inn)sjøen/elven?**	kahn mahn **baad**er ee (in)shurern/**ehl**vern
Is there a swimming pool here?	**Er det et svømme-basseng her?**	ær deh eht **svur**merbahssehng hær
Is there a skating rink near here?	**Fins det en skøyte-bane i nærheten?**	finss seh ehn **shoy**terbaaner ee **nær**hehtern
I'd like to ski.	**Jeg vil gjerne gå på ski.**	yæi vil **yæ**'ner gaw paw shee
downhill/cross-country skiing	**utforkjøring/lan-grenn**	**ewt**forkhurring/**lahng**grehn
Are there any good ski tracks (trails) nearby?	**Fins det noen gode skiløyper i nærhe-ten?**	finss deh nooern goo(d)er **shee**loyperr ee **nær**hehtern
I'd like to hire...	**Jeg vil gjerne leie...**	yæi vil **yæ**'ner **læ**ier
skates	**skøyter**	**shoy**terr
ski boots	**skistøvler**	**shee**sturvlerr
skis	**ski**	shee
I'd like to hire (rent) a bicycle.	**Jeg vil gjerne leie en sykkel.**	yæi vil **yæ**'ner **læ**ier ehn **sew**kerl

Shops, stores and services *Butikker og servicenæringer*

Where's the nearest...?	Hvor er nærmeste...?	voor ær **nær**mehster
baker's	**et bakeri**	eht baaker**ree**
bookshop	**en bokhandel**	ehn **boo**khahnderl
butcher's	**en slakter**	ehn **shlahk**terr
chemist's/drugstore	**et apotek**	eht ahpoo**tayk**
dentist	**en tannlege**	ehn **tahn**layger
department store	**et stormagasin**	eht **stoo**rmahgahsseen
grocer's	**en matvarehandel**	ehn **maat**vaarerhahnderl
hairdresser's (ladies/men)	**en frisør (dame-/herre-)**	ehn friss**urr** (**daa**mer-/**hæ**rer-)
market	**en torghandel**	ehn **torg**hahnderl
newsstand	**en aviskiosk**	ehn ah**vees**khyosk
post office	**et postkontor**	eht **post**koont**oo**r
souvenir shop	**en suvenirbutikk**	ehn sewver**neer**bewtik
supermarket	**et supermarked**	eht **sew**perrmahrkerd

General expressions *Vanlige uttrykk*

Where's the (main) shopping area?	Hvor er (det største) handlestrøket?	voor ær deh **sturs**hter **hahn**dlerstr**u**rker
Do you have any...?	Har du noen...?	har dew **noo**ern

Kan jeg hjelpe deg?	Can I help you?
Hva skal det være?	What would you like?
Hvilken... vil du ha?	What... would you like?
farge/form	colour/shape
Det er vi utsolgt for.	We're out of stock.
Skal vi bestille det?	Shall we order it for you?
Skal det være noe annet?	Anything else?
Det blir... kroner, takk.	That comes to... kroner.
Kassen er der borte.	The cash desk is over there.

Norsk

I'd like a ... one.	**Jeg vil gjerne ha en ...**	yæi vil **yæ'**ner haa ehn
big	**stor**	stoor
cheap	**rimelig**	**ree**merli
dark	**mørk**	murrk
good	**god**	goo(d)
heavy	**tung**	toong
large	**stor**	stoor
light (weight)	**lett**	leht
light (colour)	**lys**	lewss
rectangular	**rektangulær**	rehktahngewl**ær**
round	**rund**	rewn
small	**liten**	**lee**tern
square	**firkantet**	**fir**kahntert
sturdy	**robust/solid**	roo**bewst**/soo**leed**
Don't you have anything ...?	**Har du ikke noe ...?**	haar de ikker nooer
cheaper/better	**rimeligere/bedre**	**ree**merleeyerrer/**bay**drer
larger/smaller	**større/mindre**	**stur**rer/**mind**rer
How much is this?	**Hvor mye koster dette?**	voor **mew**er **kost**err **deh**ter
Please write it down.	**Kan du skrive det?**	kahn dew **skree**ver deh
I don't want to spend more than ... kroner.	**Jeg vil ikke gi mer enn ... kroner.**	yæi vil **ik**ker yee mayr ehn ... kroonerr
No, I don't like it.	**Nei, jeg liker det ikke.**	næi yæi **lee**kerr deh **ik**ker
I'll take it.	**Jeg tar det.**	yæi taar deh
Do you accept credit cards?	**Tar dere kreditt-kort?**	taar **day**rer kreh**dit**ko't
Can you order it for me?	**Kan du bestille det til meg?**	kahn dew ber**stil**ler deh til mæi

black	**svart**	svah't
blue	**blå**	blaw
brown	**brun**	brewn
green	**grønn**	grurn
grey	**grå**	graw
orange	**oransje**	oo**rahng**sh
red	**rød**	rur
white	**hvit**	veet
yellow	**gul**	gewl
light ...	**lyse ...**	**lews**ser
dark ...	**mørke ...**	**mur**rker

NUMBERS, see page 124

Chemist's (Drugstore) *Apotek*

aspirin	**aspirin**	ahspir**reen**
condoms	**kondomer**	koon**doo**merr
deodorant	**en deodorant**	ehn dehoodoo**rahnt**
insect repellent	**et insektmiddel**	eht **in**sehktmidderl
moisturizing cream	**en fuktighetskrem**	ehn **fook**tihehtskr**ay**m
razor blades	**barberblader**	bahrb**ayr**blaaderr
shampoo	**en sjampo**	ehn **shahm**poo
soap	**en såpe**	ehn **saw**per
sun-tan oil	**en sololje**	ehn **soo**lolyer
tampons	**tamponger**	tahm**pong**err
toothpaste	**en tannpasta**	ehn **tahn**pahstah

Clothing *Klær*

blouse	**en bluse**	ehn bl**ew**sser
boots	**støvler**	st**ur**vlerr
coat	**en frakk/kåpe**	ehn frahk/**kaw**per
dress	**en kjole**	ehn kh**oo**ler
pair of gloves	**et par hansker**	eht pahr **hahn**skerr
scarf	**et skjerf**	eht shærf
shirt	**en skjorte**	ehn shoo'ter
shoes	**sko**	sk**oo**
skirt	**et skjørt**	eht shur't
socks	**et par sokker**	eht pahr **sok**kerr
sweater	**en genser**	ehn **gehn**serr
swimming trunks	**et badebukse**	eht **baa**derbookser
swimsuit	**en badedrakt**	ehn **baa**derdrahkt
T-shirt	**en T-skjorte**	ehn **tay**-shoo'ter
tights	**en strømpebukse**	ehn **strurm**perbookser
trousers	**et par langbukser**	eht pahr **lahng**bookserr
Can I try it on?	**Kan jeg få prøve den?**	kahn yæi faw pr**ur**ver dehn
What's it made of?	**Hva er det laget av?**	vaa ær deh **laa**gert ahv

cotton	**bomull**	**boo**mewl
denim	**denim**	deh**neem**
lace	**knipling**	**knip**ling
leather	**lær**	l**ær**
linen	**lin**	leen
silk	**silke**	**sil**ker
suede	**semsket skinn**	**sehm**skert shin
velvet	**fløyel**	**floy**erl
wool	**ull**	ewl

Grocer's *Matvarehandel*

What sort of cheese do you have?	**Hva slags ostesorter har du?**	vaa shlakss **oos**terso'terr haa dew
half a kilo of tomatoes	**1/2 kg tomater**	ehn hahl **khee**loo too**maa**terr
a litre of milk	**1 l melk**	ehn **lee**terr mehlk
4 slices of ham	**4 skiver skinke**	feerer **shee**verr **shing**ker
some bread	**litt brød**	lit brūr
a tin (can) of peaches	**en boks fersken**	ehn bokss **fæsh**kern

Miscellaneous *Forskjellig*

I'd like a/an/some...	**Jeg vil gjerne ha...**	yæi vil y**æ'**ner haa
battery	**et batteri**	eht bahter**ree**
bottle-opener	**en flaskeåpner**	ehn **flahs**kerawpnerr
newspaper	**en avis**	ehn ah**veess**
American/English	**amerikansk/ engelsk**	ahm(eh)ri**kaansk**/ **ehng**erlsk
postcard	**et postkort**	eht **post**ko't
torch	**en lommelykt**	ehn **loom**merlewkt
I'd like a film (for this camera).	**Jeg vil gjerne ha en film (til dette apparatet).**	yæi vil y**æ'**ner haa ehn film (til **deh**ter ahpah**raa**ter)
black and white	**svart-hvitt**	**svah't**-vit
colour	**farge**	**fahr**gger
Can you repair this camera?	**Kan du reparere dette apparatet?**	kahn dew rehpah**rāy**rer **deh**ter ahpah**raa**ter
I'd like a haircut, please.	**Klipping, takk.**	**klip**ning tahk

Souvenirs *Suvenirer*

drinking horn	**et drikkehorn**	eht **drik**kerhōo'n
hunting knife	**en jaktkniv**	ehn **yahkt**kneev
reindeer skin	**et reinsdyrskinn**	ehn **ræ**insdēwrshin
sealskin slippers	**et par selskinn- støfler**	eht pahr **sāyl**shinsturflerr
troll	**et troll**	eht trol
Viking ship	**et vikingskip**	eht **vee**kingsheep

At the bank / banken

Where's the nearest bank/currency exchange office?	**Hvor er nærmeste bank/veksling-skontor?**	voor ær **nær**mehster bahngk/ **vehk**shlingskoontoor
I'd like to change some dollars/pounds.	**Jeg vil gjerne veksle noen dollar/pund.**	yæi vil yæ'ner **vehk**shler nooern dollahr/pewn
I'd like to cash a traveller's cheque.	**Jeg vil gjerne løse inn en reisesjekk.**	yæi vil yæ'ner lursser in ehn **ræ**issershehk
What's the exchange rate?	**Hva er veksling-skursen?**	vaa ær **vehk**shlingskewshern

At the post office Postkontor

I'd like to send this...	**Jeg vil gjerne sende dette...**	yæi vil yæ'ner **seh**ner dehter
airmail/express	**med fly/ekspress**	meh(d) flew/ehks**prehss**
A...-kroner stamp, please.	**Et... kroners fri-merke, takk.**	eht... -**kroo**nersh **free**mærker tahk
What's the postage for a postcard to the U.S.?	**Hva er portoen for et postkort til USA?**	vah ær **poo'**tooern for eht **post**ko't til ew-ehss-aa
Is there any post (mail) for me? My name is...	**Har det kommet noe post til meg? Mitt navn er...**	har deh **kom**mert nooer post til mæi. mit nahvn ær...

Telephoning Telefon

Where's the nearest telephone booth?	**Hvor er nærmeste telefonkiosk?**	voor ær **nær**mehster tehler**foon**khyosk
May I use your phone?	**Kan jeg få låne telefonen?**	kahn yæi faw **law**ner tehler**foon**ern
Hello. This is...	**Hallo. Dette er...**	hahloo. **deh**ter ær
I'd like to speak to...	**Kan jeg få snakke med...?**	kahn yæi faw **snah**ker meh(d)
When will he/she be back?	**Når kommer han/ hun tilbake?**	nor **kom**mer hahn/hewn til**baa**ker
Will you tell him/her I called?	**Kan du si til ham/ henne at jeg ringte?**	kahn dew see til hahm/ **heh**ner aht yæi haar ringt
Would you ask her to phone me?	**Kan du be henne om å ringe meg?**	kahn dew bay **heh**ner om aw **ring**er mæi
Would you take a message?	**Kan du ta imot en beskjed?**	kahn dew taa eemoot ehn ber**shay**

NUMBERS, see page 124

Doctor *Lege*

Where can I find a doctor who speaks English?	**Hvor kan jeg få tak i en lege som snakker engelsk?**	voor kahn yæi faw taak ee ehn l**ay**ger som sn**ah**kerr **ehng**erlsk
Where's the surgery (doctor's office)?	**Hvor er legekontoret?**	voor ær l**ay**gernkoont**oo**rer
Can I have an appointment...?	**Kan jeg få bestille en time til...?**	kahn yæi faw **tee**mer
tomorrow	**i morgen**	ee m**aw**er'n
as soon as possible	**så snart som mulig**	saw snaa't som m**ew**li

Parts of the body *Kroppsdeler*

arm	**armen**	**ahr**mern
back	**ryggen**	**rew**gern
bone	**benet (i kroppen)**	b**ay**ner (ee kr**o**ppern)
ear	**øret**	**ur**rer
eye	**øye**	**o**yer
face	**ansiktet**	**ahn**sikter
finger	**fingeren**	**fing**errern
foot	**foten**	**foo**tern
hand	**hånden**	**ho**nern
head	**hodet**	**hoo**der
heart	**hjertet**	**yæ**'ter
knee	**kneet**	kn**ay**er
leg	**benet**	b**ay**ner
lung	**lungen**	**loong**ern
mouth	**munnen**	**mew**nern
muscle	**muskelen**	**mews**kerlern
neck	**nakken**	**nah**kern
nose	**nesen**	**nay**ssern
shoulder	**skulderen**	**skewl**derrern
skin	**huden**	**hew**dern
stomach	**magen**	**maa**gern
throat	**halsen**	**hahl**sern
tongue	**tungen**	**toong**ern
I've got a/an...	**Jeg har fått...**	yæi haar fot
blister	**en blemme**	ehn **bleh**mer
bruise	**et blått merke**	eht blot **mær**ker
burn	**et brannsår**	eht **brahn**sawr
cut	**et kutt**	eht kewt
rash	**et utslett**	eht **ewt**shleht
sting	**et stikk**	eht stik
swelling	**en hevelse**	ehn **hay**verlser
wound	**et sår**	eht sawr

Could you have a look at it?	**Kan du undersøke det?**	kahn dew **ewn**ershūrker deh
It hurts.	**Det gjør vondt.**	deh yūrr voont
I feel ...	**Jeg føler meg ...**	yæi **fūr**lerr mæi
dizzy	**svimmel**	**svim**merl
nauseous	**kvalm**	kvahlm
I feel shivery.	**Jeg har kulde-gysninger.**	yæi haar **kew**leryēwsningerr
I'm diabetic.	**Jeg er diabetiker.**	yæi ær deeah**bay**tikkerr
Can you give me a prescription for this?	**Kan du gi meg en resept på dette?**	kahn dew yee mæi ehn reh**sehpt** paw **deh**ter
May I have a receipt for my health insurance?	**Kan jeg få en kvittering for sykeforsikringen?**	kahn yæi faw ehn kvit**tay**ring for **sew**kerfoshikringern

---

Hvor lenge har du følt deg slik?	How long have you been feeling like this?
Hvor gjør det vondt?	Where does it hurt?
Jeg skal ta temperaturen/måle blodtrykket.	I'll take your temperature/blood pressure.
Jeg skal gi deg en sprøyte.	I'll give you an injection.
Jeg vil ha en blodprøve/avføringsprøve/urinprøve.	I want a specimen of your blood/stools/urine.
Du bør holde sengen i ... dager.	You must stay in bed for ... days.
Du bør oppsøke en spesialist.	I want you to see a specialist.

Can you recommend a good dentist?	**Kan du anbefale en god tannlege?**	kahn dew **ahn**berfaaler ehn goo(d) **tahn**layger
I have toothache.	**Jeg har tannpine.**	yæi haar **tahn**peener
I've lost a filling.	**Jeg har mistet en plombe.**	yæi haar **mis**tert ehn **ploom**ber

What time is it? *Hvor mange er klokken?*

It's...	Den er...	dehn ær
five past one	**fem over ett**	fehm **aw**verr eht
ten past two	**ti over to**	tee **aw**verr too
a quarter past three	**kvart over tre**	kvah't **aw**verr tray
twenty past four	**tjue over fire/ti på halv fem**	khewer awverr feerer/tee paw hahl fehm
twenty-five past five	**fem på halv seks**	fehm paaw hahl sehkss
half past six	**halv sju**	hahl shew
twenty-five to seven	**fem over halv sju**	fehm **aw**verr hahl shew
twenty to eight	**ti over halv åtte/ tjue på åtte**	tee **aw**verr hahl otter/ khewer paw otter
a quarter to nine	**kvart på ni**	kvah't paw nee
ten to ten	**ti på ti**	tee paw tee
five to eleven	**fem på elleve**	fehm paw **ehl**ver
twelve o'clock	**klokken tolv**	**klok**kern tol
in the morning	**om morgenen**	om **maw'**nern
in the afternoon	**om ettermiddagen**	om **ehterr**middaagern
in the evening	**om kvelden**	om **kveh**lern
at night	**om natten**	om **nah**tern
yesterday/today	**i går/i dag**	ee gawr/ee daag
tomorrow	**i morgen**	ee **maw**er'n
spring/summer	**vår/sommer**	vawr/**som**merr
autumn/winter	**høs/vinter**	hurst/**vin**terr

Sunday	**søndag**	**surn**dah(g)
Monday	**mandag**	**mahn**dah(g)
Tuesday	**tirsdag**	**teesh**dah(g)
Wednesday	**onsdag**	**oons**dah(g)
Thursday	**torsdag**	**tawsh**dah(g)
Friday	**fredag**	**fray**dah(g)
Saturday	**lørdag**	**lur'**dah(g)
January	**januar**	yahne**waar**
February	**februar**	fehbre**waar**
March	**mars**	mahsh
April	**april**	ah**preel**
May	**mai**	maay
June	**juni**	**yew**nee
July	**juli**	**yew**lee
August	**august**	ou**gewst**
September	**september**	sehp**tehm**berr
October	**oktober**	ok**taw**berr
November	**november**	noo**vehm**berr
December	**desember**	deh**ssehm**berr

Numbers *Tall*

0	**null**	newl
1	**en**	$\overline{ay}$n
2	**to**	t$\overline{oo}$
3	**tre**	tr$\overline{ay}$
4	**fire**	feerer
5	**fem**	fehm
6	**seks**	sehkss
7	**sju**	sh$\overline{ew}$
8	**åtte**	otter
9	**ni**	nee
10	**ti**	tee
11	**elleve**	ehlver
12	**tolv**	tol
13	**tretten**	trehtern
14	**fjorten**	fyoo'tern
15	**femten**	fehmtern
16	**seksten**	sæistern
17	**sytten**	surtern
18	**atten**	ahtern
19	**nitten**	nittern
20	**tjue**	kh$\overline{ew}$er
21	**tjueen**	kh$\overline{ew}$erayn
30	**tretti**	trehti
40	**førti**	fur'ti
50	**femti**	fehmti
60	**seksti**	sehksti
70	**sytti**	surti
80	**åtti**	otti
90	**nitti**	nitti
100	**hundre**	hewndrer
1000	**tusen**	t$\overline{ew}$ssern
100,000	**hundre tusen**	hewndrer t$\overline{ew}$ssern
1,000,000	**en million**	ehn mily$\overline{oo}$n

first	**første**	furshter
second	**annen/andre**	aaern/ahndrer
third	**tredje**	tr$\overline{ay}$dyer
once	**en gang**	ehn gahng
twice	**to ganger**	t$\overline{oo}$ gahngerr
a half	**en halv**	ehn hahl
a quarter	**en fjerdedel**	ehn fy$\overline{æ}$rerd$\overline{ay}$l
a third	**en tredjedel**	ehn tr$\overline{ay}$dyerd$\overline{ay}$l
a pair	**et par**	eht pahr
a dozen	**et dusin**	eht dewsseen

Where do you come from? *Hvor kommer du fra?*

Canada	**Kanada**	**kah**nahdah
Denmark	**Danmark**	**dahn**mahrk
England	**England**	**ehng**lahn
Finland	**Finland**	**fin**lahn
Great Britain	**Storbritannia**	**stoor**brittahneeah
Iceland	**Island**	**ees**lahn
Ireland	**Irland**	**eer**lahn
New Zealand	**Ny-Zealand**	nēw-**sāy**lahn
Norway	**Norge**	**nor**gger
Scotland	**Skottland**	**skot**lahn
South Africa	**Sør-Afrika**	**sūrr**aafreekah
Sweden	**Sverige**	**svær**yer
United States	**USA**	ēw-**ehss**-aa

Signs and notices *Skilt og oppslag*

Damer	Ladies
Forsiktig	Caution
Forsiktig, trapp	Mind the step
Gratis adgang	Free admittance
Herrer	Gentlemen
Høgspenning	High voltage
I uorden	Out of order
Kaldt	Cold
Kasse	Cash desk (Cashier)
Ledig	Free/Vacant
Livsfare	Danger (of death)
Nymalt	Wet paint
Nødutgang	Emergency exit
Opptatt	Occupied
Privat	Private
Privat vei/veg	Private road
Reservert	Reserved
Røyking forbudt	No smoking
Røyking (ikke) tillatt	(Non)Smoker
Stengt	Closed
Skyv	Push
Trekk	Pull
Utgang	Exit
Varmt	Hot
Vokt deg/Dem for hunden	Beware of the dog
Åpent	Open
Åpningstider	Opening hours

Emergency *Nødsfall*

Call the police	**Ring til politiet**	ring til poolit**tee**yer
Get a doctor	**Hent en lege**	hehnt ehn **lay**ger
Go away	**Gå vekk**	gaw vehk
HELP	**HJELP**	yehlp
I'm ill	**Jeg er syk**	yæi ær sēwk
I'm lost	**Jeg har gått meg bort**	yæi haar got mæi boo't
Leave me alone	**La meg være i fred**	lah mæi **vær**er ee frāy(d)
LOOK OUT	**SE OPP**	sāy op
STOP THIEF	**STOPP TYVEN**	stop **tēw**vern
My... has been stolen.	**... er blitt stjålet.**	... ær blit **styaw**lert
I've lost my...	**Jeg har mistet ...**	yæi haar **mis**tert
handbag	**håndvesken**	**hon**vehskern
passport	**passet**	**pahs**ser
wallet	**lommeboken**	**loom**merbōōkern

Guide to Norwegian pronunciation *Uttale*

Consonants

Letter	Approximate pronunciation	Symbol	Example	
b,c,d, f,h,l, m,n,p, q,t,v,x	as in English			
g	1) before **ei, i** and **y**, generally like **y** in **y**es	y	**gi**	yee
	2) before **e** and **i** in some words of French origin, like **sh** in **sh**ut	sh	**geni**	sheh**nee**
	3) elsewhere. like **g** in **g**o	g	**gått**	got
gj	like **y** in **y**es	y	**gjest**	yehst
j	like **y** in **y**es	y	**ja**	yaa

TELEPHONING, see page 120

k	1) before **i**, and **y**, generally like **ch** in German i**ch** (quite like **h** in **h**uge, but with the tongue raised a little higher)	kh	**kino**	**kh**eenoo
	2) elsewhere, like **k** in ki**t**	k	**kaffe**	**k**ahfer
kj	like **ch** in German i**ch**	kh	**kjøre**	**kh**ürrer
r	rolled near the front of the mouth	r	**rare**	**r**aarer
rs	like **sh** in **sh**ut	sh	nor**sk**	no**sh**k
s	like **s** in **s**it	s/ss	**spise**	**s**pee**ss**er
sj	generally like **sh** in **sh**ut	sh	**stasjon**	stah**sh**oon
sk	1) before **i**, **y** and **ø**, generally like **sh** in **sh**ut	sh	**ski**	**sh**ee
	2) elsewhere, like **sk** in **sk**ate	sk	**skole**	**sk**ooler
skj	like **sh** in **sh**ut	sh	**skje**	**sh**ay
w	like **v** in **v**ice	v	**whisky**	**v**iski
z	like **s** in **s**it	s	**zoom**	**s**oom

Vowels

a	1) when long, like **a** in car	aa	**dag**	d**aa**g
	2) when short, between **a** in c**a**r and **u** in c**u**t	ah	**takk**	t**ah**k
e	1) when long, like **ay** in say, but a pure vowel, not a diphthong	āy	**sent**	s**āy**nt
	2) when followed by **r**, often like **a** in man (long or short)	ǣ æ	**her** **herre**	h**ǣ**r h**æ**rer
	3) when short, like **e** in get	eh	**penn**	p**eh**n
	4) when unstressed, like **a** in about	er	**betale**	b**er**taaler
i	1) when long, like **ee** in bee	ee	**hit**	h**ee**t
	2) when short, like **i** in sit	i	**sitt**	s**i**t

o	1) when long, often like **oo** in s**oo**n, but with the lips more tightly rounded	$\overline{oo}$	**ord**	$\overline{oo}$rd
	2) the same sound can be short, like **oo** in f**oo**t	oo	**ost**	oost
	3) when long, sometimes like **aw** in s**aw**	aw	**tog**	tawg
	4) when short, sometimes like **o** in g**o**t (British pronunciation)	o	**stoppe**	**stop**per
u	1) something like **ew** in f**ew**, or Scottish **oo** in g**oo**d (long or short)	$\overline{ew}$ ew	**mur** **busk**	m$\overline{ew}$r bewsk
	2) occasionally like **oo** in f**oo**t	oo	**nummer**	**noom**merr
y	very much like the sound described under **u** (1) above (long or short); put your tongue in the position for the **ee** in b**ee**, and then round your lips as for the **oo** in p**oo**l	$\overline{ew}$ ew	**by** **bygge**	b$\overline{ew}$ **bew**ger
æ	like **a** in **a**ct (long or short)	$\overline{æ}$	**lære**	**læ**rer
ø	like **ur** in f**ur**, but with the lips rounded (long or short)	$\overline{ur}$ ur	**dør** **sønn**	d$\overline{ur}$r surn
å	1) when long, like **aw** in s**aw**	aw	**såpe**	**saw**per
	2) when short, like **o** in g**o**t (British pronunciation)	o	**sånn**	son

Diphthongs

| au | rather like **ou** in l**ou**d, though the first part is the Norwegian ø-sound | ou | **sau** | sou |
| ei, eg, egn | like **ai** in w**ai**t, though first part is the Norwegian æ-sound | æi | **geit** **jeg** **tegne** | yæit yæi **tæi**ner |

Swedish

Some basic expressions *Användbara uttryck*

Yes/No.	**Ja/Nej.**	yaa/nay
Please.	**Var snäll och .../..., tack.**	vaar snehl ok/tahk
Thank you.	**Tack.**	tahk
I beg your pardon?	**Förlåt?**	fur'lawt

Introductions *Presentation*

Good morning.	**God morgon.**	goo(d) morron
Good afternoon.	**God middag.**	goo(d) middah(g)
Good night.	**God natt.**	goo(d) naht
Good-bye.	**Adjö.**	ahyūr
Hello/Hi!	**Hej!**	hay
My name is ...	**Mitt namn är ...**	mit nahmn ǣr
What's your name?	**Vad heter ni/du?**	vaad hāyterr nee/dēw
Pleased to meet you!	**Trevligt att träffas!**	trāyvlli(g)t aht trehfahss
How are you?	**Hur mår ni/du?**	hēwr mawr nee/dēw
Very well, thanks. And you?	**Bara bra, tack. Och ni/du?**	baarah braa tahk. ok nee/dēw
Where do you come from?	**Varifrån kommer du?**	vaarifrawn kommer dēw
I'm from ...	**Jar är från ...**	yaa(g) ǣr frawn
Australia	**Australien**	aaewstraaliern
Canada	**Kanada**	kahnahdah
Great Britain	**Storbritannien**	stōōrbrittahniern
United States	**USA**	ēwehssaa
I'm with my ...	**Jar är här med ...**	yaa(g) ǣr hǣr māyd
wife	**min fru**	min frēw
husband	**min man**	min mahn
family	**min familj**	min fahmily
boyfriend	**min pojkvän**	min poykvehn
girlfriend	**min flickvän**	min flikvehn
I'm here on business/ vacation.	**Jag är här i affärer/på semester.**	yaa(g) ǣr hǣr ee ahfǣrerr/ paw sehmehsterr

PRONUNCIATION, see page 158/EMERGENCIES, page 157

Questions *Frågor*

When?/How?	**När?/Hur?**	næær/heewr
What?/Why?	**Vad?/Varför?**	vaad/**vahr**furr
Who?	**Vem?**	vehm
Which?	**Vilken?**	**vil**kern
Where is/are ...?	**Var är/Var finns/ Var ligger ...?**	vaar æær/vaar finss/vaar **lig**gerr
Where can I find ...?	**Var hittar jag?**	vaaar **hit**tahr yaa(g)
Where can I get ...?	**Var kan jag få tag på ...?**	vaar kahn yaa(g) faw taag paw
How far?	**Hur långt?**	heewr longt
How long?	**Hur länge?**	heewr **leh**nger
How much/many?	**Hur mycket/ många?**	heewr **mewk**er(t)/**mong**ah
Can I have ...?	**Kan jag få ...?**	kahn yaa(g) faw
Can you help me?	**Kan ni hjälpa mig?**	kahn nee **yehl**pah may
Is there/Are there ...?	**Finns det ...?**	finss daay(t)
There isn't/aren't ...	**Det finns inte ...**	daay(t) finss **in**ter
There isn't/aren't any.	**Det finns ingen/ inga.**	daay(t) finss **ing**ern/**ing**ah

Do you speak ...? *Talar ni ...?*

What does this/that mean?	**Vad betyder det här/det där?**	vaa(d) ber**tew**derr daay(t) hæær/daay(t) dæær
Can you translate this for us?	**Kan ni översätta det här för oss?**	kahn nee **eer**ver'sehtah daay(t) hæær furr oss
Do you speak English?	**Talar ni engelska?**	**taa**lahr nee **ehng**erlskah
I don't speak (much) Swedish.	**Jag talar inte (så bra) svenska.**	yaa(g) **taa**lahr **in**ter (saw braa) **svehn**skah
Could you speak more slowly?	**Kan ni tala lite långsammare?**	kahn nee **taa**lah **li**ter **long**sahmahrer
Could you repeat that?	**Kan ni upprepa det där?**	kahn nee **ewp**ray'pah daay(t) dæær
Could you write it down, please?	**Skulle ni kunna skriva det?**	**skew**ler nee **kew**nnah **skree**vah daay(t)
I understand.	**Jag förstår.**	yaa(g) fur'**stawr**
I don't understand.	**Jag förstår inte.**	yaa(g) fur'**stawr** **in**ter

It's ...	Den är ...	
better/worse	**bättre/sämre**	behtrer/sehmrer
big/small	**stor/liten**	stoor/leetern
early/late	**tidig/sen**	teedi(g)/sayn
good/bad	**bra/dålig**	braa/dawli(g)
hot/cold	**varm/kall**	vahrm/kahl
near/far	**nära/långt (bort)**	nǣrah/longt (bo't)
right/wrong	**rätt/fel**	reht/fayl
vacant/occupied	**ledig/upptagen**	laydi(g)/ewptaagern

A few more useful words *Några fler användbara ord*

a little/a lot	**lite/mycket**	leeter/mewker(t)
above	**ovanför**	awvahnfurr
after	**efter**	ehfterr
and	**och**	ok
behind	**bakom**	baakom
below	**nedanför**	naydahnfurr
between	**mellan**	mehlahn
but	**men**	mehn
downstairs	**där nere**	dǣr nayrer
during	**under**	ewnderr
for	**för**	furr
from	**från**	frawn
inside	**inne**	inner
near	**nära**	nǣrah
never	**aldrig**	ahldrig
next to	**bredvid**	bray(d)veed
none	**ingen**	ingern
not	**inte**	inter
nothing	**ingenting, inget**	ingernting ingert
now	**nu**	new
on	**på**	paw
only	**bara**	baarah
or	**eller**	ehlerr
outside	**ute**	ewter
perhaps	**kanske**	kahnsher
soon	**snart**	snaa't
then	**då, sedan**	daw sehn
through	**genom**	yaynom
too	**också**	okso
towards	**mot**	moot
under	**under**	ewnderr
until	**till**	til
upstairs	**där uppe**	dǣr ewper
very	**mycket**	mewker(t)
with	**med**	mayd
without	**utan**	ewtahn

Hotel—Other accommodation *Hotell*

I have a reservation.	**Jag har beställt rum.**	yaa(g) haar berstehlt rewm
We've reserved 2 rooms.	**Vi har beställt 2 rum.**	vee haar berstehlt 2 rewm
Do you have any vacancies?	**Har ni några lediga rum?**	har nee nawgrah laydiggah rewm
I'd like a ...	**Jag skulle vilja ha ett ...**	yaa(g) skewler vilyah haa eht
single room	**enkelrum**	ehnkerlrewm
double room	**dubbelrum**	dewberlrewm
with twin beds	**med två sängar**	mayd tvaw sehngahr
with a double bed	**med dubbelsäng**	mayd dewberlsehng
with a bath	**med bad**	mayd baad
with a shower	**med dusch**	mayd dewsh
Is there ...?	**Finns det ...?**	finss day(t)
air conditioning	**luftkonditionering**	lewftkondishonnayring
a private toilet	**toalett på rummet**	tooahleht paw rewmert
a radio/television in the room	**radio/TV på rummet**	raaydo/tayveh paw rewmert
a sauna	**bastu**	bahstew
What's the price ...?	**Vad kostar det ...?**	vaad kostahr day(t)
Is there a camp site near here?	**Finns det nagon campingplats i närheten?**	finss day(t) nawgon kahmpingplahtss ee nærhaytern
Can we camp here?	**Kan vi campa här?**	kahn vee kahmpah hær
We'll be staying ...	**Vi tänker stanna ...**	vee tehnkerr stahnah
overnight only	**bara över natten**	baarah ūrverr nahtern
a few days	**några dagar**	nawgrah daa(gah)r
a week	**en vecka**	ehn vehkah

Decision *Beslut*

May I see the room?	**Kan jag få se på rummet?**	kahn yaa(g) faw say paw rewmert
That's fine. I'll take it.	**Det är bra. Jag tar det.**	day(t) ær braa. yaa(g) taar day(t)
No. I don't like it.	**Nej. Jag tycker inte om det.**	nay. yaa(g) tewkerr inter om day(t)
It's too ...	**Det är för ...**	day(t) ær fūrr
cold	**kallt**	kahlt
dark/small	**mörkt/litet**	murrkt/leetert

NUMBERS, see page 156

Do you have anything ...?	**Har ni något ...?**	haar nee **naw**got
better/bigger	**bättre/större**	**beht**rer/**stur**rer
cheaper	**billigare**	**bil**liggahrer
quieter	**tystare**	**tew**stahrer

Efternamn/Förnamn	Name/First name
Hemort/Gata/Nummer	Home town/Street/Number
Nationalitet/Yrke	Nationality/Occupation
Födelsedatum/Födelseort	Date/Place of birth
Inrest ...	Arrived on ...
Passnummer	Passport number
Ort/Datum	Place/Date
Underskrift	Signature

General requirements *Allmänna förfrågningar*

The key to room ..., please.	**Nyckeln till rum ..., tack.**	**new**ker(l)n til rewm ... tahk
Where's the ...?	**Var är ...?**	vaar ær
bathroom	**badrummet**	**baad**rewmert
dining-room	**matsalen**	**maat**saalern
emergency exit	**nödutgång**	**nūrd**ewtgawngern
lift (elevator)	**hissen**	**his**sern
Where are the toilets?	**Var är toaletten?**	vaar ær tooah**leh**tern
Where can I park my car?	**Var kan jag parkera bilen?**	vaar kahn yaa(g) pahr**kāy**rah **bee**lehn

Checking out *Avresa*

May I have my bill, please?	**Kan jag få räkningen, tack?**	kahn yaa(g) faw **raik**ningern tahk
Can you get us a taxi?	**Kan ni skaffa oss en taxi?**	kahn nee **skahf**fah oss ehn **tahk**si
It's been a very enjoyable stay.	**Det har varit en mycket trevlig vistelse.**	dāy(t) haar **vaa**rit ehn **mew**ker(t) **trāyv**li(g) **vis**terlser

Eating out *Mat och dryck*

Can you recommend a good restaurant?	**Kan ni föreslå en bra restaurang?**	kahn nee **fur**rerslaw ehn braa rehsto**rrah**ng
I'd like to reserve a table for 4.	**Jag skulle vilja beställa ett bord för 4.**	yaa(g) **skew**ler **vil**yah ber**steh**lah eht bōo͞rd fur 4
We'll come at 8.	**Vi kommer klockan 8.**	vee **ko**mmerr **klo**kkahn 8
I'd like breakfast/lunch/dinner, please.	**Jag skulle vilja ha frukost/lunch/middag, tack.**	yaa(g) **skew**ler **vil**yah haa **frew**kost/lewnsh/**mi**ddah(g) tahk
What do you recommend?	**Vad rekommenderar ni?**	vaad rehkommern**day**rahr nee
Do you have a set menu/local dishes?	**Har ni någon meny/lokal specialitet?**	haar nee **naw**gon meh**new**/loo**kaal** spehssiahli**tay**(t)
Do you have any vegetarian dishes?	**Har ni några vegetariska rätter?**	haar nee **naw**grah vehger**taa**riskah **reh**terr

---

Vad önskar ni?	What would you like?
Jag rekommenderar det här.	I recommend this.
Vad önskas att dricka?	What would you like to drink?
Vi har inte ...	We don't have ...
Önskar ni ...?	Would you like ...?

Could we have a/an ..., please?	**Kan vi få ..., tack?**	kahn vee faw ... tahk
ashtray	**en askkopp**	ehn **ahs**kop
cup	**en kopp**	ehn kop
fork	**en gaffel**	ehn **gah**fehl
glass	**ett glas**	eht glaass
knife	**en kniv**	ehn kneev
napkin (serviette)	**en servett**	ehn sehr**veht**
plate	**en tallrik**	ehn **tahl**rik
spoon	**en sked**	ehn sh**ay**d

NUMBERS, see page 156/TELLING THE TIME, page 155

Svensk

May I have some ...?	**Kan jag få lite ...?**	kahn yaa(g) faw **lee**ter
bread	**bröd**	brūrd
butter	**smör**	smūrr
lemon	**citron**	si**trōōn**
oil	**olja**	**ol**yah
pepper	**peppar**	**peh**pahr
salt	**salt**	sahlt
seasoning	**kryddor**	**krew**door
sugar	**socker**	**so**kker
vinegar	**vinäger**	vin**nai**gerr

Reading the menu *Att läsa matsedeln*

bakverk	**baak**vehrk	pastries
drycker	**drew**kkerr	drinks
efterrätter	**ehf**terrehterr	desserts
fisk	fisk	fish
frukt	frewkt	fruit
fågel	**faw**gerl	poultry
glass	glahss	ice cream
grönsaker	**grūrn**saakerr	vegetables
kött	khurt	meat
ost	oost	cheese
pastarätter	**pahs**tahrehterr	pasta
risrätter	**rees**rehterr	rice
sallader	**sahl**lahderr	salads
skaldjut	**skaal**yēwr	seafood
soppor	**sop**poor	soups
smårätter	**smaw**rehterr	snacks
smörgåsar	**smurr**gawssahr	open sandwiches
smörgåsbord	**smurr**gawsbōō'd	smörgåsbord
vilt	vilt	game
vinlista	**veen**listah	wine list
äggrätter	**ehg**rehterr	egg dishes

Breakfast *Frukost*

I'd like...	**Jag skulle vilja ha...**	yaa(g) **skew**ler **vil**yah haa
bread/butter	**lite bröd/smör**	**lee**ter brūrd/smūrr
cheese	**ost**	oost
eggs	**ägg**	ehg
ham and eggs	**skinka och ägg**	**shin**kah ok ehg
jam/roll	**lite sylt/ett små-franska**	**lee**ter sewlt/eht **smaw**frahnskah

Starters (Appetizers) *Förrätter*

grodlår	gr**oo**dlawr	frog's legs
gåslever	gawsl**ay**verr	goose liver
kaviar	kahv**y**ahr	caviar
musslor	mewsloor	mussels
ostron	**oo**stron	oysters
paté	pah**toy**	paté
sniglar	sn**ee**glahr	snails

Soups *Soppor*

I'd like some soup.	**Jag skulle vilja ha en soppa.**	yaa(g) **skew**ler vi**l**yah haa ehn **soppah**

champinjonsoppa	shamhpiny**oo**nsoppah	mushroom soup
fisksoppa	**fisk**soppah	fish soup
hummersoppa	**hew**merrsoppah	lobster soup
kålsoppa	**kawl**soppah	cabbage soup
nässelsoppa	**neh**sserlsoppah	nettle soup
oxvanssoppa	**ooks**svahnssoppah	oxtail soup

blåbärssoppa (blawb**æ**ʳssoppah)	sweet bilberry soup; served as a dessert or a vitamin-packed pick-me-up

Fish and seafood *Fisk och skaldjur*

abborre	**ah**borrer	perch
bläckfisk	**blehk**fisk	octopus
böckling	**burk**ling	smoked herring
flundra	**flewn**drah	flounder
forell	for**rehl**	trout
hälleflundra	**hehl**erflewndrah	halibut
hummer	**hew**merr	lobster
kolja	**kol**yah	haddock
krabba	**krah**bah	crab
lax	lahks	salmon
räkor	**rai**koor	prawns (shrimp)
rödspätta	r**ū**r(d)spehtah	plaice
sill	sil	herring
sjötunga	sh**ū**rtewngah	sole
tonfisk	**too**nfisk	tuna (tunny)

gravlax (**graav**lahks)	salmon marinated with salt, sugar (pepper) and dill; served with a sweet-sour mustard-vinegar-oil sauce with plenty of dill	
kräftströmming (**krehft**strurming)	Baltic herring baked with crushed tomatoes and lots of dill; served warm or cold with boiled potatoes	
stuvad abborre (**stew**vahd **ah**borrer)	perch, poached with onion, parsley and lemon; served with boiled potatoes	

baked	**ugnstekt**	ewngnstaykt
boiled	**kokt**	kookt
fried	**stekt**	staykt
grilled	**halstrad, grillad**	hahlstrahd grillahd
whole roasted	**helstekt**	haylstaykt
underdone (rare)	**blodig**	bloodig
medium	**medium**	maydeeyewn
well-done	**genomstekt**	yaynomstaykt

Meat *Kött*

beef/lamb	**oxkött/lamm**	ookskhurt/lahm
chicken/duck	**kyckling/anka**	khewkling/ahnkah
pork/veal	**fläskkött/kalv**	flehskkhurt/kahlv
biff	bif	beef steak
björnstek	byur'nstayk	roast bear
fläskkorv	flehskkorv	spicy boiled pork sausage
fläskpannkaka	flehskpahnkaakah	thick oven-baked pancake with bacon, served with cranberries
gås	gawss	goose
kalkon	kahlkoon	turkey
kalvsylta	khalvsewlta	jellied veal loaf
korv	korv	sausage
köttbullar	khurtbewlahr	meat balls
pepparrotskött	pehpahrrootskhurt	boiled beef with horseradish sauce
rökt renstek	rurkt raynstayk	roast reindeer
(rökt) skinka	(ruurkt) shinkah	(smoked) ham
älg	ehly	elk

kåldomar
(**kawl**dolmahr)

cabbage rolls, stuffed with minced meat and rice; served with cream gravy

pytt i panna
(pewt ee**pah**nah)

Swedish hash; chunks of fried meat, sausages, onions and potatoes; served with a fried egg and pickled beetroot

Vegetables and salads *Grönsaker och sallader*

beans	**bönor**	**būr**noor
beetroots	**rödbetor**	**rūr(d)bāy**toor
broccoli	**broccoli**	**brok**koli
cabbage	**kål**	kawl
carrots	**morötter**	**mōō**rurterr
cauliflower	**blomkål**	**bloom**kawl
cucumber	**gurka**	**gewr**kah
leeks	**purjolök**	**pewr**yoolūrk
lettuce	**grönsallad**	**grūrn**sahlahd
mushrooms	**svamp**	svahmp
onions	**lök**	lūrk
peas	**ärtor**	**æ'**toor
potatoes	**potatis**	poo**taa**tiss
spinach	**spenat**	speh**naat**
swede (rutabaga)	**kålrot**	**kawl**rōōt
tomatoes	**tomater**	too**maa**terr

grönsallad
(**grūrn**sahlahd)

lettuce, cucumber, tomatoes, parsley, dill with oil and vinegar dressing; accompanies the main course

hasselbackspotatis
(**hahs**serlbahkspoo-taatiss)

potatoes coated with melted butter, breadcrumbs and sometimes grated cheese, baked

kroppkakor
(**krop**kaakoor)

potato dumplings with a filling of minced bacon and onions; served with melted butter

raggmunk med fläsk
(**rahg**mewnk māyd flaisk)

potato pancake with lightly salted pork served with cranberries

skaldjurssallad
(**skaal**yew'ssahlahd)

assorted seafood salad (mostly mussels and shrimps)

västkustsallad
(**vehst**kewstsahlahd)

assorted seafood salad with mushrooms, tomatoes, lettuce, cucumber, asparagus and dill

Fruit *Frukt*

apple	**äpple**	ehpler
Arctic cloudberries	**hjortron**	yoo'tron
banana	**banan**	bahnaan
blackberries	**björnbär**	byūr'nbær
blackcurrants	**svarta vinbär**	sva'tah veenbær
bilberries (blueberries)	**blåbär**	blawbær
cherries	**körsbär**	khur'sbær
cranberries	**lingon**	lingon
gooseberries	**krusbär**	krēwsbær
grapes	**vindruvor**	veendrēwvoor
grapefruit	**grapefrukt**	"grape"frewkt
lemon	**citron**	sitrōōn
melon	**melon**	mehlōōn
orange	**apelsin**	ahperlseen
peach	**persika**	pær'sikah
pear	**päron**	pæron
plums	**plommon**	ploomon
raspberries	**hallon**	hahlon
rowanberries	**rönnbär**	rurnbær
strawberries	**jordgubbär**	yoo'dgewbahr
wild strawberries	**smultron**	smewltron

Desserts—Pastries *Efterrätter—Bakverk*

chokladmousse	shoklaa(d)mooss	chocolate mousse
glass	glahss	ice cream
jordgubbar med grädde	yoo'dgewbahr māyd grehder	strawberries with cream
kanelbulle	kahnāylbewler	cinnamon bun
mjuk pepparkaka	myēwk pehpahrkaakah	gingerbread cake
våfflor med sylt	vofloor māyd sewlt	waffles with jam
äppelkaka med vaniljsås	ehperlkaakah māyd vanilysawss	apple cake with vanilla custard

mazarin (mahssahreen)	Sweden's most beloved pastry; almond tart topped with icing
plättar (plehtahr)	small pancakes; eaten with sugar or jam, sometimes whipped cream
toscaäpplen (toskahehplern	stewed apples covered with toffee sauce and almond flakes

Drinks *Alkoholhaltiga drycker*

beer	**öl**	ūrl
(hot) chocolate	**(varm) choklad**	(vahrm) shoklaa(d)
coffee	**kaffe**	kahfer
espresso	**en espresso**	ehn ehsprehsso
with cream	**med grädde**	māyd grehder
fruit juice	**juice**	yōōss
lemonade	**en läsk**	ehn lehsk
(glass of) milk	**(ett glas) mjölk**	(eht glaass) myurlk
mineral water	**mineralvatten**	minerraalvahtern
fizzy (carbonated)	**med kolsyra**	māyd kawsēwrah
still	**utan kolsyra**	ēwtahn kawsēwrah
sugar	**socker**	sokkerr
tea	**te**	tāy
a cup of	**en kopp**	ehn kop
with lemon/milk	**med citron/mjölk**	māyd sitrōōn/myurlk
iced tea	**iste**	eestāy
wine	**vin**	veen
red/white	**rött/vitt**	rurt/vit

May I have the wine list, please?	**Kan jag få vinlistan, tack?**	kahn yaa(g) faw veenlistahn tahk
I'd like a beer, please.	**Jag skulle vilja ha en öl, tack.**	yaa(g) skewler vilyah haa ehn ūrl tahk

Bäska Droppar (behskah droppahr)	bitter-tasting aquavit, flavoured with wormwood	
Herrgårds (Aquavit) (hehrgaw^rds ahkvahveet)	flavoured with caraway seeds and whisky matured in sherry barrels	
O.P. (Anderson Aquavit) (oo pāy)	aquavit flavoured with aniseed, caraway seeds and fennel	
Punsch (pewnsh)	sweet, strong liqueur made of arrak, sugar and pure alcohol	

neat	**ren**	rāyn
on the rocks	**med is**	māyd ees
with water	**med vatten**	māyd vahtern

Complaints *Klagomål*

The meat is ...	**Köttet är ...**	khurtert ær
overdone	**för mycket stekt**	furr mewker(t) stāykt
underdone	**inte tillräckligt genomstekt**	inter tilrehkli(g)t yāynomstāykt
This is too ...	**Det här är för ...**	dāy(t) hær ær furr
bitter/salty/sweet	**beskt/salt/sött**	behskt/sahlt/surt
That's not what I ordered.	**Det där har jag inte beställt.**	dāy(t) dær haar yaa(g) inter berstehlt
The food is cold.	**Maten är kall.**	maatern ær kahl

The bill (check) *Notan*

I'd like to pay.	**Får jag betala?**	fawr yaa(g) bertaalah
What's this amount for?	**Vad står den här summan för?**	vaad stawr den hær sewmahn furr
I think there's a mistake in this bill.	**Jag tror att det är ett fel på notan.**	yaa(g) trōōr aht dāy(t) ær eht fāyl paw nōōtahn
Is everything included?	**Är allting inräknat?**	ær ahlting inraiknaht
Can I pay with this credit card?	**Kan ja betala met det här kreditkortet?**	kahn yaa(g) bertaalah māyd dāy(t) hær krehdeetkoo'tert
We enjoyed it, thank you.	**Det var mycket gott.**	dāy(t) vaar mewker(t) got

Snacks—Picnic *Mellanmål—Picknick*

I'll have one of those.	**Jag skulle vilja ha en av de där.**	yaa(g) skewler vilyah haa ehn ahv dāy dær
to the left/right	**till vänster/höger**	til vehnsterr/hūrgerr
above/below	**ovanför/nedanför**	awvahnfurr/nāydahnfurr
cheese	**ost**	oost
chips (french fries)	**pommes frites**	pom frit
Danish pastry	**wienerbröd**	veenerbrūrd
fried sausage	**en grillad korv**	ehn grillahd korv
gherkins (pickles)	**ättiksgurkor**	ehtiksgewrkah
liver paté	**leverpastej**	lāyverrpahstay
spring roll	**vårrulle**	vawrrewler

NUMBERS, see page 156

Travelling around *På resa*

Plane *Flyg*

Is there a flight to Luleå?	**Finns det något flyg till Luleå?**	finss dāy(t) **naw**got flēwg til **lēw**lāyaw
What time should I check in?	**Hur dags måste jag checka in?**	hēwr dahgss **mos**ter yaa(g) **kheh**kah in
I'd like to ... my reservation.	**Jag skulle vilja ... min reservation.**	yaa(g) **skewl**er **vil**yah ... min rehsehrvah**shōōn**
cancel	**annullera**	ahnew**lāy**rah
change	**ändra**	**ehn**drah
confirm	**bekräfta**	ber**krehf**tah

Train *Tåg*

Where's the railway station?	**Var ligger järn-vägsstationen?**	vaar **lig**gerr **yæ'n**vaigsstahshōōnern

INGÅNG	ENTRANCE
UTGÅNG	EXIT
TILL TÅGEN	TO THE TRAINS
INFORMATION	INFORMATION

Where is/are (the) ...?	**Var är ...?**	vaar **ǣr**
booking office	**biljettexpeditionen**	bil**yeht**ehkspehdish**ōō**nern
left-luggage office (baggage check)	**effektförvaringen**	eh**fehkt**furrvaaringern
lost property (lost and found) office	**hittegodsexpedi-tionen**	**hit**tergoodsehkspeh-dish**ōō**nern
luggage lockers	**förvaringsboxarna**	furr**vaa**ringsboksah'nah
platform 2	**perrong 2**	peh**rong** 2
reservations office	**biljettexpeditionen**	bil**yeht**ehkspehdish**ōō**nern
ticket office	**biljettluckan**	bil**yeht**lewkahn
waiting room	**väntsalen**	**vehnt**saalern
I'd like a ticket to Lund.	**Jag skulle vilja ha en biljett till Lund.**	yaa(g) **skewl**er **vil**yah haa ehn bil**yeht** til lewnd
single (one-way)	**enkel**	**ehn**kerl
return (round-trip)	**tur och retur**	tēwr ok reh**tēwr**
first/second class	**första/andra klass**	**fur'**stah/**ahn**drah klahss

TELLING THE TIME, see page 155

Inquiries *Förfrågningar*

When is the ... train to Uppsala?	**När går ... tåget till Uppsala?**	nær gawr... **taw**gert til **ewp**saalah
first/last/next	**första/sista/nästa**	fur'stah/**sis**tah/**neh**stah
What time does the train to Göteborg leave?	**Hur dags går tåget till Göteborg?**	hewr dahgss gawr **taw**gert til yurter**bory**
Is there a dining car/ sleeping car on the train?	**Finns det någon restaurangvagn/ sovvagn i tåget?**	finss dāy(t) **naw**gon rehsstor**rahng**vahngn/ **saw**vahngn ee **taw**gert
Is this the train to Östersund?	**Är det här tåget till Östersund?**	ær dāy(t) hær **taw**gert til urster'**sewnd**
I'd like a time-table, please.	**Skulle jag kunna få en tidtabell, tack?**	**skew**ler yaa(g) **kew**nah faw ehn **tee(d)**tahbehl tahk
Where can I find a porter?	**Var kan jag få tag på en bärere?**	vaar kahn yaa(g) faw taag paw ehn **bæ**rahrer
Can you help me with my luggage?	**Kan ni hjälpa mig med bagaget?**	kahn nee **yehl**pah may māyd bah**gaa**shert

Underground (subway) *Tunnelbana*

| Where's the nearest underground station? | **Var ligger när- maste tunnelban- estation?** | vaar **lig**gerr **nær**mahster **tew**nerlbaanerstahs**hōō**n |
| Where do I change for ...? | **Var byter jag för ...?** | vaar **bēw**terr yaa(g) furr |

Bus—Tram (streetcar) *Buss—Spårvagn*

Which tram (streetcar) goes to the town centre?	**Vilken spårvagn går till centrum?**	**vil**kern **spawr**vahngn gawr til **sehn**trewm
How much is the fare to ...?	**Hur mycket kostar det till ...?**	hewr **mew**ker(t) **kos**tahr dāy(t) til
Will you tell me when to get off?	**Kan ni säga till när jag skall stiga av?**	kahn nee **seh**yah til nær yaa(g) skah(l) **stee**gah aav

Boat service *Båt*

When does the boat for ... leave?	**När går båten till ...?**	nawr gawr **baw**tern til
How long does the crossing take?	**Hur lång tid tar överfarten?**	hewr lawng teed taar **ūr**verrfaa'tern
I'd like to take a boat trip.	**Jag skulle vilja göra en båttur.**	yaa(g) **skew**ler **vil**yah **yūr**rah ehn **bawt**tewr

Taxi *Taxi*

Where can I get a taxi?	**Var kan jag få tag på en taxi?**	vaar kahn yaa(g) faw taag paw ehn **tah**ksi
What's the fare to…?	**Vad kostar det till…?**	vaad **kos**tahr dāy(t) til
Take me to this address.	**Kör mig till den här adressen.**	khurr may til dehn hær ah**dreh**ssern
Please stop here.	**Var snäll och stanna här.**	vaar snehl ok **stah**nah hær
Could you wait for me?	**Kan ni vänta på mig?**	kahn nee **vehn**tah paw may
I'll be back in 10 minutes.	**Jag är tillbaka om 10 minuter.**	yaa(g) ær til**baa**kah om 10 mi**new**terr

Car hire (rental) *Biluthyrning*

I'd like to hire (rent) a car.	**Jag skulle vilja hyra en bil.**	yaa(g) **skew**ler **vil**yah **hew**rah ehn beel
I'd like it for a day/a week.	**Jag vill ha den en dag/en vecka.**	yaa(g) vil haa dehn ehn daa(g)/ehn **veh**kah
What's the charge per day/week?	**Vad kostar det per dag/vecka?**	vaad **kos**tahr dāy(t) pær daa(g)/**veh**kah
Is mileage included?	**Är kilometerkostnaden inräknad?**	ær khillom**māy**terr-kostnahdern **in**raiknahd
I'd like full insurance.	**Jag vill ha helför-säkring.**	yaa(g) vil haa **hāyl**fur'saikring

Road signs *Vägmärken*

CYKELBANA	Cycle path
EJ MOTORFORDON	No motor vehicles
ENSKILD VÄG	Private road
FARLIG KURVA	Dangerous bend (curve)
HUVUDLED	Main road
KÖR SAKTA	Slow down
LÄMNA FÖRETRÄDE	Give way (yield)
MOTORVÄG	Motorway (expressway)
PARKERING	Parking
TRAFIKOMLÄGGNING	Diversion (detour)
VÄGARBETE	Roadworks (men working)

TELLING THE TIME, see page 155/NUMBERS, page 156

Ni har kört fel.	You're on the wrong road.
Kör rakt fram.	Go straight ahead.
Det är där nere till vänster/höger.	It's down there on the left/right.
mitt emot/bakom ...	opposite/behind ...
bredvid/efter ...	next to/after ...
norr/söder/öster/väster	north/south/east/west

Where's the nearest filling station?	**Var ligger närmaste bensinstation?**	vaar **ligger** **nær**mahster behn**seen**stahsh $\overline{oo}$n
Fill it up, please.	**Full tank, tack.**	fewl tahnk tahk
Give me ... litres of petrol (gasoline).	**Kan jag få ... liter bensin?**	kahn yaa(g) faw ... **lee**terr behn**seen**
super (premium)/regular/unleaded/diesel	**högoktanig/lågoktanig/blyfri/diesel**	**h** $\overline{ur}$goktaanig/lawgoktaanig/**bl** $\overline{ew}$free/**dees**serl
How do I get to ...?	**Hur kommer jag till ...?**	h $\overline{ewr}$ **kom**merr yaa(g) til
I've had a breakdown at ...	**Jag har fått motorstopp vid ...**	yaa(g) haar fot **m** $\overline{oo}$to′stop veed
Can you send a mechanic?	**Kan ni skicka en mekaniker?**	kahn nee **shikk**ah ehh mehk**aa**nikkerr
Can you mend this puncture (fix this flat)?	**Kan ni laga den här punkteringen?**	kahn nee **laa**gah dehn hær pewng**tay**ringern

Landmarks *Landmärken*

bridge	**en bro**	ehn br $\overline{oo}$
forest	**en skog**	ehn sk $\overline{oo}$g
lake	**en sjö**	ehn sh $\overline{ur}$
meadow	**en äng**	ehn ehng
mountain	**ett berg**	eht **bæ**ry
path	**en stig**	ehn steeg
river	**en flod**	ehn fl $\overline{oo}$d
sea	**ett hav**	eht haav
valley	**en dal**	ehn daal
waterfall	**ett vattenfall**	eht **vah**ternfahl

Sightseeing *Sightseeing*

Where's the tourist office?	**Var ligger turistbyrån?**	vaar **ligg**err tewrist**bew**rawn
Is there an English-speaking guide?	**Finns det någon engelsktalande guide?**	finss dāy(t) **naw**gon ehngerlsktaalahnder "guide"
Where is/Where are the ...?	**Var ligger ...?**	vaar **ligg**err
botanical gardens	**botaniska trädgården**	boot**aa**niskah **trai(d)gaw**rdern
castle	**slottet**	**slott**ert
cathedral	**domkyrkan**	**doom**khewrkahn
city centre	**(stads)centrum**	**(stahds)sehn**trewm
exhibition	**utställningen**	**ewt**stehlningern
harbour	**hamnen**	**hahm**nern
museum	**museet**	mews**sāy**ert
old town	**gamla stan**	**gahm**lah staan
shopping area	**affärscentrum**	ah**fǣr**ssehntrewm
square	**torget**	**tor**yert
tower	**tornet**	**tōō**nert
zoo	**djurparken**	**yew**rpahrkern

Relaxing *Nöjen*

What's playing at the ... Theatre?	**Vad går det på ... teatern?**	vad gawr dāy(t) paw... tāy**aa**ter'n
Are there any tickets for tonight?	**Finns det några biljetter till i kväll?**	finss dāy(t) **naw**grah bil**yeh**terr til ee kvehl
What time does it begin?	**Hur dags börjar det?**	hēwr dahgss **burr**yahr dāy(t)
I'd like to reserve 2 tickets for the show on Friday evening.	**Jag skulle vilja beställa 2 biljetter till föreställningen på fredag kväll.**	yaa(g) **skew**ler **vil**yah ber**steh**lah 2 bil**yeh**terr til **fūrr**erstehlningern paw **frāy**daa(g) kvehl
Would you like to go out with me tonight?	**Skall vi gå ut i kväll?**	skah(l) vee gaw ēwt ee kvehl
Thank you, but I'm busy.	**Tack, men jag är tyvärr upptagen.**	tahk mehn yaa(g) ǣr tew**vǣr** **ewp**taagern
Is there a discotheque in town?	**Finns det något diskotek i stan?**	finss dāy(t) **naw**got disko**tāyk** ee staan
Would you like to dance?	**Skall vi dansa?**	skah(l) vee **dahn**sah
Thank you, it's been a wonderful evening.	**Tack, det har varit en underbar kväll.**	tahk dāy(t) haar **vaa**rit ehn **ewn**derrbaar kvehl

TELLING THE TIME/DAYS OF THE WEEK, see page 156

Sports *Sport*

What's the admission charge?	**Vad kostar det i inträde?**	vaad kostah dāy(t) ee intraider
Where's the nearest golf course?	**Var ligger närmaste golfbana?**	vaar liggerr nærmahster golfbaanah
Where are the tennis courts?	**Var ligger tennisbanorna?**	vaar liggerr tehnisbanoo'nah

canoeing	**kanot**	kahnōōt
car racing	**biltävling**	beeltaivling
cycling	**cykel**	sewkerl
football (soccer)	**fotboll**	fōōtbol
(horse-back) riding	**ridning**	reedning
sailing	**segling**	sāygling
skiing	**skidåkning**	sheedawkning
swimming	**simning**	simning
table tennis	**bordtennis**	bōō'dtehniss
tennis	**tennis**	tehniss

Can one swim in the lake/river?	**Kan man bada i sjön/floden?**	kahn mahn baadah ee shurn/flōōdern
Is there a swimming pool here?	**Finns det någon swimmingpool här?**	finss dāy(t) nawgon "swimmingpool" hær
Is there a skating rink near here?	**Finns det en skridskobana i närheten?**	finss dāy(t) ehn skri(d)-skoobaanah ee nærhāytern
I'd like to see an ice-hockey match.	**Jag skulle vilja se en ishockeymatch.**	yaa(g) skewler vilyah sāy ehn eeshokkimahtsh
I'd like to ski.	**Jag skulle vilja åka skidor.**	yaa(g) skewler vilyah awkah sheedoor
downhill/cross-country skiing	**utförsåkning/ längdåkning**	ēwtfur'sawkning/ lehngdawkning
I'd like to hire ...	**Jag skulle vilja hyra ...**	yaa(g) skewler vilyah hēwrah
skates	**ett par skridskor**	eht paar skri(d)skoor
skiing equipment	**skidutrustning**	sheedēwtrewstning
skis	**skidor**	sheedoor
I'd like to hire a bicycle.	**Jag skulle vilja hyra en cykel.**	yaa(g) skewler vilyah hēwrah ehn sewkerl

Shops, stores and services *Affärer och service*

Where's the nearest...?	**Var finns närmaste...?**	vaar finss **nær**mahster
baker's	**ett bageri**	eht baager**ree**
bookshop	**en bokhandel**	ehn **book**hahnderl
butcher's	**en slaktare/ett charkuteri**	ehn **slahk**tahrer/eht shahrkewter**ree**
chemist's/drugstore	**en apotek**	eht ahpoot**ayk**
dentist	**en tandläkare**	ehn **tahn(d)**laikahrer
department store	**ett varuhus**	eht **vaare**wh**ew**ss
grocer's	**en livsmedelsaffär**	ehn livsm**ay**derlsahf**ær**
hairdresser's (ladies/men)	**en frisör (dam-/herr-)**	ehn fris**urr** (daam-/hehr-)
market	**en marknad/en torghandel**	ehn **mahrk**nahd/ehn **torg**hahnderl
newsstand	**en tidningskiosk**	ehn **tee(d)**ningskhiosk
post office	**ett postkontor**	eht **post**kont**oor**
souvenir shop	**en souvenirbutik**	ehn soo**ver**neerbewteek
supermarket	**ett snabbköp**	eht **snahb**kh**ur**p

General expressions *Allmänna uttryck*

Where's the main shopping area?	**Var ligger affärscentrum?**	vaar **ligg**err ahf**æ**'ssehntrewm
Do you have any ...?	**Har ni några ...?**	haar nee **naw**grah
I'd like a ... one.	**Jag skulle vilja ha en ...**	yaa(g) **skew**ler **vil**yah haa ehn
big	**stor**	st**oo**r
cheap	**billig**	**bill**ig
dark	**mörk**	murrk
good	**bra**	braa
heavy	**tung**	tewng
large	**stor**	st**oo**r
light (weight)	**lätt**	leht
light (colour)	**ljus**	y**ew**ss
rectangular	**rektangulär**	rehktanggewl**ær**
round	**rund**	rewnd
small	**liten**	**lee**tern
square	**kvadratisk**	kvah**draa**tisk
sturdy	**kraftig**	**krah**ftig
Don't you have anything ...?	**Har ni inte någonting ...?**	haar nee **in**ter **naw**gonting
cheaper/better	**billigare/bättre**	**billig**gahrer/**beh**trer
larger/smaller	**större/mindre**	**stur**rer/**min**drer

Kan jag hjälpa er?	Can I help you?
Vad önskar ni?	What would you like?
Vilken ... önskar ni?	What ... would you like?
färg/form/kvalitet	colour/shape/quality
Det är slut på lagret.	We're out of stock.
Skall vi beställa det åt er?	Shall we order it for you?
Det blir ... kronor, tack.	That's ... crowns, please.
Kassan är där borta.	The cash desk is over there.

How much is this?	**Hur mycket kostar det här?**	hewr mewker(t) kostahr dāȳ(t) hær
Please write it down.	**Kan ni skriva det?**	kahn nee skreevah dāȳ(t)
I don't want to spend more than ... crowns.	**Jag vill inte lägga ut mer än ... kroner.**	yaa(g) vil inter lehgah ewt māȳr ehn ... krōōner
No, I don't like it.	**Nej, jag tycker inte om det.**	nay yaa(g) tewkerr inter om dāȳ(t)
I'll take it.	**Jag tar det.**	yaa(g) taar dāȳ(t)
Do you accept credit cards?	**Tar ni kreditkort?**	taar nee krehdeetkooˈt
Can you order it for me?	**Kan ni beställa det åt mig?**	kahn nee berstehlah dāȳ(t) awt may

Chemist's (drugstore) *Apotek*

aspirin	**aspirin**	ahspireen
condoms	**kondomer**	kondawmerr
deodorant	**deodorant**	dāȳodorahnt
insect repellent/spray	**ett insektsmedel/ insektsspray**	eht insehktsmāȳderl/ insehkts"spray"
moisturizing cream	**en fuktighetsbe- varande kräm**	ehn fewktighāȳtsbervaar- ahnder kraim
razor blades	**rakblad**	raakblaad
shampoo	**ett schampo**	eht shahmpoo
soap	**en tvål**	ehn tvawl
sun-tan cream	**en solkräm**	ehn sōōlkraim
tampons	**tamponger**	tahmpongerr
toothpaste	**en tandkräm**	ehn tahn(d)kraim

NUMBERS, see page 156

black	**svart**	svah^rt
blue	**blå**	blaw
brown	**brun**	br$\overline{\text{ew}}$n
green	**grön**	gr$\overline{\text{ur}}$n
grey	**grå**	graw
orange	**orange**	orahnsh
red	**röd**	r$\overline{\text{ur}}$d
white	**vit**	veet
yellow	**gul**	g$\overline{\text{ew}}$l
light ...	**ljus ...**	y$\overline{\text{ew}}$ss
dark ...	**mörk ...**	murrk

Clothing *Kläder*

blouse	**en blus**	ehn bl$\overline{\text{ew}}$ss
boots	**stövlar**	**sturv**lahr
dress	**en klänning**	ehn **kleh**ning
gloves	**ett par handskar**	eht paar **hahn(d)**skahr
jersey	**en tröja**	ehn **tru**ryah
scarf	**en scarf**	ehn skaarf
shirt	**en skjorta**	ehn **shoo**^rtah
shoes	**skor**	sk$\overline{\text{oo}}$r
skirt	**en kjol**	ehn kh$\overline{\text{oo}}$l
socks	**ett par sockor**	eht paar **so**kkoor
swimming trunks	**ett par badbyxor**	eht paar **baad**bewksoor
swimsuit	**en baddräkt**	ehn **baa(d)**drehkt
T-shirt	**en T-shirt**	ehn "T-shirt"
trousers	**ett par (lång)byxor**	eht paar **(long)**bewksoor
Can I try it on?	**Kan jag få prova den?**	kahn yaa(g) faw **pr$\overline{\text{oo}}$**vah dehn
What's it made of?	**Vad är det gjort av?**	vaad $\overline{\text{ær}}$ d$\overline{\text{ay}}$(t) y$\overline{\text{oo}}$t aav

cotton	**bomull**	**boo**mewl
denim	**denim**	deh**neem**
lace	**spets**	spehtss
leather	**läder/skinn**	**lai**der/shin
linen	**linne**	**lin**ner
silk	**siden/silke**	**see**dern/**sil**ker
suede	**mocka**	**mo**kkah
velvet	**sammet**	**sah**mert
wool	**ylle**	**ew**ler

Grocer's *Livsmedelsaffär*

What sort of cheese do you have?	**Vad har ni för sorts ostar?**	vaad haar nee fürr so'tss **oss**tahr
half a kilo of tomatoes	**ett halvt kilo tomater**	eht hahlft **khee**loo too**maa**terr
a litre of milk	**en liter mjölk**	ehn **lee**terr myurlk
4 slices of ham	**4 skivor skinka**	4 **shee**voor **shin**kah
some bread	**lite bröd**	**lee**ter brürd
a tin (can) of peaches	**en burk persikor**	ehn bewrk **pæ'**sikkor

Miscellaneous *Diverse*

I'd like a/an/some ...	**Jag skulle vilja ha ...**	yaa(g) **skew**ler **vil**yah haa
battery	**ett batteri**	eht bahter**ree**
bottle-opener	**en flasköppnare**	ehn **flahsk**urpnahrer
newspaper American/English	**en dagstidning amerikansk/ engelsk**	ehn **dahgs**tee(d)ning ahm(eh)ri**kaansk**/ **eng**erlsk
postcard	**ett vykort**	eht **vēw**koo't
torch	**en ficklampa**	ehn **fik**lahmpah
I'd like a film for this camera.	**Jag skulle vilja ha film till den här kameran.**	yaa(g) **skew**ler **vil**yah haa film til dehn hær **kaam**(er)rahn
black and white	**svart-vit**	svah't-veet
colour	**färg**	færy
Can you repair this camera?	**Kan ni laga den här kameran?**	kahn nee **laa**gah dehn hær **kaam**(er)rahn
I'd like a haircut, please.	**Klippning, tack.**	**klip**ning tahk

Souvenirs *Souvenirer*

candlestick	**en ljusstake**	ehn **yēws**staaker
ceramics	**keramik**	khehrah**meek**
clogs	**träskor**	**træs**koor
Dala horse	**en dalahäst**	ehn **daa**lahhehst
glassware	**glas**	glaass
Lapp handicrafts	**sameslöjd**	**saa**mersluryd

At the bank *På banken*

Where's the nearest bank/currency exchange office?	**Var ligger närmaste bank/ växelkontor?**	vaar **liggerr nær**mahster bahnk/**vehserlkontoor**
I'd like to change some dollars/pounds.	**Jag skulle vilja växla några dollar/ pund.**	yaa(g) **skewler vilyah vehk**slah **nawgrah dollahr/ pewnd**
I'd like to cash a traveller's cheque.	**Jag skulle vilja lösa in en resecheck.**	yaa(g) **skewler vilyah lurssah** in ehn **rayserkhehk**
What's the exchange rate?	**Vilken är växelkursen?**	vilkern **ǣr vehkserlkewˊsern**

At the post office *Post*

I'd like to send this by ...	**Jag vill skicka det här ...**	yaa(g) vil **shikkah day(t) hǣr**
airmail	**med flyg**	mayd flewg
express	**express**	ehk**sprehss**
A ...öres stamp, please.	**Ett ...öres frimärke, tack.**	eht ... **ūrrerss freemærker** tahk
What's the postage for a postcard to the U.S.A.?	**Vad är portot för ett vykort till USA?**	vaad **ǣr poˊtot fūrr** eht **vewkooˊt til ēwehssaa**
Is there any post for me?	**Finns det någon post till mig?**	finss **day(t) nawgon post til** may

Telephoning *Telefon*

Where's the nearest telephone booth?	**Var finns närmaste telefonkiosk?**	vaar finss **nærmahster tehlehfawnkhiosk**
May I use your phone?	**Får jag låna telefonen?**	fawr yaa(g) **lawnah tehlehfawnern**
Hello. This is ...	**Hallå, det här är ...**	hahlaw **day(t) hǣr ǣr**
I'd like to speak to ...	**Kan jag få tala med ...?**	kahn yaa(g) faw **taalah mayd**
When will he/she be back?	**När kommer han/ hon tillbaka?**	nǣr **kommerr hahn/hoon tilvbaakah**
Would you ask him/ her to call me?	**Skulle ni kunna be honom/henne ringa mig?**	**skewler** nee **kewnah bay honnom/hehner ringah** may
Would you take a message, please?	**Skulle ni kunna lämna ett meddelande?**	**skewler** nee **kewnah lehmnah** eht **mayday̆lahnder**

NUMBERS, see page 156

Doctor *Läkare*

Where can I find a doctor who speaks English?	**Var kan jag få tag på en läkare som talar engelska?**	vaar kahn yaa(g) faw taag paw ehn laikahrer som taalahr engerlskah
Where's the surgery (doctor's office)?	**Var ligger läkar-mottagningen?**	vaar liggerr laikahrmōōtaagningern
Can I have an appointment ...?	**Kan jag få en tid ...?**	kahn yaa(g) faw ehn teed
tomorrow	**i morgon**	ee morgon
as soon as possible	**så snart som möjligt**	saw snaʳt som muryli(g)t

Parts of the body *Kroppsdelar*

arm	**armen**	ahrmern
back	**ryggen**	rewgern
bone	**benen (i kroppen)**	bāynern (ee kroppern)
ear	**örat**	ūrraht
face	**ansiktet**	ahnsiktert
finger	**fingret**	fingrert
foot	**foten**	fōōtern
hand	**handen**	hahndern
head	**huvudet**	hēwv(ewd)ert
heart	**hjärtat**	yæʳtaht
knee	**knä(e)t**	knai(er)t
leg	**benet**	bāynert
lung	**lungan**	lewngahn
mouth	**munnen**	mewnern
muscle	**muskeln**	mewskerln
nerve	**nerven**	nærvern
nose	**näsan**	naissahn
shoulder	**skuldran/axeln**	skewldrahn/ahkserln
skin	**huden**	hēwdern
stomach	**magen**	maagern
throat	**halsen**	hahlsern
toe	**tån**	tawn
tongue	**tungan**	tewngahn
I've got a/an ...	**Jag har (fått) ...**	yaa(g) haar (fot)
bruise	**ett blåmärke**	eht blawmærker
burn	**ett brännsår**	eht brehnsawr
cut	**ett skärsår**	eht shæʳsawr
insect bite	**ett insektsbett**	eht insehktsbeht
rash	**ett utslag**	eht ēwtslaag
sting	**ett stick**	eht stik
swelling	**en svullnad**	ehn svewlnahd
wound	**ett sår**	eht sawr

Could you have a look at it?	**Skulle ni kunna titta på det?**	skewler nee kewnah tittah paw dāy(t)
It hurts.	**Det gör ont.**	dāy(t) yūrr oont
I feel ...	**Jag känner mig ...**	yaa(g) khehnerr may
dizzy	**yr**	ēwr
nauseous	**illamående**	illahmawehnder
I feel shivery.	**Jag har frossbryt-ningar.**	yaa(g) haar frosbrēwtningahr
I'm diabetic.	**Jag är diabetiker.**	yaa(g) ǣr diahbāytikkerr
Can you give me a prescription for this?	**Kan ni ge mig ett recept på det här?**	kahn nee yāy may eht rehsehpt paw dāy(t) hǣr
May I have a receipt for my health insurance?	**Kan jag få ett kvitto för min sjuk-försäkring?**	kahn yaa(g) faw eht kvitto fūrr min shēwkfur'saikring

---

Hur länge har ni känt er så här?	How long have you been feeling like this?
Var gör det ont?	Where does it hurt?
Jag skall ta temperaturen/blodtrycket.	I'll take your temperature/blood pressure.
Jag skall ge er en spruta.	I'll give you an injection.
Jag vill ha ett blodprov/avföringsprov/urinprov.	I want a specimen of your blood/stools/urine.
Ni bör ligga till sängs i ... dagar.	You must stay in bed for ... days.
Jag vill att ni vänder er till en specialist.	I want you to see a specialist.

Can you recommend a good dentist?	**Kan ni rekommen-dera en bra tandlä-kare?**	kahn nee rehkommerndāyrah ehn braa tahn(d)laikahrer
I have toothache.	**Jag har tandvärk.**	yaa(g) haar tahn(d)værk
I've lost a filling.	**Jag har tappat en plomb.**	yaa(g) haar tahpaht ehn plomb

Time and date *Klockan och datum*

It's ...	Den är ...	dehn **ær**
five past one	**fem över ett**	fehm **ūr**verr eht
ten past two	**tio över två**	teeoo **ūr**verr tvaw
a quarter past three	**kvart över tre**	kvah't **ūr**verr trāy
twenty past four	**tjugo över fyra**	khewgoo **ūr**verr **few**rah
twenty-five past five	**fem i halv sex**	fehm ee hahlv sehks
half past six	**halv sju**	hahlv shew
twenty-five to seven	**fem över halv sju**	fehm **ūr**verh hahlv shew
twenty to eight	**tjugo i åtta**	khewgoo ee ottah
a quarter to nine	**kvart i nio**	kvah't ee neeoo
ten to ten	**tio i tio**	teeoo ee teeoo
five to eleven	**fem i elva**	fehm ee **ehl**vah
noon/midnight	**klockan tolv (på dagen)/midnatt**	**klo**kkahn tolv (paw **daa**gern)/**meed**naht
in the morning	**på morgonen**	paw **mo**rronern
in the afternoon	**på eftermiddagen**	paw **ehf**terniddahn
in the evening	**på kvällen**	paw **kveh**lern
during the day	**under dagen**	ewnderr **daa**gern
at night	**på natten**	paw **nah**tern
yesterday/today	**i går/idag**	ee gawr/ee**daa**(g)
tomorrow	**i morgon**	ee **mo**rron
spring/summer	**vår/sommar**	vawr/**so**mmahr
autumn/winter	**höst/vinter**	hurst/**vin**terr

Sunday	**söndag**	surn**daa**(g)
Monday	**måndag**	mon**daa**(g)
Tuesday	**tisdag**	tees**daa**(g)
Wednesday	**onsdag**	oons**daa**(g)
Thursday	**torsdag**	too'**s**daa(g)
Friday	**fredag**	frāy**daa**(g)
Saturday	**lördag**	lūr'**daa**(g)
January	**januari**	yahnewaari
February	**februari**	fahbrewaari
March	**mars**	mah'ss
April	**april**	ah**pril**
May	**maj**	mahy
June	**juni**	**yew**ni
July	**juli**	**yew**li
August	**augusti**	ah**gew**sti
September	**september**	sehp**tehm**berr
October	**oktober**	ok**too**berr
November	**november**	noo**vehm**berr
December	**december**	dehs**sehm**berr

SWEDISH

Numbers *Räkneord*

0	**noll**	nol
1	**ett**	eht
2	**två**	tvaw
3	**tre**	trāȳ
4	**fyra**	fēwrah
5	**fem**	fehm
6	**sex**	sehks
7	**sju**	shēw
8	**åtta**	ottah
9	**nio**	neeoo
10	**tio**	teeoo
11	**elva**	ehlvah
12	**tolv**	tolv
13	**tretton**	trehton
14	**fjorton**	fyōōˊton
15	**femton**	fehmton
16	**sexton**	sehkston
17	**sjutton**	shewton
18	**arton**	aaˊton
19	**nitton**	nitton
20	**tjugo**	khēwgoo
21	**tjugoett**	khēwgoeht
30	**trettio**	trehti
40	**fyrtio**	furˊti
50	**femtio**	fehmti
60	**sextio**	sehksti
70	**sjuttio**	shewti
80	**åttio**	otti
90	**nittio**	nitti
100	**(ett)hundra**	(eht)hewndrah
1000	**(ett)tusen**	(eht)tēwssern
first/second	**första/andra**	furˊstah/ahndrah
once/twice	**en gång/två gånger**	ehn gong/tvaw gongerr
a half	**en halva**	ehn hahlvah

Where do you come from? *Varifrån kommer ni?*

Canada	**Kanada**	kahnahdah
Denmark	**Danmark**	dahnmahrk
England	**England**	englahnd
Ireland	**Irland**	irlahnd
Norway	**Norge**	noryer
Scotland	**Skottland**	skotlahnd
Sweden	**Sverige**	sværyer
United States	**USA**	ēwehssaa

Svensk

Signs and notices *Skylter och anslag*

Damer	Ladies
Drag	Pull
Ej ingång	No entrance
Herrar	Gentlemen
Hiss	Lift (elevator)
Ingång	Entrance
Kallt	Cold
Kassa	Cash desk
Ledigt	Free (vacant)
Livsfara	Danger of death
Nödutgång	Emergency exit
Öppet	Open
Reserverat	Reserved
Rökning förbjuden	No smoking
Rökning tillåten	Smoking allowed
Skjut	Push
Stängt	Closed
Stör ej	Do not disturb
Till salu	For sale
Upplysningar	Information
Upptaget	Occupied
Ur funktion	Out of order
Utgång	Exit
Varmt	Hot
Varning	Caution
Varning för hunden	Beware of the dog
Öppet	Open

Emergency *Nödsituation*

Call the police.	**Ring polisen.**	ring poleessern
Get a doctor.	**Hämta en läkare.**	hehmtah ehn laikahrer
Go away!	**Ge er i väg!**	yāy āyr ee vaig
HELP!	**HJÄLP!**	yehlp
I'm ill.	**Jag är sjuk.**	yaa(g) āer shēwk
I'm lost.	**Jag har gått vilse.**	yaa(g) haar got vilser
Leave me alone!	**Lämna mig ifred!**	lehmnah may eefrāy(d)
LOOK OUT!	**SE UPP!**	sāy ewp
STOP THIEF!	**STOPPA TJUVEN!**	stoppah khēwvern
My ... has been stolen.	**... har stulits.**	haar stēwlitss
I've lost my ...	**Jag har tappat ...**	yaa(g) haar tahpaht
handbag	**min handväska**	min hahn(d)vehskah
passport	**mitt pass**	mit pahss
wallet	**min plånbok**	min plawnbōōk

Guide to Swedish pronunciation *Uttal*

Consonants

Letter	Approximate pronounciation	Symbol	Example	
b,c,d, f,h,l, m,n,p, v,w,x	as in English			
ch	at the beginning of words borrowed from French, like **sh** in **sh**ut	sh	**chef**	sh$\overline{a}\overline{y}$f
g	1) before stressed **i, e, y, ä, ö**, and sometimes after **l** or **r**, like **y** in yet	y	**ge**	y$\overline{a}\overline{y}$
	2) before **e** and **i** in words of French origin, like **sh** in **sh**ut	sh	**geni**	sh$\overline{a}\overline{y}$nee
	3) elsewhere, like **g** in **g**o	g	**gaffel**	**g**ahferl
j, dj, g, lj, hj	at the beginning of words always like **y** in yet	y	**ja** **ljus**	yaa y$\overline{ew}$ss
k	1) before stressed **i, e, y, ä, ö**, generally like **ch** in Scottish lo**ch**, but pronounced in the front of the mouth	kh	**köpa**	**kh**$\overline{ur}$pah
	2) elsewhere, like **k** in **k**it	k	**klippa**	**k**lippah
kj	like **ch** in lo**ch**, but pronounced in the front of the mouth	kh	**kjol**	**kh**$\overline{oo}$l
qu	like **k** in **k**it followed by **v** in **v**at	kv	**Lindquist**	lin(d)**k**vist
r	rolled near the front of the mouth	r	**ryka**	**r**$\overline{ew}$kah
s	1) in the ending **-sion** like **sh** in **sh**ut	sh	**mission**	mi**sh**$\overline{oo}$n
	2) elsewhere, like **s** in **s**o	s/ss	**ses**	s$\overline{a}\overline{y}$ss
	3) the groups **sch, skj, sj, stj** are pronounced like **sh** in **sh**ut	sh	**schema**	**sh**$\overline{a}\overline{y}$mah

sk	1) before stressed **e, i, y, ä, ö**, like **sh** in sh**u**t	sh	**shänk**	shehnk
	2) elsewhere, like **sk** in sk**i**p	sk	**skola**	sk**oo**la
t	1) in the ending **-tion** like **sh** in sh**u**t or **ch** in ch**a**t	sh tsh	**station** **nation**	stah**sh**oo̅n naht**sh**oo̅n
	2) elsewhere, like **t** in top	t	**tid**	teed
tj	like **ch** in Scottish loch, but pronounced in the front of the mouth; sometimes with a **t**-sound at the beginning	kh	**tjäna**	**kh**ainah
z	like **s** in so	s	**zenit**	s**ay̅**nit

Vowels

a	1) when long, like **a** in car	aa	**dag**	daa(g)
	2) when short, between **a** in c**a**t and **u** in c**u**t	ah	**tack**	tahk
e	1) when long, like **ay** in say	a̅y̅	**sen**	s**ay̅**n
	2) when followed by **r**, like **a** in m**a**n; long or short	æ̅	**erfara**	**æ̅**rfaarah
	3) when short, like **e** in get	eh	**beck**	behk
	4) unstressed, like **a** in about	er	**betala**	b**er**taalah
ej	like **a** in mate	ay	**nej**	nay
i	1) when long, like **ee** in bee	ee	**vit**	veet
	2) when short, between **ee** in m**ee**t and **i** in h**i**t	i	**hinna**	hinnah
	3) in a few words, e.g. in the personal pronoun **mig**, like **a** in mate	ay	**mig**	may

o	1) when long, often like $\overline{oo}$ in soon, but with the lips more tightly rounded	**oo**	**sko**	sk$\overline{oo}$
	2) the same sound can be short	oo	**solid**	soo**leed**
	3) when long, sometimes like **aw** in r**aw**, but with the tongue a little higher in the mouth and the lips closely rounded	aw	**son**	sawn
	4) when short, sometimes like **o** in h**o**t	o	**korrekt**	korr**ehkt**
u	1) when long, like Swedish **y**, but with the tongue a little lower in the mouth, and with a puff of breath at the end	$\overline{ew}$	**hus**	h$\overline{ew}$ss
	2) when short, a little more like the **u** of p**u**t	ew	**full**	fewl
y	like German **ü** in **ü**ber, or French **u** in **u**ne; round your lips and try to say **ee** as in b**ee**	$\overline{ew}$ ew	**vy** **syster**	v$\overline{ew}$ **sew**sterr
å	1) when long, like **aw** in r**aw**, but with the tongue a little higher in the mouth and the lips closely rounded	aw	**gå**	gaw
	2) when short, like **o** in h**o**t	o	**sång**	song
ä	1) when followed by **r**, like **a** in m**a**n, long or short	$\overline{æ}$ æ	**ära** **värka**	$\overline{æ}$rah **vær**kah
	2) elsewhere, like **e** in g**e**t; long or short	ai eh	**läsa** **bäst**	**lais**sah behst
ö	like **ur** in f**ur**, but with the lips rounded and without any r-sound; long or short; when followed by **r**, it is pronounced with the mouth a little more open	$\overline{ur}$ ur	**röd** **köld** **öra**	r$\overline{ur}$d khurld $\overline{ur}$rah

English–Danish dictionary

c common gender	*nt* neuter	*pl* plural

A

able, to be kunne 4
above ovenpå 5
accept, to tage 21
address adresse *c* 15
admittance adgang *c* 29
after efter 5, 17
air conditioning klimaanlæg *nt* 6
airmail luftpost *c* 24
American amerikansk 23
amount beløb *nt* 13
and og 5
any nogen 4, 6
anything noget 7, 21
anywhere et eller andet sted 19
April april 27
arm arm *c* 25
art gallery kunstgalleri *nt* 17
ashtray askebæger *nt* 8
aspirin aspirin *c* 22
at ved 5
August august 27
Australia Australien 3
autumn *(fall)* efterår *nt* 27

B

back ryg *c* 25
back, to be komme tilbage 24
bad dårlig 5
baker's bager *c* 20
bank bank *c* 24
basic anvendelig 3
bath bad *nt* 6
bathroom badeværelse *nt* 7
be, to være 4
bed seng *c* 6, 26
beer øl *nt* 13
before *(time)* før 5
behind bagved 17
below nedenunder 5
better bedre 5, 7, 21
between mellem 5
bicycle cykel *c* 18
big stor 5, 20
bill *(check)* regning *c* 7, 13
bitter bitter 13
black and white *(film)* sort/hvid 23
black sort 21
blood blod *nt* 26

blood pressure blodtrykket *nt* 26
blouse bluse *c* 22
blue blå 21
boat båd *c* 15
boat service bådfart *c* 15
body legeme *nt* 25
bone knogle *c* 25
booking office pladsreserveringen *c* 14
bookshop boghandel *c* 20
boots støvler *c/pl* 22
botanical gardens botaniske have *c* 17
boyfriend kæreste *c* 3
bra bh *c* 22
breakdown motorstopp *nt* 16
breakfast morgenmad *c* 8
bridge bro *c* 18
brown brun 21
bruise blåt mærke *nt* 25
burn brandsår *nt* 25
bus bus *c* 15
busy optaget 18
but men 5
butcher's slagter *c* 20

C

call, to *(help)* tilkalde 30
call, to *(telephone)* ringe 24
camera kamera *nt* 23
camp, to kampere 6
campsite campingplads *c* 6
can *(tin)* dåse *c* 23
Canada Canada 3
cancel annullere 14
car bil *c* 16
car hire *(rental)* biludlejning *c* 16
cash desk kasse *c* 20, 29
castle borg *c* 17
cathedral domkirke *c* 17
caution forsigtig 29
change ændre 14
change, to *(money)* veksle 24
cheap billig 5, 7, 20
check in, to checke ind 14
check out, to rejse 7
chemist's (drugstore) apotek *nt* 20, 22
child barn *nt* 3
city centre byens centrum *c* 17
close, to lukker 17

clothing klæder c 22
cold koldt 5, 6, 13, 29
colour farve 20, 23
come, to komme 8
condoms kondomer nt/pl 22
confirm bekræfte 14
cotton bomuld c 22
credit card kreditkort nt 13, 21
crossing overfart c 15
cup kop c 8
currency exchange office vekselkontor nt 24
cut snitsår nt 25
cycling cykling c 19

D
dance, to danse 18
danger fare c 29
dark mørk 6, 20
date dato c 7, 27
date of birth fødelsdato c 7
day dag c 6, 16, 26
December december 27
decision beslutning c 6
denim denim c 22
Denmark Danmark 29
dentist tandlæge c 20, 26
deodorant deodorant c 22
department store stormagasin nt 20
diabetes sukkersyge c 26
diesel diesel c 16
dining-room spisesale c 7
dinner middag c 8
discotheque diskotek nt 18
dish ret c 8
dizzy svimmel 26
doctor læge c 25, 30
doctor's office (surgery) konsultation 25
dollar dollar c 24
double bed dobbeltseng c 6
double room dobbeltværelse nt 6
down ned 5
downstairs nedenunder 5
dress kjole c 22
drink drikkevare c 13
drugstore (chemist's) apotek nt 20

E
ear øre nt 25
early tidligt 5
east øst 17
eight otte 28
emergency exit nødudgang c 7, 29

emergency nødstilfælde nt 30
England England 29
English (language) engelsk 4, 17, 15, 23, 30
enjoy, to nyde 13
enjoyable nyd 7
entrance fee entré c 17
entrance indgang c 14, 29
evening aften c 18, 27
exchange rate vekselkursen c 24
exit udgang c 14, 29
expensive dyr 5
express expres 24
expression udtryck nt 3, 20
eye øje nt 25

F
face ansigt nt 25
family familie c 3
February februar 27
few, a et par 6
filling station benzinstation c 16
filling (tooth) plombe c 26
film film c 23
find, to finde 4, 16, 25, 30
fine godt 3, 6
finger finger c 25
Finland Finland 29
first class første klasse c 14
first første 15, 28
first name fornavn nt 7
five fem 28
flight fly nt 14
food mad c 13
foot fod c 25
football (soccer) fodbold c 19
forbidden . . . forbudt 29
forest skov c 18
fork gaffel c 8
four fire 28
free (vacant) ledigt 5
free of charge gratis 29
Friday fredag 27
from fra 5

G
general almindelig 7, 20
gentlemen (toilets) herrer c/pl 29
get, to få 4, 15
get, to (fetch) skaffe 7
girlfriend kæreste c 3
glass glas nt 8
gloves handsker c/pl 22
go away. to gå væk 30
go out, to (rendez-vous) gå ud 18

golf course golfbane *c* 19
good afternoon god dag 3
good god 5, 8, 20, 26
good morning god morgen 3
good night god nat 3
good-bye farvel 3
Great Britain Storbritannien 3, 29
green grøn 21
grey grå 21
grocer's købmand 20; madvarer *c* 23
guide guide *c* 17

H
hairdresser frisør *c* 20
half, a halv *c*, halvt *nt* 28
hand hånd *c* 25
handbag håndtaske *c* 30
harbour havn *c* 15, 17
have, to have 6, 7, 23
he han 24
head hoved *nt* 25
health insurance sygeforsikring *c* 26
heart hjerte *nt* 25
heavy tung 21
hello hallo 24; hello 3
help! hjælp! 30
help, to hjælpe 4, 20
her hende 24
here her 15
hi hej 3
him ham 24
hire, to leje 16, 19
holidays ferie *c* 3
home town by *nt* 7
horse racing hestevæddeløb *nt* 19
hot varm 5, 6, 29
how far hvor langt 4
how hvordan 4
how long hvor længe 4, 14, 15, 26
how much hvor meget 4, 17, 18
hundred hundrede *nt* 28
hurt, to gøre ondt 26
husband mand *c* 3

I
ill syg 30
in i 5
information information *c* 14, 29
injection indsprøjtning *c* 26
inquiries forespørgsler *c/pl* 14
insect bite insektbid *nt* 25
insect spray insekt-spray *nt* 22
inside indenfor 5
introductions præsentationer *c/pl* 3

Ireland Irland 29
island ø *c* 18

J
January januar 27
jersey ulden trøje *c* 22
journey *(trip)* tur *c* 14
July juli 27
June juni 27

K
key nøglen *c* 7
kilo kilo(gram) *nt* 23
knee knæ *nt* 25
knife kniv *c* 8

L
lace knipling *nt* 22
ladies *(toilets)* damer *c/pl* 29
lake sø *c* 18, 19
landmark landmærke *nt* 18
large stor 21
last sidste 15
late sent 5
laundry service tøjvask *c* 6
leather læder *nt* 22
leave, to afgår 15
left venstre 17
left-luggage office *(baggage check)* bagageopbevaring *c* 14
leg ben *nt* 25
letter *(mail)* brev *nt* 24
lift *(elevator)* elevator *c* 7
light *(colour)* lys 21
light *(weight)* let 21
like to, to lyst have 18
linen lærred *nt* 22
litre liter *c* 16, 23
local lokal 8
look at, to *examine)* se på 26
lose, to tabe 30
lost faret vild 30
lost property *(lost and found)* office hittegodskontor *nt* 14
luggage locker bagageboks *c* 14
lunch frokost *c* 8
lung lunge *c* 25

M
mail post *c* 24
March marts 27
market torvet *nt* 17
match kamp *c* 19

May maj 27
me mig 4
mean, to betyde 4
mechanic mekaniker *c* 16
meet, to træffe 3
mend, to *(fix)* reparere 17
mileage kilometerpenge *c* 16
milk mælk *c* 23
million million *c* 28
mistake fejl *c* 13
moisturizing cream fugtighedscreme *c* 22
Monday mandag 27
morning morgen *c* 27
mountain bjerg *nt* 18
mouth mund *c* 25
muscle muskel *c* 25
museum museum *nt* 17
my min 7

N
napkin *(serviette)* serviet *c* 8
nationality nationalitet *c* 7
nausea *(nauseous)* kvalme *c* 26
near nær 5
nearest nærmeste 16, 19, 20, 24
never aldrig 5
New Zealand New Zealand 29
newsagent bladhandler *c* 20
newspaper avis *c* 23
next næste 15
next to ved siden af 17
night nat *c* 27
nine ni 28
no nej 3
noisy støjende 6
north nord 17
Norway Norge 29
nose næse *c* 25
not ikke 4, 5
nothing ikke noget 5
notice opslag *nt* 29
November november 27
now nu 5
number *(house)* nummer *nt* 7

O
occupation stilling *c* 7
occupied optaget 5, 29
October oktober 27
on på 5
once en gang 28
one en 28
only kun 5
open åben 17, 29

opposite overfor 17
or eller 5
orange orange 21
order, out of i uorden 29
order, to bestille 13, 20, 21
outside udenfor 5

P
pardon, I beg your undskyld 3
parents forældre *pl* 3
park, to parkere 7
parking parkering *c* 16
part del *c* 25
passport pas *nt* 7, 30
path sti *c* 18
pay, to betale 13
per day pr. dag *c* 16
perhaps måske 5
petrol *(gasoline)* benzin *c* 16
place of birth fødested *nt* 7
place sted *nt* 7, 16
plane fly *nt* 14
plate tallerken *c* 8
platform perron *c* 14
play, to spille 18
please vær så venlig 3
police politi *nt* 30
post office posthus *nt* 20, 24
postage porto *c* 24
postcard postkort 24
pound *(sterling)* pund *nt* 24
prescription recept *c* 26
private privat 29
pull, to trække 29
puncture *(flat)* punktering *c* 17
push, to skubbe 29

Q
quality kvalitet *c* 20
quarter kvart *nt* 27
question spørgsmål *nt* 4
quiet rolig 7

R
radio radio *c* 6
rash udslæt *nt* 25
razor blades barberblade *pl* 22
receipt kvittering *c* 26
recommend, to anbefale 8, 26
rectangular rektangulær 21
red rød 21
regular *(petrol)* normal 16
repeat, to gentage 4
requirements forespørgsler *pl* 7

reservation bestilling *c* 14
reserve, to bestille 8, 18
reserved reserveret 29
restaurant restaurant *c* 8
return *(round trip)* retur 14
riding *(horse-back)* ridning *c* 19
right *(correct)* rigtigt 5
right *(direction)* højre 17
river flod *c* 18, 19
road sign vejskilt *nt* 15
road vej *c* 29
road works vejarbejde *pl* 16
room service service på værelset *c* 6
room værelse *nt* 6
round rund 21

S

sale udsalg *nt* 29
salty saltet 13
Saturday lørdag *c* 27
scarf tørklæde *nt* 22
Scotland Skotland 29
sea hav *nt* 18
seat plads *c* 18
second anden/andet 28
second class anden klasse *c* 14
see, to se 6
send, to sende 16, 24
September september 27
serve, to servere 8
set menu dagens ret *c* 8
seven syv 28
shampoo shampoo *c* 22
shape form *c* 20
she hun 24
shirt skjorte *c* 22
shivers *(shivery)* kuldegysninger *pl* 26
shoe sko *c* 22
shop *(store)* butik *c* 20
shopping area forretningskvarter *nt* 20; indkøbscentret *nt* 17
shoulder skulder *c* 25
shower bruser *c* 6
sign skilt *nt* 29
signature underskrift *c* 7
silk silke *c* 22
single room enkeltværelse *nt* 6
single *(one way)* enkelt 14
six seks 28
skates skøjter *c/pl* 19
skating rink skøjtebane *c* 19
ski ski *c* 19
skiing skiløb *nt* 19
skiing, cross-country langrend *nt* 19
skiing, downhill styrtløb *nt* 19
skiing equipment skiudstyr *nt* 19

skin hud *c* 25
skirt nederdel *c* 22
slice skive *c* 23
slowly, more langsom 4
small lille 5, 21; lyst 6; mindre 21
smoking rygning *c* 29
soap sæbe *c* 22
socks sokker *c/pl* 22
soon snart 5, 25
sort slags *c* 23
South Africa Sydafrika 29
south syd 17
souvenir shop souvenirbutik *c* 20
souvenir souvenir *nt* 23
speak, to tale 4, 24, 25
specialist speciallæge *c* 26
specimen prøve *c* 26
spoon ske *c* 8
sport sport *c* 19
spring forår *nt* 28
square firkantet 21
stamp frimærke *nt* 24
stay ophold *nt* 7
stay, to blive 6
steal, to stjæle 30
sting stik *nt* 25
stock, out of udsolgt 20
stomach mave *c* 25
stop, to standse 15
store *(shop)* butik *c* 20
straight ahead ligeud 17
street gade *c* 7
sturdy solid 21
suede ruskind *nt* 22
summer sommer *c* 28
sun-tan cream solcreme *c* 22
Sunday søndag *c* 27
super *(petrol)* super 16
supermarket supermarked *nt* 20
surgery *(doctor's office)* konsultation *c* 25
surname navn *nt* 7
Sweden Sverige 29
sweet sødt 13
swelling hævelse *c* 25
swimming svømning *c* 19
swimming pool svømmebasin *nt* 19
swimming trunks badebukser *pl* 22
swimsuit badadragt *c* 22

T

T-shirt T-shirt *c* 22
table bord *nt* 8
take, to tage 6, 14, 15, 21

English–Finnish dictionary

A

able, to be voida 34
above -n yllä/yli 35, 44
accept, to hyväksyä 53
address osoite 47
admission charge pääsymaksu 51
admittance pääsy 61
after *(time)* -n jälkeen 35
air conditioning ilamastointi 36
airmail lentoposti 56
American amerikkalainen 55
amount summa 44
and ja 35
any yhtään 34
anything else entä muuta/saako olla muuta 52
anything mitään 37
anywhere jossain 51
apple omena 51
April huhtikuu 59
arm käsivarsi 57
arrive, to saapua 46
ashtray tuhkakupi 38
aspirin aspiriini 54
at -n kohdalla 35
August elokuu 59
Australia Australia 33
autumn *(fall)* syksy 59

B

back selkä 57
back, to be *(return)* tulla takaisin 47, 56
bad huono 35
baker's leipomo 52
bank pankki 56
basic perus- 33
bath kylpy 36
bathroom kylpyhuone 37
battery paristo 55
be, to olla 34
bed vuode 36, 56
beer olut 43
before *(time)* ennen -a 35
begin, to alkaa 50
behind -n takana/taakse 35, 49
below -n alla/alle 35, 44
better parempi 35, 37, 53
between -n välissä/välillä 35
beware varoa 61
bicycle (polku)pyörä 51
big suuri 35; iso 53
bigger suurempi 37
bill *(check)* lasku 37, 44

bitter kitkerä 44
black and white *(film)* mustavalkoinen 55
black mustaa 53
blood veri 58
blood pressure verenpaine 58
blouse puseron 54
blue sinistä 53
boat lautta 47
boat service vesiliikenne 47
body ruumis 57
bone luu 57
booking office lipunmyynti 45
bookshop kirjakauppa 52
boots saappaat 54
botanical gardens kasvitieteellinen puutarha 49
boyfriend poikaystävä 33
bra rintaliivit 65
brakes jarruja 48
breakfast aamiainen 38
bridge silta 48, 50
brown ruskeata 53
bruise mustelma 57
burn palohaava 57
bus bussi 46
business trip liikematka 33
but mutta 35
butcher's lihakauppa 52

C

call, to *(help)* kutsua 62
call, to *(telephone)* soittaa 56
camera kamera 55
camp, to leiriytyä 36
campsite leirintäälue 36
can *(tin)* tölkki 56
Canada Kanada 33
cancel peruuttaa 45
car auto 47
car hire *(rental)* auton vuokraus 47
cash desk kassa 52, 61
castle linna 49
cathedral tuomiokirkko 49
caution varo 61
change muuttaa 45
change, to *(money)* vaitoraha 56
charge maksu 47
cheap halpa 35, 53
cheaper halvempi 37
check in, to ilmoittautua 45
check out, to lähteä 37
chemist's *(drugstore)* apteekki 52, 54
city centre keskusta 49
close, to sulkea 49

clothing vaatetus 54
coach (long-distance bus) bussi 46, 47
cold kylmä 35, 44, 62
colour väri 52, 55
come, to tulla 38
condoms kondomeja 54
confirm vahvistaa 45
cotton puuvillaa 54
credit card luottokortti 44, 53
crossing ylitys 47
cruise risteily 47
cup kuppi 38
currency exchange office
  valuutanvaihtopaikka 56
cut (viilto)haava 57
cycle racing pyöräkilpailut 51

D
dance tanssi 50
danger vaara 61
dark pimeä 36; tumma 35, 53
date päivä 37; päivämäärä 59
date of birth syntymäaika 37
day päivä 36, 47, 58, 59
December joulukuu 59
decision päätös 36
denim farkkukangasta 54
Denmark Tanska 61
dentist hammaslääkäri 52, 58
deodorant deoderanttia 54
department store tavaratalo 52
diabetic sokeritautinen 58
diesel dieselöljyä 48
dining-room ruokasali 37
dinner päivällinen 38
discotheque disko 50
dizzy huimaus 58
doctor lääkäri 57, 62
doctor's office (surgery) vastaanotto 57
dog koira 61
dollar dollari 56
double bed kaksoisvuode 36
double room kahden hengen huone 36
down alas/alhaalla 35
downstairs alakerrassa 35
dress leningin 54
drink juoma 43
drive, to ajaa 48
drugstore (chemist's) apteekki 52
during aikana 35

E
ear korva 57
early aikainen 35
east itä 49
eight kahdeksan 60
emergency hätä 62
emergency exit hätäuloskäynti 37, 61
England Englanti 61

English (language) englantilainen 34, 49,
  55, 57
entrance fee pääsymaksu 49
entrance sisään(käynti) 46, 61
evening ilta 50, 59
exchange rate vaihtokurssi 56
exhibition näyttely 49
exit ulos(käynti) 45, 61
expensive kallis 35
express pika 56
expression ilmaisu 33, 52
eye silmä 57

F
face kasvot 57
family perhe 33
far kaukana 35
fare maksu 46, 47
February helmikuu 59
few, a muutama 35, 36
fill up, to täyttää 48
filling station bensiiniasema 48
filling (tooth) paikka 58
film filmi 55
find, to löytää 34, 57
fine (well) hyvä 33, 36
finger sormi 57
Finland Suomi 61
Finnish (language) suomi 34
first ensimmäinen 46, 61
first class ensimmäinen luokka 45
first name etunimi 37
fitting room sovituskoppi 54
five viisi 60
fjord vuono 50
flight lento 45
food ruoka 44
foot jalka 57
football (soccer) jalkapallo 51
for -n suuntaan/-n sijaan 35
forbidden ... kielletty 61
forest metsä 50
fork haarukka 38
four neljä 60
free (of charge) vapaa 61
free (vacant) vapaa 35
Friday perjantai 60
from -n suunnasta 35
frost damage kelirikko 48

G
general yleinen 37, 52
gentlemen (toilets) miehille 61
get, to (taxi) hankkia 37, 47
get off, to (transport) nousta pois 46
girlfriend tyttöystävä 33
give, to antaa 58; saada 44, 48
glacier jäätikkö 50
glass lasi 38

gloves hansikkaat 54
go away! mankää tiehenne! 62
go out, to *(rendez-vous)* lähteä ulos 50
golf course golf-rata 51
good hyvä 35, 38, 53, 58
good afternoon (hyvää) päivää 33
good morning (hyvää) huomenta 33
good night hyvää yötä 33
good-bye näkemiin 33
Great Britain Iso Britannia 61
green vihreää 53
grey harmaata 53
grocer's sekatavarakauppa 52, 55
guide opas 49

H
hair-cut tukanleikku 55
hairdresser kampaaja 52
half, a puolikas 61
hand käsi 57
handbag käsilaukku 62
harbour satama 47, 49
have, to -lla on 36, 37, 55; saada 34
he hän 56
head pää 57
health insurance sairausvakuutus 58
heart sydän 57
heavy painava 53
hello hei 33, 56
help, to auttaa 34, 46, 52
help! apua! 62
her hänelle 56
here täällä 47
hi terve 33
him hänelle 56
hire, to vuokrata 47, 51
holiday loma 33
home town kotikaupunki 37
hot kuuma 35, 62
how kuinka 34
how far kuinka kaukana 34
how long kuinka kauan 34, 46, 47, 58
how many kuinka monta 34, 50, 53
how much kuinka paljon 34; paljonko 49, 53
hundred sata 60
hurt, to koskee 58
husband aviomies 33

I
ice hockey jäähockey 15
ill sairas 62
in -n sisässä/-llä 35
include, to sisällyttää 47
included sisältyy 44
information neuvonta 45, 62
injection ruiske 58
inquiries tiedusteluja 46
insect bite hyönteisen purema 57

insect repellent hyttysöljyä 54
inside sisään/sisälle 35
insurance vakuutus 47
introductions esittely 33
Ireland Irlanti 61
island saari 50

J
January tammikuu 59
jersey villatakin 54
journey *(trip)* matka 46
July heinäkuu 29
June kesäkuu 59

K
key avain 37
kilo kilo 55
knee polvi 57
knife veitsi 38

L
lace pitsiä 54
ladies *(toilets)* naisille 62
lake järvi 50, 51
landmark maamerkki 50
large suurta kokoa 53
last viimeinen 46
late myöhäinen 35
leather nahkaa 54
leave, to lähteä 46, 47
left vasen 44, 49
left-luggage office *(baggage check)* matkatavarasäilytys 45
leg sääri 57
lift *(elevator)* hissi 37, 62
light *(colour)* vaalea 35, 53; *(weight)* kevyt 53
like, to pitää 53
like to, to haluta 50
linen pellavaa 54
litre litra 48, 55
little, a vähän 35
local paikallinen 38
look at, to *(examine)* katsoa 53
lose, to kadottaa 62
lost eksynyt 62
lost property *(lost and found)* **office** löytötavaratoimisto 45
lot, a paljon 35
luggage lockers säilytyslokerot 45
lunch lounas 38
lung keuhko 57

M
mail posti 56
main tärkein 52

March maaliskuu 59
mark *(currency)* markka 52
market (kauppa)tori 49
match ottelu 51
May toukokuu 59
me minut, minulle 34, 47
mean, to tarkoittaa 34
mechanic korjaaja 48
mend, to *(fix)* korjata 48
menu ruokalista 38
message viesti 56
midnight keskiyö 59
mileage kilometrimäärä 47
milk maito 55
million miljoona 60
minute minuutti 47
mistake virhe 44
moisturizing cream kosteusvoidetta 54
moment, at the hetkellä 52
Monday maanantai 60
morning aamulla 59
mountain vuori 50
mountaineering vuoristokiipeily 51
mouth suu 57
muscle lihas 57
museum museo 49
my minun 37

N
name nimi 56
napkin *(serviette)* lautasliina 38
narrow kapea 48
nationality kansallisuus 37
nauseous pahoinvointi 58
near lähellä/lähelle 35
nearest lähin 48, 51, 52, 56
nerve hermo 57
never ei koskaan 35
New Zealand Uusi-Seelanti 61
newspaper sanomalehti 55
newsstand lehtikioski 52
next seuraava 46, 47
next to vieressä 35, 49
night yö 59
nine yhdeksän 60
no ei 33
noisy meluisa 36
none ei yhtään 35
noon keskipäivä 59
north pohjoinen 49
Norway Norja 61
nose nenä 57
not ei 34, 35
nothing ei mitään 35
notice varoitus 61
November marraskuu 59
now nyt 35
number *(house)* numero 37

O
occupation ammatti 37
occupied varattu 35, 62
October lokakuu 59
on -n päällä/päälle 35
once kerran 61
one yksi 60
only vain 35, 36
open avoinna 62
open, to avata 49
opposite vastapäätä 49
or tai 35
orange oranssia 53
order, to tilata 44, 52, 53
order, out of epäkunnossa 62
outside ulkona/ulos 35
overnight yhden yön 36

P
pardon anteeksi 33
park, to pysäköidä 37
parking pysäköimtipaikka 48
part osa 57
passport passi 37, 62
pay, to maksaa 44
penni *(currency)* penni 56
perhaps ehkä 35
petrol *(gasoline)* bensiini 48
picnic piknik 44
place paikka 37
place of birth syntymäpaikka 37
plane lento(kone) 45
plate lautanen 38
platform laituri 45
play, to esittää 50
please olkaa hyvä 33
police poliisi 62
porter kantaja 46
post posti 56
postcard postikortti 56
post office posti 52, 56
pound *(sterling)* punta 56
prescription resepti 58
price hinta 36
private oma 36; yksityinen 62
pull, to vetää 62
puncture *(flat)* puhjennut rengas 48
push, to työntää 62

Q
quality laatu 52
quarter neljännestä/vartin 59
question kysymys 34
quieter rauhallisempi 37

R
radio radio 36

rash ihottummaa 57
razor blades partakoneen teriä 54
receipt kuitti 58
recommend, to suositella 38, 58
rectangular suorakulmainen 53
red punaista 53
regular *(petrol)* matalaoktaanista 48
repeat, to toistaa 34
requirements tarpeita 37
reservation varaus 36, 45
reservations office paikanvaraus 45
reserve, to varata 38, 50
reserved varattu 62
restaurant ravintola 38
return ticket *(round trip)* menopaluu 45
riding *(horse-back)* ratsastus 15
right *(direction)* oikea 35, 44, 49
river joki 50, 51
road tie 49, 62
road sign liikennemerkki 48
road works tietyö 48
room huone 36
round pyöreä 53

S
sale alennusmyynti/ale 62
salty suolainen 44
Saturday lauantai 60
sauna saunaa 36
scarf huivin 54
Scotland Skotlanti 61
sea meri 50
seat paikkaa 50
second toinen 61
second class toinen luokka 45
see, to nähdä 36
send, to lähettää 48, 56
September syyskuu 59
set menu vakiolista 38
seven seitsemän 60
shampoo shampoota 54
shape muoto 52
she hän 56
shirt paidan 54
shivery puistatuksi 58
shoes kengät 54
shop *(store)* myymälä 52
shopping area ostosalue 49, 2
shoulder olkapää 57
show näytös 50
shower suihku 36
sign kyltti 61
signature allekirjoitus 37
silk silkkiä 54
since alkaen 35
single room yhden hengen huone 36
single ticket *(one-way)* menolippu 45
six kuusi 60
skates luistimet 51

skating rink luistinrata 51
ski, to hiihtää 51
ski jumping mäkihyppy 51
skiing hiihto 51
skiing, cross-country murtomaahiihto 51
skiing, downhill laskettelu 51
skiing equipment hiihtovarusteet 51
skin iho 57
skirt hameen 54
skis sukset 51
slice siivu 55
slowly hitaasti 48
small pieni 35, 36, 53
smoking tupakointi 62
snack välipala 44
soap saippuaa 54
socks (nilkka)sukat 54
soon pian 35
sort laatu 55
south etelä 49
South Africa Etelä-Afrikka 61
souvenir muistoesine 55
souvenir shop matkamuistomyymälä 52
speak, to puhua 34, 56, 57
specialist erikoislääkäri 58
specimen näyte 58
speed limit nopeusrajoitus 48
speed skating pikaluistelu 51
spoon lusikka 38
sport urheilu 51
spring kevät 59
square neliskulmainen 53
stamp postimerkki 56
stay, to pysyä 58; viipyä 36
steal, to varastaa 62
sting pistos 57
stock, out of ei varastossa 52
stomach *(inside/outside)* maha/vatsa 57
stop, to *(catch)* ottaa kiinni 62; pysäkki 47
store *(shop)* myymälä 52
straight ahead suoraan eteenpäin 49
street katu 37
sturdy tanakka 53
suede mokkaa 54
summer kesä 59
sun-tan cream aurinkovoidetta 54
Sunday sunnuntai 60
super *(petrol)* korkeaoktaanista 48
supermarket valintamyymälä 52
surgery *(doctor's office)* vastaanotto 57
surname sukunimi 37
Sweden Ruotsi 61
sweet makea 44
swelling turvotusta 57
swim, to uida 51
swimming uinti 51
swimming pool uimaallas 51
swimming trunks uimahousut 54
swimsuit uimapuvun 54

table 172 **zoo**

T

table pöytä 38
take, to *(buy, accept)* ottaa 36, 53
take, to *(time)* kestää 46, 47
tampons tampooneja 54
taxi taksi 37, 47
telephone puhelin 56
television televisio 36
tell, to kertoa 56
temperature lämpö 58
ten kymmenen 60
tennis tennis 51
tennis court tennis-kenttä 51
test, to kokeilla 48
thank you kiitos 33
theatre teatteri 50
then sitten 35
thief varas 62
third kolmas 61
this tämä 53
three kolme 60
throat *(inside/outside)* kurkku/kaula 57
through läpi 35
Thursday torstai 60
ticket lippu 45
ticket office lipputoimisto 45
tights sukkahousut 54
time kello 59
tin *(can)* tölkki 55
to -n kohdalle 35
today tänään 59
toilet(s) WC(:t) 36, 37
tomorrow huomenna 57, 59
tongue kieli 57
tonight tänä iltana 50
too liian 36, 64
too *(also)* myös 35
toothache hammassärky 58
toothpaste hammastahnaa 54
torch taskulamppu 53
touch, to koskea 61
tourist office matkailutoimisto 48
towards -a kohti 35
tower torni 49
town kaupunki 50
town centre kaupungin keskusta 46
tram *(streetcar)* raitiovaunu 46
translate, to kääntää 34
trousers *(pitkät)* housut 54
try on, to sovittaa 54
T-shirt T-paidan 54
Tuesday tiistai 60
twice kahdesti 61
twin beds kaksi vuodetta 36
two kaksi 60

U

under alla/alle 35
understand, to ymmärtää 34
United States USA (Yhdysvallat) 33

unleaded lyijytöntä 48
until asti 35
up ylös/ylhäällää 35
upstairs yläkerrassa 35
use, to käyttö 56
useful hyödyllinen 35

V

vacancies, no täynnä 62
vacancy vapaa huone 36
vacant vapaa 62
vegetarian kasvissyöjä 38
velvet samettia 54
very tosi 35

W

wait, to odottaa 47, 62
waiting room odotushuone 45
wallet lompakko 62
want, to haluta 50
water vesi 34
waterfall vesiputous 50
Wednesday keskiviikko 60
week viikko 36, 47
west länsi 49
what mitä 34, 52
when milloin 34, 49
where missä 33, 34, 45, 49
which mikä, kumpi 34
white valkoista 53
who kuka 34
why miksi 34
wife vaimo 33
wine viini 34
winter talvi 59
with mukana 33; -n kanssa 35
without ilman 35
wonderful ihana 50
wool villaa 54
word sana 35
worse huonompi 35
wound haava 57
write down, to kirjoittaa 53
wrong *(incorrect)* väärä 35, 49

Y

yellow keltaista 53
yes kyllä 33
yesterday eilen 59
yet vielä 35

Z

zero nolla 60
zoo eläintarha 49

English–Icelandic dictionary

f feminine   *m* masculine   *nt* neuter

A

able, to be að geta 66
above fyrir ofan 76
accept, to að taka 85
address heimilisfang *nt* 79, 80
admittance aðgangur *m* 94
after fyrir aftan 80
air conditioning loftræsting *f* 68
airmail flugpóstur *m* 88
a lot mikið 67
American amerísk 87
amount upphæð *f* 76
and og 67
anti-freeze frostlögur *m* 80
any einhver 68
anything eitthvað 69, 84
appointment viðtalstími *m* 89
April apríl *m* 91
arm handleggur *m* 89
arrive, to að koma 78
ashtray öskubakki *m* 70
aspirin aspirín *m* 86
August ágúst *m* 91
Australia Ástralía 93
autumn *(fall)* haust *nt* 92

B

back bak *nt* 89
bad slæmur 67
baggage farangur *m* 78
baker's bakarí *nt* 84
balcony svalir *f* 68
bank banki *m* 88
bath bað *nt* 68
bathroom baðherbergi *nt* 69
battery *(car)* rafgeymir *m* 80
battery *(small)* rafhlöður *f* 87
be, to að vera 66
beach strönd *f* 81
bed rúm *nt* 68, 90
beer bjór *m* 75
begin, to að byrja 82
behind á eftir 67
below undir 67, 76
better betri 67, 69
between á milli 67
beware varist 94
bicycle hjól *nt* 83
big stór 67, 69, 85

bill *(check)* reikningur *m* 69, 76
bitter beiskur 85
black svartur 85
black and white (film) svart-hvít
  (filma) 87
blood blóð *nt* 90
blood pressure blóðþrýstingur *m* 90
blouse blússa *f* 86
blue blár 85
boat bátur *m* 78
boat service báta þjónusta *f* 78
body líkami *m* 89
bone bein *nt* 89
bookshop bókaverslun *f* 84
boots stígvél *nt* 86
botanical gardens grasagarður *m* 81
boyfriend vinur *m* 65
bra brjóstahaldari *m* 86
brake fluid bremsuvökvi *m* 80
brakes hemlar *m* 79
breakdown bilun *f* 80
breakfast morgunverður *m* 70
bridge brú *f* 79, 81
brown brúnn 85
bruise skráma *f* 89
burn brunasár *nt* 89
bus vagn *m* 78
business viðskipti *nt* 65
busy upptekinn 82
but en 67
butcher's kjötbúð *f* 84
buy, to að kaupa 87

C

call, to *(telephone)* að hringja 88, 94
camera myndavél *f* 87
camp, to að tjalda 68
campsite tjaldstæði *nt* 68
can *(tin)* dós *f* 87
Canada Kanada 93
cancel afpöntun *f*, afturköllun *f* 77
car bíll *m* 79
car hire *(rental)* bílaleiga *f* 79
cash desk kassi *m* 84, 93
cathedral dómkirkja *f* 81
caution varúð *f* 94
change breyting *f* 77
change, to *(money)* að skipta 88
charge greiðsla *f* 79

ICELANDIC DICTIONARY

Íslensk Orðabók

cheap ódýr 67, 69, 85
check, to að athuga 80
check in, to að skrá sig inn 77
check out, to að skrá sig út 69
chemist's *(drugstore)* apótek *nt* 84, 86
cinema bíó *nt* 82
city centre miðbær *m* 81
close, to að loka 81
clothing fatnaður *m* 86
coach *(long-distance bus)* rúta *f*, langferðabíll *m* 77
coat kápa *f* 86
cold kaldur 67, 69, 76, 94
colour litur *m* 84
colour *(film)* lit *(filma)* 87
come, to að koma 65, 70
condoms smokkur *m* 86
confirm að staðfesta 77
confirmation staðfesting *f* 68
coolant kælivökvi *m* 80
cotton bómull *f* 86
credit card greiðslukort *nt* 76, 85
crossing ferð *f* 78
crown *(currency)* króna *f* 84, 88
cup bolli *m* 70
currency exchange office gjaldeyrisafgreiðsla *f* 88
cut skurður *m* 89
cycle racing hjólreiðakeppni *f* 83

D
dance dansleikur *m* 82
danger hætta *f* 93
dark dimmur 69, 85
date dagsetning *f* 69, 91
day dagur *m* 68, 79, 90, 91
December desember *m* 91
decision ákvörðun *f* 68
delicatessen sérverslun *f* með tilbúinn mat *m* 84
denim denímefni *nt* 86
Denmark Danmörk 93
dentist tannlæknir *m* 84, 90
deodorant svitakrem *nt* 86
department store stórverslun *f* 84
diabetic sykursýkis- 90
diesel díselolía *f* 80
dining-room stofa *f* 69
dinner kvöldverður *m* 70
discoteque diskótek *nt* 82
dish réttur *m* 70
dizzy með svima 90
doctor læknir *m* 94
doctor's office *(surgery)* læknisstofa *f* 89
dog hundur *m* 94

dollar dollari *m* 88
double tveggjamanna 68
double bed hjónarúm *nt* 68
down niður 67
downstairs niðri 67
dress kjóll *m* 86
drink drykkur *m* 75
drive, to að aka 79
drugstore *(chemist's)* apótek *nt* 84
during á meðan 67, 91

E
ear eyra *nt* 89
early snemma 67
east austur 80
eight átta 92
emergency neyðarástand 94
emergency exit neyðarútgangur *m* 69
England England 93
English ensk 87
English *(language)* enska *f* 66, 81, 89
enjoy, to að njóta 76
enjoyable ánægjulegur 69
entertainment skemmtanir *f* 82
entrance inngangur *m* 77, 94
evening kvöld *nt* 82, 91
exchange rate gengi *nt* 88
exhibition sýning *f* 81
exit útgangur *m* 77; útgöngudyr *f* 94
expensive dýr 67
express hraðpóstur *m* 88
eye auga *nt* 89

F
face andlit *nt* 89
family fjölskylda *f* 65
far langt 67
fax símbréf *nt* 88
February febrúar *m* 91
fee gjald *nt* 81
feel, to að finna 90
few fáir 67, 68
fill up, to að fylla 79
filling *(tooth)* fylling 90
filling station bensínstöð *f* 79
film filma 87
find, to að finna 80,
fine *(well)* vel 65; *(good)* ágætt 68
finger fingur *m* 89
Finland Finnland 93
first fyrstur 78, 93
first class fyrsta farrými *nt* 77
first name skírnarnafn *nt* 69
fishing veiðar *f* 83
fitting room mátunarklefi *m* 85

five fimm 92
fjord fjörður nt 81
flight flug nt 77
food matur m 76
foot fótleggur m 89
football (soccer) fótbolti m 82, 83
forbidden bannaður 94
fork gaffall m 70
four fjórir 92
free laus 94
Friday föstudagur m 91
from frá 67
frost frost nt 79
fur hat loðhattur m 86

G

general almennur 69, 84
gentlemen (toilets) herrasnyrting f 93
get, to að fá 66; (fetch) að ná í 69, 79
get off, to (transport) að fara út úr 78
geyser goshver m 81
girlfriend vinkona f 65
give, to að gefa 76, 80, 90
glacier jökull m 81
glass glas nt 70
gloves hanskar m 86
go away, to fara til 94
go out, to (rendez-vous) að fara út 82
golf course golfvöllur m 82
good afternoon góðan dag m 65
good góður 67, 70, 85, 90
good morning góðan dag m 65
good night góða nótt f 65
good-bye bless 65
Great Britain Stór Bretland 93
green grænn 85
grey grár 85
grocery grænmetisverslun f 84, 87
guide leiðsögumaður m 81

H

hair-cut klipping f 87
hairdresser hárgreiðslustofa f 84
half hálfur 93
hand hönd f 89
handbag handtaska f 94
harbour höfn f 78, 81
have, to að hafa 68, 69, 87
he hann 88
head höfuð nt 89
health insurance sjúkratrygging f 90
heart hjarta nt 89
heavy þungur 85
hello halló 65, 88

help, to að hjálpa 66, 78, 84
help! hjálp! 94
her henni 88
here hér 68, 79
hi hæ 65
him honum 88
hire, to að leigja 79, 83
holiday frí nt 65
home town heimabær m 69
horse-back riding reiðmennska f 83
hot heitur 67, 69, 93
how hvernig 66
how far hversu langt 66
how long hvað lengi 66, 78, 85, 90
how much hvað mikið 66, 81, 82, 85
hundred hundrað 92
hurt, to að finna til 90
husband eiginmaður m 65

I

ice hockey íshokkí nt 83
Iceland Ísland 93
Icelandic Íslensk 65
ill veikur 94
include, to að vera innifalið 79
included innifalið 76
information upplýsingar f 77, 94
injection að fá sprautu f 90
inquiries upplýsingar f 78
insect bite skordýrabit nt 89
insect repellent skordýrafæla f 86
inside inni 67
introduce, to að kynna fyrir 65
introductions kynningar f 65
Ireland Írland 93
island eyja f 81

J

January janúar m 91
jersey prjónapeysa f 86
journey (trip) ferð f 78
July júlí m 91
June júní m 91

K

key lykill m 69
kilo kíló nt 87
km kílómetrar m 79
knee hné nt 89
knife hnífur m 70
krona (currency) krona f 88

L

lace blúnda *f* 86
ladies *(toilets)* kvennasnyrting *f* 94
lake stöðuvatn *nt* 81, 83
landmark kennileiti *nt* 81
large stór 85
last síðastur 78
late seint 67
leather leður *nt* 86
leave alone, to að skilja eftir 94
leave, to að fara 78
left vinstri 76, 80
left-luggage office *(baggage check)* óskilafarangur *m* 77
leg fótur *m* 89
letter *(mail)* bréf *nt* 88
lift *(elevator)* lyfta *f* 69, 94
light *(colour)* ljós 85, *(weight)* léttur 85
like, to að líka við 85
linen lín *nt* 86
liquor store vínbúð *f* 84
litre líter *m* 80, 87
little, a lítið 67
local þjóðar- 70
look at, to *(examine)* að skoða 90
lost property (lost and found) office tapað fundið 77
lost villtur 94
luggage farangur *m* 94
luggage lockers geymsluskápar *m* 77
lunch hádegisverður *m* 70
lung lungu *nt* 89

M

mail póstur *m* 88
main aðal 84
March mars *m* 91
market markaður *m* 81
match leikur *m* 82
May maí *m* 91
me mér 66, 79
mean, to að þýða 66
mechanic viðgerðarmaður *m* 80
mend, to *(fix)* að gera við 80
menu matseðill *m* 70, 71
message skilaboð *nt* 88
midnight miðnætti *nt* 91
mileage kílómetragjald *nt* 79
milk mjólk *f* 87
million miljón *f* 93
minute mínúta *f* 79
mistake mistök 76
moisturizing cream rakakrem *nt* 86
moment augnablik *nt* 84
Monday mánudagur *m* 91
more meira 66
morning morgunn *m* 91
mountain fjall *nt* 81
mountaineering fjallganga *f* 83
mouth munnur *m* 89
muscle vöðvi *m* 89
museum safn *nt* 81
my mitt, minn 65, 69

N

name nafn *nt* 68, 69, 88
napkin *(serviette)* servétta *f*, munnþurrka *f* 70
narrow þröngur 79
nationality þjóðerni *nt* 69
nauseous óglatt 90
near nálægt 67, 79, 82, 84 ,88
nerve taugar *f* 89
never aldrei 67
New Zealand Nýja Sjáland 93
newsagent blaðasala *f* 84
newspaper dagblað *nt* 87
next næstur 78
night nótt *f* 92
nine níu 92
no nei 65
noisy hávær 69
noon hádegi *nt* 91
north norður 80
Norway Noregi 93
nose nef *nt* 89
not ekki 66, 67
nothing ekkert 67
notice tilkynning *f* 93
November nóvember *m* 91
now núna 67
number *(house)* númer *nt*, húsnúmer *nt* 69

O

occupation starf *nt* 69
occupied upptekinn 67, 93
October október *m* 91
oil olía *f* 80
old gamall 67
once einu sinni 93
one einn 92
only aðeins 67, 68
open opið 94
open, to að opna 81
or eða 67
orange appelsínugulur 85
order, out of bilað 93
order, to að panta 76, 84, 85
outside úti 67

ICELANDIC DICTIONARY

overnight eina nótt f 68

P

park, to að leggja bíl 69
parking bílastæði nt 79
part hluti m 89
passport vegabréf nt 69, 94
path stígur m 81
pay, to að borga 76
per day á dag m 79
perhaps ef til vill 67
petrol (gasoline) bensín nt 79, 80
picnic lautarferð f 76
place staður m 69, 80
place of birth fæðingarstaður m 69
plane flugvél f 77
plate diskur m 70
platform pallur m 77
play, to að leika 82
please afsakið 65
pleased ánægður 65
point of interest athyglisverður staður m 81
police lögregla f 94
porter dyravörður m 78
post office pósthús nt 84, 88
postage póstburðargjald nt 88
postcard póstkort nt 88
pound (sterling) pund nt 88
prescription lyfseðill m 90
price verð nt 68
private einka- 68, 93
public almennings- 88
pull, to að draga 93
puncture (flat) sprungið dekk nt 80
push, to að ýta 94

Q

quality gæði nt 84
quarter fjórðungur m 93; (hour) korter nt 91
question spurning f 66
quieter rólegri 69

R

radio útvarp nt 68
rash útbrot nt 89
razor blades rakvélablöð nt 86
receipt kvittun f 90
recommend, to að mæla með 70, 90
rectangular rétthyrndur 85
red rauður 85
registered mail ábyrgðarpóstur m 88
regular (petrol) venjulegt bensín nt 80

repeat, to að endurtaka 66
requirements kröfur f 69
reservation pöntun 68, 77
reservations office pantanir f 77
reserve, to að panta 70, 82
reserved frátekinn 93
restaurant veitingastaður m 70
return (round trip) báðar leiðir f 77
riding (horse-back) reiðmennska 83
right (correct) réttur 67, 78; (direction) hægri 76, 80
river á f 81, 83
road vegur m 80, 93
road sign vegvísir m 79
room herbergi nt 68
round kringlóttur 85

S

sale útsala f 94
salty saltur 76
Saturday laugardagur m 91
sauna gufubað nt 68
scarf slæða f 86
Scotland Skotland 93
sea sjór m 81
seat sæti nt 82
second annar 93
second class annað farrými nt 77
see, to að sjá 68
see, to (visit) að heimsækja 90
send, to að senda 80, 88
September september m 91
serve, to að þjóna 70
service þjónusta f 76
set menu fastur matseðill m 70
seven sjö 92
shampoo sjampó nt 86
shape lögun f 84
she hún 88
shirt skyrta f 86
shivery skjálfandi 90
shoe skór m 86
shop verslun f 81, 84
shopping area verslunarsvæði nt 84
shoulder öxl f 89
show sýning f 82
show, to að sýna 85
shower sturta f 68
sign merki nt 93
signature undirskrift f 69
silk silki nt 86
since síðan 67
single einsmanns 68
single (one-way) aðra leiðina f 77
six sex 92
skates skautar m 83

Íslensk Orðabók

skating rink skautasvell *nt* 83
ski skíði *nt* 83
ski, to að skíða 83
ski jumping skíðastökk *nt* 83
skiing skíðamennska *f* 83
skiing, cross-country skíðaganga *f* 83
skiing, downhill brun *nt* 83
skiing equipment skíðabúnaður *m* 83
skin húð *f* 89
skirt pils *nt* 86
slice sneið *f* 87
slowly hægt 66, 79
small lítill 67, 69, 85
smoking reykingar 94
snack smáréttir *m* 76
soap sápa *f* 86
sock sokkar *m* 86
soon bráðum 67
sort tegund *f* 87
South Africa Suður Afríka 93
south suður 80
souvenir minjagripur *m* 87
souvenir shop minjagripaverslun *f* 84
speak, to að tala 66, 88
specialist sérfræðingur *m* 90
specimen sýni *nt* 90
speed limit hraðatakmarkanir *f* 79
speed skating skautahlaup *nt* 83
spoon skeið *f* 70
sport íþróttir *f* 82
spray, insect skordýraeitur *nt* 86
spring vor *nt* 92
square ferhyrndur 85
stamp frímerki *nt* 88
stay dvöl *f* 69
stay, to að dvelja 68, 90
sting sár *nt* eftir stungu *f* 89
stock, out of ekki fáanlegur 84
stolen stolinn 94
stomach magi *m* 89
stop, to að stoppa 79, 94
store *(shop)* verslun *f* 84
straight ahead beint áfram 80
street gata *f* 69
suede rúskinn *nt* 86
summer sumar *nt* 92
sun-tan cream sólkrem *nt* 86
Sunday sunnudagur *m* 91
super *(petrol)* súper bensín *nt* 80
supermarket stórmarkaður *m* 84
surgery *(doctor's office)* læknisstofa *f* 89
Sweden Svíþóð 93
sweet sætur 76
swelling bólga *f* 89
swim, to að synda 83
swimming sund *nt* 83

swimming pool sundlaug *f* 83
swimming trunks sundskýla *f* 86
swimsuit sundbolur *m* 86

T
table borð *nt* 70
take, to að taka 68, 78
tampons tíðatappar *m* 86
taxi leigubíll *m* 69, 79
telegram skeyti *nt* 88
telephone sími *m* 88
television sjónvarp *nt* 68
tell, to að segja frá 88
temperature hiti *m* 90
ten tíu 92
tennis court tennisvöllur *m* 82
tennis tennis *m* 83
test, to að prófa 79
thank you takk fyrir 65
thanks takk 65
theatre leikhús *nt* 82
then þá 67
these þessir hérna 76
thief þjófur *m* 94
third þriðji 93
third, a þriðjungur *m* 93
those þessir þarna 76
three þrír 92
throat háls *m* 89
through í gegnum 67
Thursday fimmtudagur *m* 91
ticket miði *m* 77, 82
ticket office miðasala *f* 77
tights sokkabuxur *f* 86
time tími *m* 91
tin *(can)* dós *f* 87
today í dag *m* 92
toilets snyrtingar *f* 68, 69
tomorrow á morgun *m* 89, 92
tongue tunga *f* 89
tonight í kvöld *nt* 82
too of 69, 76; *(also)* líka 67
toothache tannpína *f* 90
toothpaste tannkrem *nt* 86
torch blys 87
touch, to að snerta 89
tour ferð *f* 78
tourist office ferðaskrifstofa *f* 81
towards í áttina til 67
town borg *f* 82
town centre *(downtown)* miðbær *m* 78
tram *(streetcar)* sporvagn *m* 78
translate, to að þýða 66
travel, to að ferðast 77
trousers síðbuxur *f* 86

try on, to að máta 85
T-shirt bolur *m* 86
Tuesday þriðjudagur *m* 91
twice tvisvar 93
twin beds tvö rúm *nt* 68
two tveir 92
tyre pressure loftþrýstingur *m* í dekkjum *nt* 80

U
under undir 67
underpants undirbuxur *f* 86
understand, to að skilja 66
unleaded blýlaust 80
up upp 67
upstairs uppi 67
use, to að nota 88
useful gagnlegur 67

V
vacancy laust pláss *nt* 68, 93
vacant laus 67, 94
vacation *(holiday)* frí *nt* 65
vegetarian grænmetisæta *f* 70
velvet flauel *nt* 86
very mjög 67
view útsýni *nt* 68

W
wait, to að bíða 79 ,94
waiting room biðstofa *f* 77
wallet seðlaveski *nt* 94
want, to að vilja 82
water vatn *nt* 75
waterfall foss *m* 81

Wednesday miðvikudagur *m* 91
week vika *f* 68, 79
west vestur 80
what hvað 66, 84
wheel chains keðjur *f* 80
when hvenær 66, 81
where hvar 65, 77, 81
which hver 66
white hvítur 85
who hver 66
why hvers vegna 66
wife eiginkona *f* 65
windscreen water gluggaúði *m* 80
wine vín *nt* 75
winter vetur *m* 92
with með 65, 67
without án 67
wonderful dásamlegur 82
wood skógur *m* 81
wool ull *f* 86
word orð *nt* 67
worse verri 67
wound sár *nt* 89
write down, to að skrifa niður 85
wrong rangur 67, 80

Y
yellow gulur 85
yes já 65
yesterday í gær 92
young ungur 67
your þinn

Z
zero núll 92
zoo dýragarður *m* 81

English–Norwegian dictionary

c common gender   *nt* neuter   *pl* plural

A

able, to be kunne 98
above over 99; ovenfor 109
accept, to ta 117
address adresse *c* 111
admission inngangsbillett *c* 115
after etter 99, 113
air conditioning air-conditioning 100
airmail med fly 120
a lot mye 99
American amerikansk 119
amount beløp 109
and og 99
any noe 100, 116
anything noe 101, 117
anywhere noe sted 115
appointment time *c* 121
April april *c* 123
arm arm *c* 121
ashtray askebeger *nt* 102
aspirin aspirin *c* 118
at ved 99
August august 123
Australia Australia 97
autumn høst *c* 123

B

back rygg *c* 121
back, to be komme tilbake 111, 120
bad dårlig 98
baker's bakeri *nt* 116
bank bank *c* 120
basic vanlige 97
bath bad *nt* 100
bathroom bad *nt* 101
battery batteri *nt* 119
be, to være 98
bed seng *c* 100, 122
beer øl *nt* 108
before *(time)* før 99
begin, to begynne 114
behind bak 99, 113
below under 99; nedenfor 109
better bedre 98, 101, 117
between mellom 99
bicycle sykkel *c* 115
bicycling sykling *c* 115
big stor 98, 117
bigger større 101
bill regning *c* 101, 109
bitter besk 108
black svart 117
black and white *(film)* svart-hvitt 119

blister blemme *c* 121
blood blod 122
blood pressure blodtrykk *nt* 122
blouse bluse *c* 118
blue blå 117
boat båt *c* 111
boat trip båttur *c* 111
body kropp *c* 121
bone ben *nt* 121
booking office billettkontor *nt* 110
bookshop bokhandel *c* 116
boot støvel *c* 118
botanical gardens botanisk hage *c* 113
bottle flaske *c* 108
boyfriend venn *c* 97
breakdown motorstopp *c* 113
breakfast frokost *c* 102, 103
brown brun 117
bruise blått merke *nt* 121
burn brannsår *nt* 121
bus buss *c* 111
business forretning *c* 97
busy opptatt 114
but men 99
butcher's slakter *c* 116

C

call, to *(phone)* ringe 120, 126
camera apparat *nt* 119
camp site campingplass *c* 100
camp, to campe 100
can *(tin)* boks *c* 119
Canada Kanada 97
cancel annullere 110
car bil *c* 101, 112
car hire *(rental)* bilutleie 112
cash desk kasse *c* 116, 125
castle slott *nt* 113
cathedral domkirke *c* 113
caution forsiktig 125
change, to *(money)* veksle 120
change, to *(transport)* bytte 111
cheap billig 98; rimelig 101, 117
check in, to sjekke inn 110
check out, to reise 101
chemist's *(drugstore)* apotek *nt* 116, 118
city centre sentrum *nt* 113
close, to stenge 113
clothing klær *pl* 118
coat *(man's)* frakk *c* 118; *(woman's)* kåpe *c* 118
cold kald 98, 108, 125
colour farge *c* 116, 119

come, to komme 97, 102
condom kondom *nt* 118
confirm bekrefte 110
cost, to koste 100, 117
cotton bomull 118
credit card kredittkortet 109, 117
crossing *(maritime)* overgfart *c* 111
crown *(currency)* krone *c* 116, 120
cup kopp *c* 102, 108
currency exchange office vekslingskontor *nt* 120
customs toll *c* 112
cut kutt *nt* 121

D
dance, to danse 114
danger fare *c* 125
dark mørk 100, 117
date *(day)* dato *c* 101
day dag *c* 100, 112, 122
December desember *c* 123
decision beslutning *c* 100
denim denim 118
Denmark Danmark 125
dentist tannlege *c* 116, 122
deodorant deodorant *c* 118
department store stormagasin *nt* 116
detour *(diversion)* omkjøring *c* 112
diabetic diabetiker *c* 122
diesel diesel 112
dining car spisevogn *c* 111
dining-room spisesalen *c* 101
dinner middag *c* 102
discoteque diskotek *nt* 114
dish rett *c* 102; spesialitet 102
dizzy svimmel 122
doctor lege *c* 121, 126
doctor's office *(surgery)* legekontor *nt* 121
dog hund *c* 125
dollar dollar *c* 120
double dobbel 100
double bed dobbeltseng *c* 100
down ned 99
downstairs nede 99
dress kjole *c* 118
drink drikkevare *c* 108
drink, to drikke 102
drive, to kjøre 112
drugstore *(chemist's)* apotek *nt* 116

E
ear øre *nt* 121
early tidlig 98
east øst 113
eight åtte 124
emergency nødsfall *nt* 126
emergency exit nødutgang *c* 101, 125
England England 125
English engelsk 119; *(language)* engelsk

98, 113, 121
enjoyable hyggelig 101
entrance inngang *c* 110
evening kveld *c* 114, 123
exchange rate vekslingskurs *c* 120
exhibition utstilling *c* 113
exit utgang *c* 110, 125
expensive dyr 98
express ekspress 120
expression uttrykk 97, 116
eye øye *nt* 121

F
face ansikt *nt* 121
family familie *c* 97
far fjern 99
farm bondegård *c* 114
February februar *c* 123
feel, to føle seg 122
ferry ferge *c* 111
few par 100
filling *(tooth)* plombe *c* 122
filling station bensinstasjon *c* 112
film film *c* 119
find, to finne 98; få 121
fine *(OK)* brå 100
finger finger *c* 121
finish, to slutte 114
Finland Finland 125
first første 111, 124
first class første klasse *c* 110
first name fornavn *nt* 101
fishing fiske *nt* 115
five fem 124
fjord fjord *c* 114
flight fly *nt* 110
food mat *c* 108
foot fot *c* 121
football *(soccer)* fotball *c* 115
forest skog *c* 114
fork gaffel *c* 102
four fire 124
Friday fredag *c* 123
from fra 97, 99

G
general allmenn 101, 116
gentlemen *(toilets)* herrer *c/pl* 125
get, to komme til 112
get, to *(fetch)* skaffe 101; få tak i 111
get off, to *(transport)* gå av 111
girlfriend venninne *c* 97
give, to gi 122
glass glass *nt* 102
gloves hanske *c* 118
go away! gå vekk! 126
go out, to *(rendez-vous)* gå ut 114
golf course golfbane *c* 115

good bra 98, 102, 117, 122
good afternoon god dag 97
good morning god morgen 97
good night god natt 97
good-bye adjø 97
Great Britain Storbritannia 97, 125
green grønn 117
grey grå 117
grocery matvarehandel *c* 116, 119
guide guide *c* 113

H
hair-cut klipp *c* 119
hairdresser *(ladies)* damefrisør *c* 116
hairdresser *(men)* herrefrisør *c* 116
half en halv 124
hand hånd *c* 121
handbag håndveske *c* 126
harbour havn *c* 113
have, to få 98; har 100, 101, 119, 120
he han 120
head hode *nt* 121
health insurance sykeforsikring *c* 122
heart hjerte *nt* 121
heavy tung 117
hello hallo 97, 120
help, to hjelpe 98, 116
help! hjelp! 126
her hennes 120
here her 111
hi hei 97
him ham 120
hire, to leie 112, 115
holiday *(vacation)* ferie *c* 97
home town hjemsted *nt* 101
hot varm 98, 125
hotel hotell *c* 100
how far hvor langt 98, 112
how hvor 98
how long hvor lang 98, 111, 122
how much hvor mye 98, 117
hundred hundre 124
hurt, to gjøre vondt 122
husband mann *c* 97

I
ice hockey ishockey *c* 115
Iceland Island 125
ill syk 126
in i 99
include, to inkludere 112
included inkludert 109
information informasjon *c* 110
injection sprøyte *c* 122
inquiries forespørsel *c* 110
insect repellent insektmiddel *nt* 118
inside inne 99
insurance forsikring *c* 112
introduction *(social)* presentasjon *c* 97

Ireland Irland 125
island øy *c* 114

J
January januar *c* 123
July juli *c* 123
June juni *c* 123

K
key nøkkel *c* 101
kilo kilo *nt* 119
knee kne *nt* 121
knife kniv *c* 102
krone *(money)* krone *c* 117

L
lace knipling *c* 118
ladies *(toilets)* damer *c/pl* 125
lake *(inn)*sjø *c* 115
landmark landemerke *nt* 114
large stor 117
last siste 110, 111
late sen 98
leather lær *nt* 118
leave, to gå 111
leave alone, to la være i fred 126
left venstre 109, 113
left-luggage office *(baggage check)*
 bagasjeoppbevaring *c* 110
leg ben *nt* 121
letter *(mail)* brev *nt* 120
lift *(elevator)* heis *c* 101
light *(colour)* lys 117; *(weight)* lett 117
like, to like 117
linen lin *nt* 118
litre liter *c* 112, 119
little, a lite 99
local lokal 102
look at, to *(examine)* undersøke 122
lost mistet 126
lost, to be gå seg bort 126
lost property (lost and found) office
 hittegodskontor *nt* 110
luggage lockers oppbevaringsboks *c* 110
lunch lunsj *c* 102
lung lunge *c* 121

M
mail post *c* 120
main størst 116
many mange 98
March mars *c* 123
market torghandel *c* 113
match *(sport)* kamp *c* 115
May mai *c* 123
me meg 98
meadow eng *c* 114

NORWEGIAN DICTIONARY

mean, to bety 98
mechanic mekaniker *c* 113
meet, to treffes 97
mend, to *(fix)* reparere 113
menu spisekart *nt* 103
message beskjed *c* 120
mileage kjørelengde *c* 112
milk melk *c* 119
million million 124
mineral water mineralvann *nt* 108
minute minutt *nt* 111
mistake feil *c* 109
moisturizing cream fuktighetskrem *c* 118
Monday mandag *c* 123
more litt 98
morning morgen *c* 123
mountain fjell *nt* 114
mouth munn *c* 121
muscle muskel *c* 121
museum museum *nt* 113
my min, mitt, mine 97

N

name navn *nt* 97, 120; *(surname)* etternavn *nt* 101
napkin *(serviette)* serviett *c* 102
nationality nasjonalitet *c* 101
nauseous kvalm 122
near nær 99, 112, 115, 116, 120
neck nakke *c* 121
never aldri 99
New Zealand Ny-Zealand 125
newspaper avis *c* 119
newsstand aviskiosk *c* 116
next neste 110, 111
next to ved siden av 99, 113
night natt *c* 123
nine ni 124
no nei 97
no ... *(forbidden)* ... forbudt 112
noisy støyende 100
none ingen 99
north nord 113
Norway Norge 125
Norwegian *(language)* norsk 98
nose nese *c* 121
not ikke 98, 99
nothing ingenting, ikke noe 99
notice *(sign)* oppslag *nt* 125
November november *c* 123
now nå 99

O

occupation *(profession)* yrke *nt* 101
occupied opptatt 99
October oktober *c* 123
on på 99
once en gang 124

one en 124
only bare 99, 100
open, to åpne 113
opposite midt imot 113
or eller 99
orange oransje 117
order, out of i uorden 125
order, to bestille 108, 116, 117
outside ute 99
overnight natten over 100

P

pair par *nt* 118
pardon unnskyld 97
park, to parkere 101
parking parkering *c* 112
part del *c* 121
passport pass *nt* 101, 126
path sti *c* 114
pay, to betale 109
per day pr. dag 112
perhaps kanskje 99
petrol *(gasoline)* bensin *c* 112
picnic picnic *c* 109
place sted *nt* 101
place of birth fødested *nt* 101
plane fly *nt* 110
plate tallerken *c* 102
platform *(station)* perrong *c* 110
play, to *(theatre)* spille 114
please vær (så) snill å ...,... takk 97
pleased hyggelig 97
police politi *nt* 126
post office postkontor *nt* 116, 120
postage porto *c* 120
postcard postkort *nt* 120
pound *(money)* pund *nt* 120
prescription resept *c* 122
private privat 125
pull, to trekke 125
puncture *(flat)* punkteringen 113
push, to *(open)* skyv 125

Q

quarter of an hour kvarter *nt* 123
question spørsmål *nt* 98
quiet rolig 101

R

radio radio *c* 100
rash utslett *c* 121
rate *(of exchange)* kurs *c* 120
razor blade barberblad *nt* 118
receipt kvittering *c* 122
recommend, to anbefale 102, 122
rectangular rektangulær 117
red rød 117

Norsk ordliste

regular *(petrol)* normal 112
repeat, to gjenta 98
reservation reservasjon *c* 110
reserve, to bestille 100, 102, 114
reserved reservert 125
restaurant restaurant *c* 102
return ticket *(round trip)* tur-returbillett *c* 110
right *(direction)* høyre 109, 113; *(correct)* riktig 99
river elv *c* 114, 115
road vei *c* 125
road sign trafikkskilt *nt* 112
road works veiarbeid, vegarbeid 112
room rom *nt* 100, 101
round rund 117

S

salty salt 108
Saturday lørdag *c* 123
sauna badstue *c*, sauna *c* 100
scarf skjerf *nt* 118
Scotland Skottland 125
sea sjø *c* 114
second annen, andre 124
second class andre klasse *c* 110
see, to se 100
send, to sende 113, 120
September september *c* 123
set menu meny *c* 102
seven sju 124
shampoo sjampo *c* 118
shape form *c* 116
she hun 120
shirt skjorte *c* 118
shoe sko *c* 118
shop *(store)* butikk *c* 116
shopping area handlestrøk *nt* 116
shoulder skulder *c* 121
show *(theatre)* forestilling *c* 114
shower dusj *c* 100
sign *(notice)* skilt *nt* 125
signature underskrift *c* 101
silk silke *c* 118
since siden 99
single enkel 100
single ticket *(one-way)* enkeltbillett *c* 110
six seks 124
skate skøyte *c* 115
skating rink skøytebane *c* 115
ski ski *c* 115
ski, to gå på ski 115
ski boots skistøvel *c* 115
ski jumping skihopping *c* 115
skiing, cross-country langrenn *nt* 115
skiing, downhill utforkjøring *c* 115
skin hud *c* 121
skirt skjørt *nt* 118
sleeping car sovevogn *c* 111
slice skive *c* 119

slowly langsom 98; sakte 112
small liten 98, 100, 117
smoking røyking *c* 125
snack småretter *c/pl* 109
soap såpe *c* 118
socks sokk *c* 118
soon snart 99, 121
sort slags *nt/pl* 119
south sør 113
South Africa Sør-Africa 125
souvenir suvenir *c* 119
souvenir shop suvenirbutikk *c* 116
speak, to snakke 98, 120, 121
specialist spesialist *c* 122
specimen *(medical)* prøve *c* 122
speed skating skøyteløp 115
spoon skje *c* 102
sport sport *c* 115
spring vår *c* 123
square *(town)* plass *c*, torg *nt* 113
square *(shape)* firkantet 117
stamp *(postage)* frimerke *nt* 120
stay opphold *nt* 101
stay, to bli 100
sting stikk *nt* 121
stock, out of utsolgt 116
stolen stjålet 126
stomach mage *c* 121
stop, to stanse 111
stop thief! stopp tyven! 126
store *(shop)* butikk *c* 116
straight ahead rett frem 113
sturdy robust, solid 117
suede semsket skinn 118
summer sommer *c* 123
sun-tan oil sololje *c* 118
Sunday søndag *c* 123
super *(petrol)* super 112
supermarket supermarked *nt* 116
surgery *(doctor's office)* legekontor *c* 121
Sweden Sverige 125
sweet søt 108
swelling hevelse *c* 121
swim, to svømme 115
swimming svømming *c* 115
swimming pool svømmebasseng *nt* 115
swimming trunks badebukse *c* 118
swimsuit badedrakt *c* 118

T

table bord *nt* 102
take, to ta 100, 117
tampons tampong *c* 118
taxi drosje *c* 101, 111
telephone booth telefonkiosk *c* 120
telephone telefon *c* 120
television TV *c* 100
tell, to si 120
temperature temperatur *c* 122
ten ti 124

tennis tennis *c* 115
tennis court tennnisbane *c* 115
thank, to takke 97
thanks takk 97
theatre theater *nt* 114
then da 99
there der 98
thief tyv *c* 126
think, to tror 109
third tredje 124
this denne 111
three tre 124
throat hals *c* 121
through gjennom 99
Thursday torsdag *c* 123
ticket billett *c* 110, 114
ticket office billettluke *c* 110
tights strømpebukse *c* 118
time *(clock)* klokken 123
tin *(can)* boks *c* 119
today i dag 123
toilets *(restroom)* toalett *nt* 100, 101
tomorrow i morgen 121, 123
tongue tunge *c* 121
tonight i kveld 114
too for 100, 108; *(also)* også 99
toothache tannpine *c* 122
toothpaste tannpasta *c* 118
torch *(flashlight)* lommelykt *c* 119
tourist office turiskontor *nt* 113
towards mot 99
town by *c* 114
town centre sentrum *nt* 111
train tog *nt* 110
tram *(streetcar)* trikk *c* 111
translate, to oversette 98
trousers langbukser *c/pl* 118
try on, to prøve 118
T-shirt T-skjorte *c* 118
Tuesday tirsdag *c* 123
twice ganger 124
two to 124

U
under under 99
underground *(subway)* t-bane *c* 111
underground station t-banestasjon *c* 111
understand, to forstå 98
United States USA 97
unleaded blyfir 112
until til 99
up opp 99
upstairs oppe 99
us oss 101

useful nyttig 99

V
vacancy ledige rom *nt* 100
vacant ledig 99
vacation ferie *c* 97
valley dal *c* 114
vegetarian vegetar(isk) 102
very meget 99

W
waiting room venterom *nt* 110
wallet lommebok *c* 126
water vann *nt* 108
waterfall foss *c* 114
Wednesday onsdag *c* 123
week uke *c* 100, 112
well bra 97
west vest 113
what hva 98, 116
when når 98, 113
where hvor 97, 98, 110, 113
which hvilken 98
white hvit 117
who hvem 98
why hvorfor 98
wife kone *c* 97
wine vin *c* 108
winter vinter *c* 123
with med 97, 99
without uten 99
wonderful veldig hyggelig 114
wool ull *c* 118
word ord *nt* 99
worse verre 98
wound sår *nt* 121
write, to skrive 117
wrong *(incorrect)* feil 99, 113

Y
yellow gul 117
yes ja 97
yesterday i går 123
yet ennå 99

Z
zero null 124
zoo dyrehage *c* 113

English–Swedish dictionary

c common gender   *nt* neuter   *pl* plural

A

able, to be kunna 130
above ovanför 131, 141
accept, to ta emot 149
address adress *c* 144
after efter 131, 145
air conditioning luftkonditionering *c* 132
airmail med flyg 152
a lot mycket 131
American amerikansk 151
amount summa *c* 141
and och 131
any några 130, 132
anything något 133; någonting 148
apple äpple *nt* 151
appointment tid *c* 153
April april 155
arm arm *c* 153
ashtray askkopp *c* 134
aspirin aspirin *c* 149
August augusti 155
Australia Australien 129
autumn *(fall)* höst 155

B

back rygg *c* 153
back, to be *(return)* vara tillbaka 144; komma tillbaka 152
bad dålig 131
baggage bagage *nt* 143
baker's bageri *nt* 148
bank bank *c* 152
basic användbar 129
bath bad *nt* 132
bathroom badrum *nt* 133
battery batteri *nt* 151
be, to vara 130
bed säng *c* 132, 154
beer öl *c* 140
begin, to börja 146
behind bakom 131, 145
below nedanför 131, 141
better bättre 131, 133, 148
between mellan 131
beware varning för 157
bicycle cykel *c* 147
big stor 131, 148
bigger större 133
bill *(check)* nota *c* 141; räkning *c* 133
bitter besk 141
black svart 150
black and white *(film)* svart-vit 151

blood blod *nt* 154
blood pressure blodtryck *nt* 154
blouse blus *c* 150
blue blå 150
boat båt *c* 143
boat service båt *c* 143
body kropp *c* 153
bone ben *nt* 153
booking office biljettexpedition *c* 142
bookshop bokhandel *c* 148
boots stövlar *c/pl* 150
botanical gardens botanisk trädgård *c* 146
boyfriend pojkvän *c* 129
breakdown motorstopp *nt* 145
breakfast frukost *c* 134
bridge bro *c* 145
brown brun 150
bruise blåmärke *nt* 153
burn brännsår *nt* 153
bus buss *c* 143
business affär *c* 129
busy upptagen 146
but men 131
butcher's slaktare *c*, charkuteri *nt* 148

C

call, to *(help, telephone)* ringa 152, 157
camera kamera *c* 151
camp, to campa 132
campsite campingplats *c* 132
can *(tin)* burk *c* 151
cancel, to annullera 142
Canada Kanada 129
car bil *c* 144
car hire *(rental)* biluthyrning *c* 144
car racing biltävling *c* 147
cash desk kassa *c* 149, 157
castle slott *nt* 146
cathedral domkyrka *c* 146
caution varning *c* 157
change, to ändra 142
change, to *(money)* växla 152
cheap billig 148
cheaper billigare 133
check in, to checka in 142
check out, to checka ut 133
chemist's *(drugstore)* apotek *nt* 148, 149
children barn *nt/pl* 129
city centre (stads)centrum *nt* 146
clothing kläder *pl* 150
cold kall 131, 132, 141, 157
colour färg *c* 149, 151
come from, to komma från 129

SWEDISH DICTIONARY

come, to komma 134
condoms kondomer *c/pl* 149
confirm, to bekräfta 142
cotton bomull *c* 150
credit card kreditkort *nt* 141,149
crossing överfart *c* 143
crown *(currency)* krona *c* 149, 152
cup kopp *c* 134
currency exchange office växelkontor *nt* 152
cut skärsår *nt* 153
cycling cykel *c* 147

D
dance, to dansa 146
danger fara *c* 157
dark mörk 132, 148
date datum *nt* 133, 155
date of birth födelsedatum *nt* 133
day dag *c* 132, 144, 154, 155
December december 155
decision beslut *nt* 132
denim denim *c* 150
Denmark Danmark 156
dentist tandläkare *c* 148, 154
deodorant deodorant *c* 149
department store varuhus *nt* 148
diabetic diabetiker *c* 154
diesel diesel *c* 145
dining room matsal *c* 133
dinner middag *c* 134
discotheque diskotek *nt* 146
dish rätt *c* 134
dizzy yr 154
doctor läkare *c* 153, 157
doctor's office *(surgery)* läkarmottagning *c* 153
dog hund *c* 157
dollar dollar *c* 152
double bed dubbelsäng *c* 132
double room dubbelrum *nt* 132
downstairs där nere 131
dress klänning *c* 150
drink dryck *c* 140
drugstore *(chemist's)* apotek *nt* 148, 149
during under 131, 155

E
ear öra *nt* 153
early tidig 131
east öster 145
eight åtta 156
emergency nödsituation *c* 157
emergency exit nödutgång *c* 133, 157
England England 156
English *(language)* engelsk 130, 146, 151, 153
enjoy, to njuta 141
enjoyable trevlig 133

entrance ingång *c* 142, 157
evening kväll *c* 146, 155
exchange rate växelkurs *c* 152
exhibition utställning *c* 146
exit utgång *c* 142, 157
express express 152
expression uttryck *nt* 129, 148
eye öga *nt* 153

F
face ansikte *nt* 153
family familj *c* 129
fare pris *nt* 143, 144
February februari 155
feel, to känna sig 154
few, (a) några 131, 132
fill up, to tanka 145
filling *(tooth)* plomb *c* 154
filling station bensinstation *c* 145
film film *c* 151
find, to hitta 130, 153
fine *(well)* bra 129, 132
finger finger *nt* 153
first class första klass *c* 142
first först 143, 156
first name namn *nt* 133
five fem 156
flight flyg *nt* 142
food mat *c* 141
foot fot *c* 153
football *(soccer)* fotball *c* 147
for för 131
for sale til salu 157
forbidden förbjuden 157
forest skog *c* 145
fork gaffel *c* 134
four fyra 156
free *(vacant)* ledig 131, 157
Friday fredag 155
from från 131

G
general allmän 133, 148
gentlemen *(toilets)* herrar 157
get, to få tag på 130
get, to *(fetch)* skaffa 133, 144
get lost, to vilsegången 157
get off, to *(transport)* stiga av 143
girlfriend flickvän *c* 129
give, to ge 145, 154
glass glas *nt* 134
gloves handskar *c/pl* 150
go away, to gå väg 157
go out, to *(rendez-vous)* gå ut 146
golf course golfbana *c* 147
good afternoon god middag 129
good bra 131, 134, 148, 154

Svensk ordista

good morning god morgon 129
good night god natt 129
good-bye adjö 129
green grön 150
Great Britain Storbrittanien 129
grey grå 150
grocer's livsmedelsaffär c 148, 151
guide guide c 146

H
hair-cut klippning c 151
hairdresser frisör c 148
half halva c 156
hand hand c 153
handbag handväska c 157
harbour hamn c 146
have, to ha 130, 132, 133, 151
he han 152
head huvud nt 153
health insurance sjukförsäkring c 154
heart hjärta nt 153
heavy tung 148
hello hallå 129, 152
help! hjälp! 157
help, to hjälpa 130, 143, 149
her hennes 152
here här 132, 144
hi hej 129
him honom 152
hire, to hyra 144, 147
holiday helgdag c 129
home town hemort c 133
hot varm 131, 157
how hur 130, 143, 145, 149, 154
how far hur långt 130
how long hur länge 130, 143, 154
how much hur mycket 130, 149
how many hur många 130
hundred hundra 156
hurt, to göra ont 154
husband man c 129

I
ice hockey ishockey c 147
ill sjuk 157
include, to ingå 144
included inräknad 141
information information c 142; upplysning c 157
injection spruta c 154
inquiries forfrågningar c/pl 143
insect bite insektsbett nt 153
insect repellent insektsspray c 149
insect spray insektsspray c 149
inside inne 131
insurance försäkring c 144
introduce, to presentera 129

introductions presentation c 129
Ireland Irland 156

J
January januari 155
jersey tröja c 150
July juli 155
June juni 155

K
key nyckel c 133
kilo kilo nt 151
knee knä nt 153
knife kniv c 134

L
lace spets c 150
ladies (toilets) damer 157
lake sjö c 145, 147
landmark landmärke nt 145
large stor 148
last sista 143
late sen 131
leather läder nt, skinn nt 150
leave, to lämna 143
leave alone, to lämna ifred 157
left vänster 141, 145
left-luggage office (baggage check) effektförvaring c 142
leg ben nt 153
letter (mail) brev nt 152
lift (elevator) hiss c 133, 157
light (colour) ljus 148; (weight) lätt 148
like, to tycka om 149
linen linne nt 150
litre liter c 145, 151
little, a lite 131
local lokal 134
look at, to (examine) titta på 154
lose, to tappa 157
lost property (lost and found) office hittegodsexpedition c 142
luggage bagage nt 157
luggage lockers förvaringsbox c 142
lunch lunch c 134
lung lunga c 153

M
made of gjort av 150
mail post c 152
March mars 155
May maj 155
me mig 130, 144
mean, to betyda 130
mechanic mekaniker c 145
meet, to träffa 129

SWEDISH DICTIONARY

mend, to *(fix)* laga 145
menu meny *c* 134; matsedel *c* 135
message meddelande *nt* 152
midnight midnatt *c* 155
mileage kilometerkostnad *c* 144
milk mjölk *c* 151
minute minut *c* 144
mistake fel *nt* 141
moisturizing cream fuktighetsbevarande kräm *c* 149
Monday måndag 155
more mer 130
morning morgon *c* 155
mountain berg *nt* 145
mouth mun *c* 153
muscle muskel *c* 153
museum museum *nt* 146
my min, mitt *(pl* mina) 129, 133

N
name namm *nt* 129, 132
napkin *(serviette)* servett *c* 134
nationality nationalitet *c* 133
nauseous illamående 154
near nära 131, 145, 147
nearest närmaste 148, 152
nerve nerv *c* 153
never aldrig 131
newspaper tidning *c* 151
newsstand tidningskiosk *c* 148
next nästa, 143
next to bredvid 131, 143
night natt *c* 155
nine nio 156
no nej 129
none ingen 131
noon klockan tolv (på dagen) 155
north norr 145
Norway Norge 156
nose näsa *c* 153
not inte 130, 131
nothing ingenting, inget 131
notice anslag *nt* 157
November november 155
now nu 131
number *(house)* nummer *nt* 133

O
occupation yrke *nt* 133
occupied upptagen 131, 157
October oktober 155
oil olja *c*
on på 131
once en gång 156
one ett 156
only bara 131, 132
open öppet 157
opposite mitt emot 145

or eller 131
orange orange 150
order, out of ur funktion 157
order, to beställa 141, 149
outside ute 131
overnight över natt 132

P
pardon förlåt 129
parents föräldrar *c/pl* 129
park, to parkera 133
parking parkering *c* 144
part del *c* 153
passport pass *nt* 133, 157
path stig *c* 145
pay, to betala 141
per day per dag 144
perhaps kanske 131
petrol bensin *c* 145
picnic picknick *c* 141
place of birth födelseort *c* 133
place ort *c* 133
plane flyg *nt* 142
plate tallrik *c* 134
platform perrong *c* 142
play, to spela 146
please var snäll och ... 129
pleased trevligt 129
police polis *c* 157
porter bärare *c* 143
post office postkontor *nt* 148; post *c* 152
postage porto *nt* 152
postcard vykort *c* 152
pound *(sterling)* pund *c* 152
prescription recept *nt* 154
price pris *nt* 132
private privat 132
pull, to dra 157
puncture *(flat)* punktering *c* 145
push, to trycka 157

Q
quality kvalitet *c* 149
quarter fjärdedel *c* 155, 156
question fråga *c* 130
quieter tystare 133

R
radio radio *c* 132
rash itslag *nt* 153
razor blades rakblad *nt* 149
receipt kvitto *nt* 154
recommend, to föreslå 134; rekommendera 154
rectangular rektangulär 148
red röd 150
regular *(petrol)* lågoktanig 145
repeat, to upprepa 130

Svensk ordista

theatre teater *c* 146
then då, sedan 131
there där 130
thief tjuv *c* 157
think, to tro 141
third tredje 156
third tredjedel *c* 156
this den här, det här 149
those de där 141
three tre 156
throat hals *c* 153
through genom 131
Thursday torsdag 155
ticket biljett *c* 142, 146
ticket office biljettluckan *c* 142
time tid *c* 155
tin *(can)* burk *c* 151
today idag 155
toilet toalett *c* 132, 133
tomorrow i morgon 153, 155
tongue tunga *c* 153
tonight i kväll 146
too för 132, 141; *(also)* också 131
toothache tandvärk *c* 154
toothpaste tandkräm *c* 149
torch ficklampa *c* 151
tourist office turistbyrå *c* 146
towards mot 131
town stad *c* 146
town centre centrum *nt* 143
tram *(streetcar)* spårvagn *c* 143
translate, to översätta 130
travel, to resa 142
trousers (lång)byxor *nt/pl* 150
try on, to prova 150
Tuesday tisdag 155
twice två gånger 156
twin beds två sängar *c/pl* 132
two två 156

U
under under 131
understand, to förstå 130
United States USA 129
unleaded blyfri 145
until till 131
upstairs där uppe 131
use, to använda 152
useful användbar 131

V
vacancy ledigt rum *nt* 132, 157
vacant ledig 157
vegetarian vegetarisk 134
velvet sammet *c* 150
very mycket 131

W
wait, to vänta 144
waiting room väntsal *c* 142
wallet plånbok *c* 157
water vatten *nt* 140
waterfall vattenfall *nt* 145
Wednesday onsdag 155
week vecka *c* 132, 144
west väster 145
what vad 130, 149
when när 130
where var 129, 130, 142, 146
which vilken 130
white vit 150
who vem 130
why varför 130
wife fru *c* 129
wine vin *nt* 140
winter vinter 155
with med 129, 131
without utan 131
wonderful underbar 146
wool ylle *nt* 150
word ord *nt* 131
worse sämre 131
wound sår *nt* 153
write down, to skriva 149
wrong *(incorrect)* fel 131, 145

Y
yellow gul 150
yes ja 129
yesterday i går 155

Z
zero noll 156
zoo djurpark *c* 146